Parrots

The author with flock members Juno and Lime

Parrots:
The Flock Among Us

John Steckley
Photos by Angelika Steckley

Rock's Mills Press
Oakville, Ontario
2017

Published by
ROCK'S MILLS PRESS
www.rocksmillspress.com

Copyright © 2017 John Steckley.
All rights reserved. Published by arrangement with the author.

For information, contact the publisher at
customer.service@rocksmillspress.com
or visit us online at www.rocksmillspress.com.

CONTENTS

1. Fledgling Ideas ... *1*
2. Conures ... *20*
3. Quakers ... *39*
4. Amazons ... *68*
5. Africans ... *88*
6. Cockatiels and Other Cockatoos ... 108
7. Juno the Celestial Parrot ... *133*
8. The Whole Flock ... *148*
    Bibliography ... *169*
    Index ... *171*

Parrots

Chapter One
FLEDGLING IDEAS

Humans have long recognized the intelligence of parrots. In *Moralia*, the Greek philosopher/historian Plutarch (45–125 A.D.) wrote:

> ... as for starlings and crows and parrots which learn to talk and afford their teachers so malleable and imitative a vocal current to train and discipline, they seem to me to be champions and advocates of the other animals in their ability to learn, instructing us in some measure that they too are endowed both with rational utterance and with articulate voice... (as quoted in Boehrer 2015:9).

I am happy to say that my time spent with parrots and writing this book leads me to concur with Plutarch. Much more recently, Deborah Duffy, an animal behavior researcher at the University of Pennsylvania, had this to say about Alex, the African Gray studied and loved by Irene Pepperberg: "He was an ambassador of non-human animals, showing us that you don't need to have a brain that looks human to possess complex cognitive abilities" (in Pepperberg 2008:13).

Parrots have taught me much about the potential for intelligence in 'aviankind.' They are good spokesbirds for their class. They definitely are "endowed both with rational utterance and with articulate voice." And I like to think of our aviary as an embassy where compelling examples of the cognitive abilities of non-humans are on display.

In researching this book, my reading about other intelligent birds and the relationships they have with humans taught me much about parrots and my relationship to them. That being said, Bernd Heinrich's insightful *Mind of the Raven* provides an apt disclaimer for this book: "Ultimately, knowing all that goes on in their brains is, like infinity, an unreachable destination. The interesting part is the journey" (xxi).

Welcome to my journey with our parrots.

What is a Parrot?

What is a parrot? It is a bird (which is a class of animal) that belongs to the order of Psittaciformes, just as a human is a mammal that belongs to the order Primates. Birds belonging to this order live on every continent, although the ones in North America (with the exception of Mexico) and Europe are feral, birds brought in from other parts of the world that escaped or were released. In Asia they live primarily in south and southeast Asia. Classification of parrots has been going through a series of changes over the last two decades. The classification system that I find most handy divides them into four different families (you can find it at creagrus.home.montereybay.com/parrots.html):

- Cacatuidae includes Australasian parrots, primarily cockatoos, as you can guess from the name of the family.
- Psitticidae includes in its number the parrots of the Americas, otherwise known as New World parrots and two African genera.
- Psittaculidae is comprised of the rest of the Asian and African parrots, including the ringnecks found in South Asia and along a narrow strip of Africa. These are birds so often seen in YouTube videos.
- Finally, there is Strigopidae, parrots often found running around in New Zealand, including the famous kakapo (from the Maori 'kaka', meaning 'parrot', and 'po', night), which is a ground-dwelling parrot.

This book will focus on the first two groups, as those are the families (in addition to ours) to which our parrots belong.

There are three general characteristics that all parrots share. One is that they have hooked beaks, which as you will see in a later chapter are good at hooking keys off laptop computers. A second is the presence of the cere (based on a Latin word for wax), which is a waxy, fleshy area at the base of their upper mandible or beak. The nostril holes of the parrot are found there. Humans have only one mandible, which is our lower jaw. We can't move our upper jaw (or maxilla). Because parrots have an upper mandible, too, they can open their upper beaks very wide. When Gus, our cockatiel, whistles high notes, his upper mandible makes a significant upward movement. Third, like owls and woodpeckers, parrots have what are called zygodactyl feet, with two toes pointing forward and two pointing backward. Because their talons have several joints, this enables parrots to grasp and handle objects adroitly, in something of the same way that primates can with their opposable thumbs pressing in the opposite direction of their fingers. As you will see in the next chapter, Stanee, our green-cheeked conure, was able to use a tool because of this capacity.

What to Expect in this Book:
The Story of Five Parrots on the Floor

There are five parrots in front of me on the floor in a caged-in area that used to be half of our living room. Two of them, Stanee and Louis, are conures, both with the slender bodies and red tails that give them a name that means 'flame tails'. There are two Quaker parrots, Quigley and Tikkifinn, closely related to the conures but a little stockier as suits the cooler climate of their ancestral home. Both are gray in the front; Quigley (a male) is green of head and back, while Tikkifinn (a female) is blue in both those places. The fifth parrot, Sam, is bigger, and hails from Africa, far from Quigley and Tikkifinn's South American origins. Sam has a gray head, a big black beak that poses a constant threat to his human companions, and a V-shaped marking down his centre, green above, orange below.

I didn't see them land from their usual places on perches and on top of cages, but I'm almost completely sure of the order they landed in, and why. I can do this because they are part of my flock, and they are the subject of this book. If you want to know the story of why I'm sure about this, then read the book! If you want to cheat, flip to the last chapter. The answer is there (somewhere).

My Rationale for Writing the Book

"The person who imagines that a parrot is a parrot and nothing more will soon find that he or she has made a very great mistake" (W. T. Greene, *The Grey Parrot and How to Manage It*, 1924, as quoted in *Dudley and Gilderoy*, by Algernon Blackwood, 1929: 7)

One reason I am writing this book is the second-class—in fact, third-class—status of parrots in Canada and the United States. Parrots are ghettoized as "exotics," "small pets," or "other pets." They get treated as if they were illegal immigrants not worthy of the respect or care enjoyed by the "top two" pet animals, dogs and cats. For instance, a nearly universal complaint made by people in North America with parrots is the lack of an avian veterinarian in their area. On the Facebook page for Quaker parrots that I belong to, I have read many stories of people having to drive for three or four hours to see an avian vet. That is way too long to travel with a sick or wounded bird. The veterinary school in Ontario, based at the University of Guelph, only interns one aviary vet every year, which is far too few. I hope that the administrators of the program read this book and give their policy second thoughts. Parrots are important companions for humans. They need more vets who know how to take care of them!

On the weekend that I wrote the first draft of this introduction a "mega-adoption" of cats and dogs was held at Exhibition Place in Toronto. It was a worthy event, surely, but, quite predictably, there was no mention of parrots, no actions taken to assist or adopt abandoned birds. This kind of attitude needs to change, and I hope that this book goes at least a little way to effecting that change. This book is for the birds, the hooked-bill birds. They can and often do speak for themselves when you are in their company, but there is a need for more writers to speak for them on the printed page. They need avian sociologists as interpreters. They need a publicist to make people more aware of their intelligence and their social nature.

Are parrots really exotic pets? I would like to make two points. One concerns the argument that as "exotic animals" parrots should not be purchased as pets. A good rebuttal to this argument comes from Betty Jean Craige in her book *Conversations with Cosmo: At Home with an African Grey Parrot.* After an article about Cosmo appeared in an Atlanta paper, a subsequent letter to the editor made the "exotic animal" argument. Her response was one with which I wholeheartedly concur: "I agree that we should desist in the capturing of wild birds—everywhere. But keeping domestically bred pet birds is not, in my opinion, a sin. I have come to believe that the responsible ownership of parrots can serve well both parrots and humans. (Craige 2010:32)

Secondly, our birds are all Canadian-born, as I suspect most parrots in Canada are, and most of the others are probably from the U.S., hardly an "exotic" birthplace. They are second-, third-, fourth- and "more-" generation Canadians, so they should be respected like any other pets born and raised in Canada. For that matter, how many Canadians own breeds of dog that were first domesticated in Canada? To the best of my knowledge, the only such surviving breed is the Qimmiq or Canadian Inuit dog, and not a lot of people south of the Arctic own those. The vast majority of dogs Canadians own are the descendants of immigrants, just like most humans and all parrots. They are *all* exotics in some sense, and domesticated as well. And what about cats? Aren't they exotic? The same is true of them. No wild cats were domesticated here in North America. The first domesticated cats in Canada arrived in the seventeenth century with the French. The Wendat (Huron) people used the same name for cats as for weasels, and not just because they can weasel their way into our hearts. (We have a cat called "Brenda" who has done just that.)

Having had many kinds of pets throughout my life—fish, turtles, salamanders, frogs, cats, and dogs—I can say from experience that parrots fulfill the role of companion just as well as my other creature friends. Some days, in fact, I would have to say they do it better than the others. No insult intended to our dogs and cat, but they do not stand on my head and lightly preen my forehead, one of the most calming experiences that I know. Our border-collie cross and dachshund do wag their tails, and Brenda purrs when she comes to visit me early in the morning. Those actions are also good for my emotional state, but not the same as being preened by a parrot. Anthropologists use the term "grooming" for such mutual bonding behaviour. It's something that we primates should understand. We preen each other too. Just watch mother humans seeing their children off to school, especially kindergarten in early September, and you can easily see that.

Writing About Animals

My first two formal attempts at writing about animals were nothing original nor very good. They reflected my passions, not any talent that I had or any great effort that I made. They were taken almost word-for-word from short books I had read on the subject. In my defense, I did not know what plagiarism was at the time. I was writing a grade five project. I wrote about weasels and turtles, who were the wild animals I could get closest to during my weekend expeditions to the neighbourhood stream and swamp. Weasels fascinated me then and still do—particularly the least weasel (yes, that's its name, kind of insulting, like lesser apes!) that we saw at a leash-free park a few years ago, and the ferrets that we see in the local pet store. As for turtles, well, my best writing about them came at age 11 when I wrote of a female midland painted turtle in my diary. Watching that turtle lay her eggs was for me a rare and spectacular event. Staring at the spot in later days, wishfully envisioning baby turtles digging their way out, didn't make them hatch. I did not know enough about reptile reproduction at the time to understand that the eggs would never hatch, as she lacked a mate.

After writing the second grade-five project, I added a note to my teacher saying that I wanted to write books about animals in the future. My teacher was impressed, if possibly in a bemused way. He wrote that my goal was "admirable" or some other such teacherly encouraging adjective. I wouldn't have thought at the time it would take so long to reach my goal. But a dream delayed is still a dream come true.

In 1985, a quarter-century later, I had obtained a job working on contract for the Wildlife Branch of the Ontario Ministry of Natural Resources. The Wildlife Branch had a responsibility to provide teachable material on wildlife for children in grades four to six. It was a useful means of teaching students about biology. There was a new wildlife program, called Project Wild, developed in the western states, that was being introduced into the province. Workshops were held for people wanting to use the program in class or run workshops on their own. Once trained, I got to travel around the province training others—lots of fun. I also finally got to write about animals—even more fun.

My first task was to write the text for a poster on winter birds of Ontario, a project I dearly loved. I began to develop a style of mixing science with humour (one museum biologist referred to my writing as "corny," which I took as a compliment) in these pieces. One was on starlings, a bird almost universally ignored or disliked. Even then, I was writing about the underdog (or the "underbird") in a positive way. Here is the first paragraph:

> The starling is a good example of an immigrant success story. Not many years after fewer than 100 birds were released in New York's Central Park in 1890, they were successfully competing with native species of birds across the continent. The key to their success is their adaptabil-

ity, their capacity to learn to live in a broad variety of habitats. (Steckley 1986, in Ontario Ministry of Natural Resources, Poster 3423)

Reading *Arne the Darling Starling*, by Margarete Sigi Corbo and Diane Marie Barras (1983) 30 years later, was a joy for me, and vindicated Plutarch's inclusion of starlings among the spokesbirds for animals.

My first animal book came out in 2015: *Gibbons: The Invisible Apes* (Rock's Mills Press). The idea for it arose from a textbook that I wrote on physical anthropology. As part of my research, I wanted to get to know gibbons better, and decided after meeting my first two that a book should come out of it. Experiencing a long-held dream come true made me want to experience it again, so here we are.

Parallel Lives: Mammals and Birds

I have long been interested in animal biology, as you can readily see. The job described above was really one meant for a biologist. I talked my way into it because of my lifelong interest in animals, my extensive reading of Stephen Jay Gould's essays, and my ability to spin words, even in interviews. For a course that I taught in physical anthropology (I am now retired) I talked a lot about animal biology, most notably about primates, human and non-human. I am confident in saying my textbook on the subject has more references to parrots than any other physical anthropology textbook, and perhaps any textbook on any subject. A picture and description of Louis, our rose-crowned conure, is featured in a section on "What is a species?" He is very photogenic and easy to write about, as you will see in the next chapter.

Only recently, however, did I come up with what to me is a new idea about the "parallel lives" of birds and mammals. Like many others, I thought of birds in terms of the Great Chain of Being, that traditional (and flawed) notion originating with the ancient Greeks that places pond scum at the bottom of the heap and humans at the top (to oversimplify). That positions birds one step below mammals, closer to reptiles than we are. But after living with parrots over these last few years I have come to rethink my ideas.

Now I think of birds as parallel to mammals, cousins with the same grandparents—the aforementioned reptiles—whose differences from us are in some ways less significant than our similarities. Birds are, like us, endotherms, or warm-blooded. Reptiles are cold-blooded, or exothermic. Birds are good parents (unlike our reptile grandparents, who laid eggs and abandoned them to their fate), and, like mammals, form strong attachments to both their mates and their young. Parrots, the corvids (crows, jays, magpies, ravens, rooks and some others), gulls, hawks and other species rank high on the bird intelligence scale, as we do for mammals. Their brain-to-body ratio, a key measure of intelligence, is said to be equal to that of the great apes and whales. That says a lot—and so do they. True, mourning doves don't seem to think much, but on the mammal side there are rabbits and muskrats, not to mention those humans who think that whales are fish, gorillas are monkeys and that sasquatch is for real. In an earlier draft of this book, I wrote that "mice and sparrows seem pretty much equal to me on this parallel scale." Since then, however, I've read Chris Chester's brilliant *Providence of a Sparrow: Lessons from a Life Gone to the Birds* (2004), which caused me to raise my estimate of the intelligence of the common English (or house) sparrow.

Author's Perspective:
Anthropomorphism, Anthropodenial and Critical Anthropomorphism

There have historically been two extremes of writing about animals, both of them inaccurate in their own way. One is known as anthropomorphism, which involves the projection of human abilities, emotions and behaviours onto non-human animals without providing any scientific proof. It is meant as a sharp criticism, coming from old-time scientists, usually male. Anthropomorphism is implied when scientists use phrases such as "only anecdotal evidence."

There are many examples of anthropomorphism, from talking animals in movies and television commercials (especially those whose mouths move like human mouths) to people talking about their animals in ways that make a late-comer to a conversation think it's a human under discussion. For instance, when I first observed Honey, a white-handed gibbon who lived in a small rehabilitation zoo in southern Ontario, I thought for a brief moment that she "looked lonely" because she was alone in her compound, something I had never seen before. But after a few seconds, I watched her and her neighbour, a green monkey, walk over to the compound's mesh wall and preen each other. I'd call my first impression a misread on my part.

The opposite extreme, mechanomorphism, suggests that animals can only be understood in terms of genetically programmed actions and automatic responses to rewards and punishments—that everything animals do is instinctive, not learned or creative. Primate specialist Frans de Waal criticizes this viewpoint as being an example of anthropodenial, which he defined as "a blindness to the humanlike characteristics of others animals, or the animal-like characteristics of ourselves" (de Waal 1997:51).

Let's take the example of jealousy. I believe that anyone who denies the existence of this purportedly "human" emotion in other animals needs to observe carefully interactions between humans and their pets. Lime, our yellow-headed Amazon, sometimes exhibits jealousy when she sees another of our parrots getting attention from me or perching on my shoulder. She has demonstrated her jealousy by flying directly at the shoulder with the other bird on it, causing the other bird to fly away. I don't see that as a genetically programmed reaction.

I believe that there is a middle road between the two inaccurate extremes: critical anthropomorphism. This involves accepting that humans and non-humans share abilities, emotions and behaviours, but doing so with a keen, critical, scientific eye. Jane Goodall did this when she demonstrated that a troop of chimpanzees made tools, using hammer and anvil rocks to crack particularly hard nuts. Goodall showed that juveniles learned how to make tools by watching older chimpanzees, and also observed other chimpanzee troops that hadn't made the same discovery. Tool use by Stanee, our green-cheeked conure, provides another good example of critical anthropomorphism that I discuss in chapter two.

Parrot Books

I do not generally like books about parrots, or material about parrots on websites. There are a number of reasons for my dislike. One is that the books tend to take a "how-to" approach, particularly focusing on how to make parrots stop biting. More useful advice in this regard would be entitled "How to stop doing dumb things that predictably make your parrot bite you, you fool." Another reason is this. Writers about parrots (particularly their own parrots) tend to measure their pet's intelligence purely by its ability to talk and to do tricks. Those are the things people ask me about when they hear that I have parrots. I do not believe that a pet's capacity to do things that we want it to do should be the sole yardstick for intelligence. Perhaps I am biased in this as I do not like to do what other people (particularly college administrators and politicians) want me to do. Compliance isn't intelligence. Close observation of birds solving problems they have encountered in "natural" (as opposed to experimentally contrived) settings provides the best measure of their intelligence. As communication with humans is one aspect of parrots' lives, then their words—as well as their other modes of communication, their utterances that are *not* words—are one (but only one) reflection of their intelligence. Parrots devise their own meaningful communication sounds for their humans. It's up to us to learn what meaning they intend to assign to those utterances.

In Joanna Burger's *The Parrot Who Owns Me*, which I highly recommend, we see how her long experience with parrots converted her from being a behaviorist (as she was taught in school to be) to someone who saw beyond animals' reactions to rewards and punishments to perceive an independent intelligence and human-like set of emotions. Part of my dislike for "how-to" books comes from my long-held criticism of behaviorism as a viable psychological tool for understanding humans (or, for that matter, the rats and pigeons behaviorists initially studied). More humanistic forms of psychology give individuals more credit for individual action or agency. More "avianistic" (to coin a term) ways of studying parrots teach us more than behaviorism can.

As an anthropologist, I put more faith in field studies about primates than I do in lab studies. I feel the same way when it comes to studying parrots. Our aviary is not a laboratory; it is the "natural" habitat for our flock. We don't conduct experiments on them; we try to understand them, just as they try to understand us. We confuse each other sometimes. But we also have increased our ability to understand what the other is trying to say.

Does Your Parrot Talk?

As soon as people find out that I live with parrots, they almost always ask, "Do your parrots talk?" I dislike that question because it demonstrates our society's lack of understanding of parrots. My usual answer is "They do, but we are still learning how to understand them."

There are better answers, but they are longer. Take, for example, the words of Polynesia (called that no doubt because the name begins with "Poly"), the female African grey who taught Dr. John Dolittle in Hugh Lofting's classic *The Story of Doctor Dolittle*. Polynesia began her linguistic tutelage of Dr. Dolittle in the following way:

POLYNESIA

> "Did you know that that animals can talk?"
>
> "I knew that parrots can talk," said the Doctor.
>
> "Oh, we parrots can talk in two languages—people's language," said Polynesia proudly. "If I say 'Polly wants a cracker,' you understand me. But hear this: '*Ka-ka oi-ee, fee-fee?*'"
>
> "Good gracious!" cried the Doctor. "What does that mean?"
>
> "That means 'is the porridge hot yet' in bird language." (Lofting 1988: 11)

Another good answer comes from Chris Chester, in his aforementioned book about B, his house sparrow. Although we have had sparrows at our bird feeders for years, I only just learned that sparrows are good imitators. Along with many other types of birds, they learn to sing and chirp in their regional dialect of sparrow. And they have been scientifically demonstrated to be able to copy the sounds or calls of other species of birds (the scientific term for that is "allospecific calls") (see Pepperberg 1999:17 and 23). When you read this, I hope you say to yourself, "If a sparrow can do this much, imagine what a parrot can do!" This is not meant as a putdown of sparrows.

> As B matured and became personally interested in my behavior, his clucking grew more complex, developing into a muttered stream-of-consciousness commentary he sometimes carried on with himself when I'm inattentive to his agenda or when he's busy with something new, puzzling, or that he finds objectionable. . . . I've read different estimates on the number of vocalizations house sparrows are capable of producing, with the high end ranging between fifteen and twenty. I'd say one hun-

dred or more is closer to the mark, many of them with specific meanings I've been able to decipher—'please,' 'thank you,' 'don't move,' 'come back,' to name a few. (Chester 2004:61)

While I think he might be overestimating a bit, I still believe that he is right about there being more than just 15 or 20 vocalizations.

Yet another answer comes from one of my heroes, Aldo Leopold, master conservationist. I recently discovered that he wrote about parrots. I shouldn't have been surprised. The article was entitled "The Thick-Billed Parrot in Chihuahua" (1937). He was writing about the *Rhychopsitta pachyrhynch*, known by the local Mexicans as *guacamaja*, the only indigenous North American parrot except for the now extinct Carolina parakeet. Leopold composed the following passage, writing after he had his breakfast and the birds had theirs:

> . . . as you begin the steep ascent out of the canyon, some sharp-eyed parrot, perhaps a mile away, espies this strange creature puffing up the trail where only deer or lion, bear or turkey are licensed to travel. Breakfast is forgotten. With a whoop and a shout the whole gang is awing and coming at you. As they circle overhead *you wish fervently for a parrot dictionary*. Are they demanding what-the-devil business have you in these parts? Or are they, like an avian chamber- of-commerce, merely making sure you appreciate the glories of their home town, its weather, its citizens, and its glorious future as compared with any and all other times and places whatsoever? It might be either or both. And there flashes through your mind the sad premonition of what will happen when the road is built and this riotous reception committee first greets the tourist-with-a-gun. (Leopold 1937:9; emphasis mine)

The "sad premonition" proved prophetic. The thick-billed parrot is now an endangered species, presumed hunted-out in Arizona. Parrots respond to a wounded or dying flock member by staying close by, making themselves easy targets. This is probably one major reason why the Carolina parakeet became extinct so quickly.

I won't so much be presenting a parrot dictionary here in this book as a short phrasebook for each bird. Sam's schmecking noise has two meanings: "I like the taste of that" and "I want another Cheerio." The second meaning is emphasized by the relatively rapid repeating of the sound, perhaps accompanied by a short, shrill whistle of insistence: "I want another Cheerio, NOW."

Lime's two-tone whistle is a call of welcome, a question asking where I am, a contact call (to use the technical term) and an answer to a request for such a response. Her hello-ho-ho is different from her regular "hello" in that her feathers are fluffed and her eyes, too, show emotion. This happens when she has escaped from the aviary and is in the high-hanging bin of big spoons, when

I come in from getting the mail, when I surprise her by coming to the aviary when she doesn't expect me to, and when she has flown to the bin of spoons from my shoulder (and my office) for a second or third time. I suspect it is a hello of uncertainty or surprise.

Gus has a chirp that tells me that there was something wrong with the timing of my putting him in his cage at night (for example, when he is put into his cage earlier than he thinks is appropriate). Louis has a cry for help uttered when he is wet from a bath, has hit the floor because he can't fly in such a state, and he needs a lift from Angie or me. Tikkifinn's soft muttering with head movements left and right indicate (I think) that she is happy that I am talking to her.

Now the expected (sort-of) answer to the just-as-expected question. Six out of nine of our birds do "talk human," some more than others. As for the two who don't: the cockatiel does not speak English, but he can whistle a conversation with the best of them, and has many ways of communicating to me what he is feeling. I am proud to say that I don't usually get it wrong. But I am still making mistakes and learning. Stanee, the alpha female of the flock, like many a conure has a trill that tells you she is happy. Sometimes I will go a long time without hearing it, but when I do, I expect her to fly to my shoulder, and suspect that she will preen the back of my head. I've never heard her speak a human word. She doesn't need to for her to communicate with me.

Before we end this section, I have to address one more related issue. Parrots don't parrot. (I once thought that that would be a good title for the book.) By that I mean that they do not mindlessly mimic what they hear. This was proved conclusively by Irene Pepperberg's work with Alex and other African greys. Parrots may use words that their owners teach them, but those words may well have a context and a meaning for the parrots that we have to learn to comprehend. Further, they can sometimes demonstrate that they understand context and general meaning much in the way that we do when learning a language. In volume 3 of his *Parrots in Captivity*, W. T. Greene, unfortunately equating intelligence with use of human speech, gave two examples. The second might be more rumour than fact, but it is a good story:

> Do Parrots ever talk intelligently? That is to say, do they ever make intelligent use of their acquired vocabulary? We think so. Thus our lamented Goffin [a species of cockatoo] never screamed for "Potato" except when he spied that esculent [vegetable fit to be eaten] upon the table; and it was certainly something like intelligence that prompted another talented bird to say, "Serve him right!' when his mistress . . . asked: 'Oh, Polly, why did you bite my boy?' for the urchin had been teasing the poor bird unmercifully and had got not more than his deserts, when 'Polly' suddenly nipped and drew blood from the offending finger." (Green 1884c:viii)

I agree with the parrot. It did serve the boy right.

In his epic *King Solomon's Ring*, Konrad Lorenz recorded the following story:

> The well-known Berlin ornithologist, Colonel von Lukanus, ... possessed a grey parrot which became famous through a feat of memory. Von Lukanus kept ... a tame hoopoe named 'Höpfchen.' The parrot, which could talk well, soon mastered this word. Hoopoes unfortunately do not live long in captivity, though grey parrots do; so, after a time 'Höpfchen' went the way of all flesh and the parrot appeared to have forgotten his name, at any rate, he did not say it any more. Nine years later, Colonel von Lukanus acquired another hoopoe and, as the parrot set eyes on him for the first time, he said at once, and then repeatedly, 'Höpfchen'... 'Höpchen'..." (Lorenz 1952:101)

Here is a simple example of a parrot's expansion of the original meaning of a human phrase. Sam, our Senegal rescue, says "good night." He almost exclusively says it only at night. He typically says it when I am in the process of putting the birds to cage (what I call "beddy bird time"). He may say it when he steps up on the stick. (I don't dare offer him my finger.) However, he is most likely to say it right after I have put him on the perch in his cage on which he sleeps. One evening (I describe it in detail later) we had a fight. His biting and my bleeding were involved. I was very angry with him and I showed it. Once he was put in his cage, he repeatedly said "good night" to me, and I answered back just as often. He did so more than ten times, which was not typical at all; in fact, that experience has yet to be repeated. I feel that he was making sure that we were still connected as friends. It might be a bit of a stretch to call it an apology, but it is hard to tell. He is also known to say "good night" when I am staying late in the aviary. Once he said it right after the usual time that he goes to his cage. I think he was hinting that he wanted to go to sleep, and wanted me and the lights out. Intelligent, big-brained animals need their sleep. And they are not afraid who knows it. (In keeping with that thought, 'good night' sometimes is heard when the light is turned on early in the morning, too.)

Being Pooped On

For parrot owners, having someone shit on you is not just a metaphor, it is a frequent—in my case daily—occurrence. This idea seemed disgusting when we got our first parrot. The only other time a bird had pooped on me was while I was sitting under a tree reading around about the first time I dropped out of graduate school. It was a good metaphor for my state of mind and career at that time.

Don't let this potential fecal downfall discourage you from having a parrot as a pet. You get used to it awfully quickly. You do learn to check your hair and clothing before you leave your home for the great world outside. With the little birds, such as Juno, our parrotlet, and even Louis, our rose-crowned conure, I don't even notice being pooped on when it happens. Here is an example. I was going to a job interview. Earlier that day Louis had been on my arm. I noticed, before walking into the interview room, that I had Louis poop on my shoulder. Fortunately, I was early, so I could rush to the bathroom (fitting given what I was doing and why) and clean it off. It had been well over an hour since I had left the house.

Now, I do notice when the poop perpetrator is Lime, our Amazon, because it is warm and runny (sorry about writing that), but other than rushing for paper towels (an important parrot accessory) to clean it off with, I soon forget the experience. My final words on the subject for prospective parrot owners are, simply: Don't worry about it. You'll get used to it. It's kind of like changing baby diapers, although the thought of that grosses me out.

Parrots Are Not Dogs

In Norwegian mystery writer Karin Fossum's *Black Seconds*, a pet-store owner tells a detective that "People don't realize how difficult parrots are to handle. When they get them home they're disappointed when they discover they can't take the bird out of the cage and stroke it." (Fossum 2002:143)

Well, in time you may be able to, but it takes a lot of work and patience.

One of the first lessons the new parrot owner needs to learn is that parrots are *not* dogs. Having had dogs almost half of my life, it took me a while to learn that basic fact. I like the way that Joanna Burger expresses this important distinction in *The Parrot Who Owns Me*:

> Your average parrot is not your average dog. Dogs have been bred to seek approval from just about anybody. Not parrots. You must go slow. Trust must be earned. Parrots want to make their own friends at their own speed; pushing them provokes fear or aggression. They have quick, wicked tempers. In the wild, I've watched them happily preen, strung out along a branch; suddenly one bird will lunge at another for no apparent reason. (Burger 2002:39)

Putting this in my own particular (peculiar) way, here are 13 ways in which dogs and parrots are different:

1. Your parrot is more likely to bite you that your dog is. You need to learn to watch for warning signs. There are also locations where they do not wish to be disturbed.

2. Dogs are generally much more forgiving than parrots are (at least they forgive faster). But when a parrot forgives you it is a powerful and memorable experience to be truly enjoyed.

3. It is usually easier to pet a dog than to pet a parrot. But when you are able

to pet a parrot without being bitten, it is a wonderful gift. And some parrots cuddle (e.g., umbrella cockatoos).

4. Your parrot can sit on your shoulder or head, your dog can't or shouldn't. It's just wrong.

5. A parrot will never crowd you out of your bed. A flock of parrots (or even one bird) will crowd you if you are eating something. I hardly ever eat in the aviary anymore, except breakfast, a meal in which Cheerios are shared.

6. Dogs can be housebroken (even some dachshunds). Toilet-trained parrots are an urban legend. Don't believe it.

7. You can take a dog for a walk, but you can only take a parrot for a lift (on your shoulder or head).

8. Parrots will literally walk all over you. Dogs will only metaphorically walk all over you.

9. A parrot can laugh at your jokes. A dog will only give you a look.

10. Dogs shed. Parrots present you with gifts of feathers (and down).

11. Dogs usually try hard to please you. Parrots usually try hard to make you please them.

12. Punish a dog and it usually asks to be forgiven. Punish a parrot and it will punish you back.

13. A dog is much more likely to do tricks on command for an audience than a parrot is. Big parrots know that if they scream at you, they will get the attention they want without having to do any tricks..

But birds are also like dogs in a number of ways. They bond readily, and are good companions when they do. They are intelligent, and, as social animals, they are good at reading human body language and moods. Both make provide good therapy for humans.

Believe it or not, parrots also share some traits with cats:

1. They can be fussy about what they eat. This seems to be especially true when pellets that are recommended by veterinarians are offered to them. A purely sunflower seed diet is bad for parrots, but they won't thank you for offering them pellets that are not sunflowers.

2. They like to knock things over and watch them fall. This is especially the case when those things make a loud noise when they crash to the floor.

3. They can be sneaky.

4. They can be aloof.

5. They can take a long time to forgive.

6. They know how to entertain themselves, but often need good toys to do so

7. They can be bored. Which brings us to our next topic—

Parrots and Cages

She's only a bird in a gilded cage,
A beautiful sight to see.

You may think she's happy and free from care.
She's not, though she seems to be.
—Arthur J. Lamb and Harry Von Tilzer, "Only a Bird in a Gilded Cage" (1900)

I imagine that many new new parrot owners recall this refrain before they purchase their first bird.

My analogy is this. Imagine you are on a flight across the world. You are wedged into your seat because you took the cheapest flight possible. You have no companions to talk to. You don't have anything to read, watch, or listen to. And you're not particularly tired. That is the day-to-day life of a parrot who lives without parrot company, is never permitted to leave his or her cage, has no interesting toys in the cage, and who interacts little with his or her owner. Just imagine it!

Parrots are not decorations. They are intelligent social animals who need the same mental stimulation as humans. Parrots, like humans are easily bored. Boredom is one of the leading causes of parrots plucking themselves until major patches of skin are left with no feathers to cover them. Humans in the same situation might drink to excess or deliberately cut themselves.

It is good for parrots to have parrot company and also lots of interaction with their humans. Lime, our female yellow-headed Amazon, is getting the latter right now, as she is perched on my bald head preening herself. Periodically, I reach up and give her a scritch. Both of us are enjoying the experience.

Think of all the interactive toys that new human parents who can afford them (both the babies *and* the toys) surround their babies with. It is necessary stimulation. Children who have been raised in institutions (orphanages and the like) have much less chance of receiving the stimulation that a healthy human intellect needs—and suffer for it.

Sam, our rescue Senegal, demonstrated to us the harm that an unstimulating environment can do to a parrot. Sam was severely socially and emotionally abused when we got him, something he will never completely shake. He spent days we can't number alone in a cage that held only him, water and sunflower seeds. The room was usually dark. There were many birds trapped in the room with him, but the possibility of interaction with them was low. He didn't pluck himself, but he carries with him irrational fears that he will never be rid of. And he is a fear-biter.

Currently we have nine parrots. We do not recommend such a large number to the faint of heart who don't like doing a lot of cleaning every day. They are a flock, and engage in a lot of social interaction with each other (some of it negative, such as tail-pulling). No one is completely left out. Even the outliers, Lime the Amazon and Gus the cockatiel, have bonded with each other. All the birds enjoy time both in and out of the cage every day. Our eldest son divided our former living room in half: aviary and living room. Seven out of the nine parrots spend most of their day in the aviary, outside of their cages. Quigley, a Quaker parrot, is different from the others in that he is quite cage-territorial, and spends more time in his cage than any of the birds. The eighth bird is our parrotlet, Juno, who is in his cage outside of the aviary most of the day. We are afraid that if he were in the aviary, he might be injured by one of the much bigger birds, although we have recently been leaving him in there for up to an hour, with no negative results. But Juno gets serious shoulder time with both Angie and I, and spends a good deal of time admiring the open cutlery drawer (for reasons that we don't pretend to understand). The ninth bird is the intensely human-social Poccopeck, who similarly admires our two glass plates in the cupboard.

First Fictional Experiences with Parrots

Although as a child I was not filled with the desire to own a parrot, and I never brought a wounded bird home, birds were still part of my life as a child. The two that come to mind are the fictional parrots Kiki and Captain Flint.

Kiki appeared in the children's adventure children's stories written by British author Enid Blyton from 1944 to 1955, books I devoured as a child. The "Fabulous Five" children who were the heroes of the eight novels included Jack, who possessed a very talkative, attitude-laden parrot, the aforementioned Kiki. She was the first one to speak in the first novel, *Island of Adventure*. I well remember her comments: "Shut the door, idiot," "Wipe your feet," "Where are your manners?" and "Where is your handkerchief?"—the dictatorial words of the adults responsible for Jack and the others. I cannot remember whether the books ever said what species Kiki was, but from the volume of her utterances, the fact she had a crest on the top of her head, and because she was red and gray, I suspect that she was a gang-gang cockatoo (*Callocephalon fimbriatum*). And it was in those books that I was also introduced to puffins—not parrots but close, at least in terms of appearance.

Another fictional parrot I encountered early in life was Captain Flint, the bird owned by the dreaded pirate Long John Silver (an early hero of mine) in the Robert Louis Stevenson novel *Treasure Island*. Like Kiki, and despite the name, Captain Flint (named after Long John's former captain) was female. She uttered such stereotypical pirate lines as "pieces of eight," "shiver me timbers" and "walk the plank." Long John Silver claimed that she was about 200 years old, and had been the companion bird of a number of famed captains before him. Again, there is no mention of species, but illustrations I have seen, plus the fact she was a pirate parrot, makes me believe that she was an Amazon. (That was certainly the case in the classic 1950 Disney movie.) She got the last word in at the novel's close: "Pieces of eight, pieces of eight." I like to think of Lime, our yellow-headed Amazon, as Captain Flint, which makes me Long John Silver. As I write this, I am thinking of teaching her to say "pieces of eight, pieces of eight." But I would have to say it with deep emotion for her to feel it

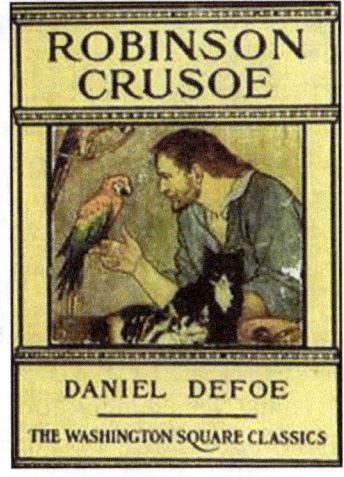

FICTIONAL PARROTS:
Top, N.C. Wyeth illustration from 1911 edition of *Treasure Island*; right, cover of early twentieth-century edition of *Robinson Crusoe*.

would be worth learning, as you'll see in a later chapter.

We know that there is an association in contemporary minds of pirates and parrots, and not just because the two words sound a lot alike. —And not just because, since 1979, the mascot of the Pittsburgh Pirates baseball team has been the "Pirate Parrot." English pirates of the seventeenth century did have parrots on board, but these were more a commodity than a companion. The wealthy in seventeenth century England paid good money for parrots.

Stevenson said that he got the idea for the companion parrot from Daniel Defoe's *The Life and Adventures of Robinson Crusoe*, first published in 1719. In the almost 300 years since *Robinson Crusoe* was published, numerous editions have featured a parrot on the cover, usually looking like some species of macaw. In the book Crusoe captures a young parrot by knocking it down with a stick, taking "some years" before he teaches it to speak. The parrot learns how to call Crusoe by name, and how to loudly say his own name, "Poll." At one point in the story Crusoe is asleep, to be awakened by the words, "Robin, Robin, Robin Crusoe: poor Robin Crusoe! Where are you, Robin Crusoe? Where are you? Where have you been?" It was Poll.

Later in the novel, Crusoe acquired other parrots, and actually, horrifically, shot and ate one to show "his man" Friday how a gun worked. But when he left (in 1686 in the story) he took one parrot with him. I assume it was Poll.

In case you are wondering whether *Robinson Crusoe* provides the earliest association between the name Poll and parrots, it does not. In Ben Jonson's *Epigrams*, published in 1616, we find the following two references, although their meaning is hard for me to pin down accurately. First, in the epigram entitled "Inviting a Friend to Supper," Jonson speaks about what they will and will not have, and declares: "And we will have no Pooly, or Parrot by." I can't say whether the denied parrot was not to be eaten, or not to be a guest! Then, in a short epigram entitled "On Court-Parrat," Jonson curiously wrote: "To pluck down mine, / Poll sets up me wits still, / Still, 'tis his luck / to praise me 'gainst his will." Perhaps Jonson had taught the parrot something positive to say about him, something the bird might not have believed. And is pluck used sarcastically?

There are a number of theories about the connection between the name "Poll(y)" and parrots. My belief is that it comes from the term "poll," meaning head (as in the bird name "redpoll," a type of finch). As parrots' heads are larger relative to their bodies than those of most birds, and because particularly big-headed parrots such as African Greys were among the first that English speakers encountered, this explanation makes sense to me.

First Non-Fictional Parrots

The first real parrot I ever met—and for a long time the only one—was my great aunt Nell's budgie "Richard." Perhaps it would be more appropriate to say her *budgies* "Richard." For as long as I knew her, Aunt Nell had a bird called

Richard. There was a series of them—I have no idea how many or when she got the first. Now, there was most probably a story here that I and my sisters would have loved to have known. Aunt Nell never married. She was a nurse for most of her life, and one of a generation of Canadian women whose lives were affected by a shortage of men in the population in the years after the First World War because of the high number of deaths in battle and in the Spanish flu epidemic that broke out near the end of the war. She was one of a group of great aunts of mine who were intelligent, educated women who never married, but were loved by generations to come, the children and grandchildren of their siblings. We thought of Aunt Nell as the nicest woman in the world. We would liked to have asked her why she named every bird Richard, but that seemed rude. Was there a soldier she cared for who died in the war? We will never know. But if so, some man's loss was a gain for her budgies and her great-nephews and nieces. If we ever have a budgie, we will name it Richard (even if it's a female).

The second parrot I got to know in person, and the first that my wife Angie and I got to know together, was Koko, a male yellow-headed Amazon. We would go into the pet store where he lived to buy food for our dogs and cats, and were enthralled by this big beautiful bird. From watching and interacting with him we moved on to observing the other parrots in the store, the ones that were for sale. He was the bait, and we were the unwary fish entranced by the flashy green and yellow lure. It was from him that I learned how to read the moods of Lime, our future yellow-headed Amazon, a very important skill set if you are going to have a parrot, especially a large one with a big beak. If the tail flares out like a geisha's fan, the head feathers rise up, and the pupils dilate, you had better watch out. Koko was the first parrot to bite me. But no pain, no learning gain.

I still visit Koko when we go to that pet store. The first thing I do after entering is to walk over to his cage. If there is no flare of the tail and no rise of the crest, I open the cage up, and we greet each other with a shake of a talon and a finger. He walks over to get closer to me, sometimes anticipating the finger-and-talon shake by extending his left talon. I lean forward to get closer to him. It is a mutual connection.

He did bite me once: hard. He had been moved out of his comfort spot, his cage, and was walking around on top of a cage in the back of the pet store, rather than his usual position in the front by the window. It was my foolishness, not his fault. The next time we met he was back in his cage, and we greeted each other with our usual friendship finger-talon shake. I always look forward to seeing him, and like to think that he feels the same way.

And now on to the birds who have come into our home and our hearts. I am the narrator, but they are the ones who are really telling the stories.

Chapter Two
Conures

Introduction

I am sitting in the aviary watching a hockey game. Two small parrots, both conures, fly over to land on me. One lands on my head, the other on my back just beneath my neck. Both start moving their beaks and tongues up and down on my skin, having an almost instant calming effect on me. The trill uttered by the one on my back enhances that effect. Neither one speaks human, but they really don't have to. I understand some of their many communications. The one on the top of my head is Louis; the one on my back is Stanee. I don't even have to look at them to know who they are. The different ways their flights sound, where they landed and the way they preen me tell me all I need to know to identify them.

What is a Conure?

Conure is a name that not all bird-specialist biologists or ornithologists have an easy time with. For it has changed meaning over the years and it rivals parakeet (see the next chapter) as an imprecise term for small- to medium-sized parrots. The name comes from two words in ancient Greek, *kōnos* meaning 'cone' and *oura* meaning 'tail'. "Cone tail" describes their short body and long tail structure pretty well. They were originally native to South America, but now are typically born and raised in North America, as they are a very popular bird among aviculturists (people who raise birds) and parrot owners.

There are two speciose genera (that is, genera bearing many species) of conure: *Pyrrhura* and *Aratinga*. All three conures discussed in this chapter belong to *Pyrrhura*. The term comes from two Greek roots, *pyrr* for 'fire' (as in 'pyromaniac') and *oura*, again for tail (also in the Greek-based word 'squirrel'). Pyrrhura, then, are "fire tails." By their all red tails you shall know them.

Green-Cheeked Conures

Green-cheeked conures are called *Pyrrhura molinae*, and are sometimes known as Molina's conure. The species label comes from the name of Chilean-born Jesuit Father Juan Ignacio Molina (1740–1829). When his religious order was expelled from Chile, he fled to Italy, where he became a professor of natural science. Like many a Jesuit, he was a gifted scholar and writer, and published the first book on the natural history of the plants and animals of Chile in 1782. He also gave several species of birds their scientific names.

Green-cheeked conures are pretty much the default birds in pet stores in Canada. Most of the stores we have been in that sell parrots have a least one of the species for sale. And almost all these birds seem to be fascinated with human fingernails, at least in my experience interacting with them in stores. But being common does not make them any less special than other species of parrots. The same applies to budgies, even though I have never really gotten to know one, not even Aunt Nell's Richards. And it certainly doesn't apply to cockatiels either. The price isn't the social value of the bird.

One of my favourite features of green-cheeked conures is their trill. You know that a conure is nearby when you hear that sound. It seems to me to be a conure's version of a cat's purr. You know they are feeling happy, and if you are like me, you know that they are making you feel happy.

Then there is the light-coloured circle that surrounds their eyes, their eye-rings (technically called the periophthalmic ring). Conures and their larger cousins the macaws have this feature. With our Stanee and Louis, this ring is white, as it is in a number of conure species. It makes them look like they are wearing glasses, or have chosen a very pale shade of heavy makeup. It certainly draws attention to their eyes.

CLASSIFICATION OF GREEN-CHEEKED CONURES

Order	Psittaciformes (i.e., parrots)
Superfamily	Psittacoidae
Family	Psittacidae
Subfamily	Arinae
Tribe	Arini
Genus	Pyrrhura
Species	Molinae

Shoulder Bird Experience and Benji, Our First Bird

Before talking about Benji, I want to share with you Chris Chester's beautiful description of the shoulder bird experience. In his case it was B, his house sparrow:

> After staring at me for a minute, B flew from the bookcase to my shoulder and has, in a manner of speaking, never really left it. I can

close my eyes or stare into space and relive the surprise and delight of an instant when the order of things reversed and a bird flew to me instead of away. Since that day, I've tried without success to explain the significance of that moment in a way that makes sense to those of my friends who view this whole "bird thing" as proof I'm delusional. It's easy enough to find words and phrases: "Profound experience, life-altering even, magical, charming, sublime, intense, unforgettable, amazing, truly amazing, incredibly amazing, so amazing I couldn't believe it, amazing when I think about it…." (Chester 2004:59)

I get it. And Benji was the first bird to present the gift of that feeling to me. He was my first shoulder bird. He was also the first parrot we brought home. He was a colourful yellow-sided variant of the green-cheeked conure. His bright spirit glowed like his feathers. When I first saw him, I was charmed by his practice of putting his talons on the side of his face, a gesture of contentment and happiness. I had never seen it before, but that was probably at least in part because I hadn't observed parrots very carefully before. Whenever I see it now, I cannot help but think of Benji. I call it a Benji scritch. No matter how many times I see it, it will always remind me of him.

We lost him after only three days of having him at home. We were still in a period of excitement of having our first parrot at home. He was killed by our high-prey-drive border collie, Egwene. The conflicting feelings I had were difficult to cope with. Egwene was a very close animal companion. It was like having a sister kill a brother. We buried Benji in the backyard in a spot I sometimes visit. He will never leave my heart, nor his spirit my shoulder.

The birds had a small measure of revenge a few months later. Lime, our Amazon, was learning to fly, and quite often hit the floor when trying to do so. Egwene was stalking the newly floor-crashing bird when she was attacked by three little birds that pecked furiously at her head, two conures and a Quaker. Egwene retreated.

I wrote a poem about Benji that I cannot find. All that I can remember about it is saying that, after losing Benji, it was the first time in my life that my right shoulder was a lonely place. The shoulder loneliness persisted for a while, as our next two birds were not, at that time, what I would call shoulder birds, though years later both would become such. Quigley, our next bird, was learning to climb and to fly when we first acquired him—that was his priority in his first days and weeks with us, not sitting still on my shoulder. Our second bird, Stanee, was developing the aloofness that we still often see. She definitely would not have made a good pirate's companion, unless he needed some tough-love mothering. She has over-preened the top of our Senegal Sam's head (his top head feathers approach baldness), and it hurts sometimes when she preens my face. But if you want your nails done, if you desire what I call a 'pet-acure', she's your bird.

Louis (to whom you will be introduced more formally later on in this chapter) was the first to take back my right shoulder as a place where a friend liked to stay. Louis did a lot in helping me cope with the loss of Benji. I will always miss our first parrot. My shoulders will always bear the light weight of his soul.

Today as I write this, Louis has done me and my shoulder a great favour. He had just taken a bath, and got so soaked that he could not achieve liftoff from the floor. Sam was bullying him into the corner because Sam is at his most ruthless on the ground. (My toes have borne witness to that on a number of occasions.) I heard Louis giving off his complaint/distress call, so I rushed over to him, and lifted him up to the central cage/feeding station. About 10 minutes later I heard it again, more frantic this time. Sam had cornered him on the floor where the aviary mesh meets the window. I got Louis to step up, and took him with me to my office. He stayed there on my shoulder for over half-an-hour, longer than he had ever done so outside the aviary. During his first few minutes in my office, he did not signal to the others, something he usually does when he is outside the aviary. He stood fairly still except for some shakes to dry himself off. He even preened me a bit, something he only occasionally does when he is outside the aviary. Shoulder birds don't get any better than Louis. But I would have to wait for that experience.

Early Days with Stanee
STANEE ENTERS OUR HOUSEHOLD

We had known her by the name "Stan" at the pet store where we got Benji and Quigley (the Quaker Parrot featured in the next chapter). The people at the pet store thought that she was a male. And we did too. Perhaps it was because Stanee is such a tough bird, and they feared her somewhat. It was only after we got to know her, particularly her broodiness at various times and her close relationships with male birds, that we figured out her true gender. She can be one tough parrot. That is not an uncommon feature of green-cheeked conures. On one website we read that "Green-cheeked conures are also known for being gutsy. Some owners have witnessed them fearlessly taunting larger pet-birds in the house…" (see, for example, www.birdchannel.com/bird-species/profiles/green-cheeked-conure-2.aspx).

One sign of Stanee's green-cheeked conure gutsiness is the way that she bullies Lime, our Amazon, who is much bigger than her. When she does so, she is not just being a flock mother (which she is), but a kind of police officer too. Sometimes she drives Lime away when she feels that Lime is threatening Angie or Stanee's inner flock (made up of her, Louis, Sam and sometimes Tikkifinn), but occasionally she will drive Lime from place to place in a clear show of dominance: mother, police officer, and boss. One night she, Sam and Tikkifinn were all in Sam and Stanee's cage. There seemed to be no problem with the arrangement. But I was putting the birds into their cages for the night and needed to get Tikkifinn out of the cage. I used a stick for her to step up upon, but she was resisting. Stanee watched this for a few seconds and then decided that she was duty-bound to enforce the rules. She drove Tikkifinn out of the cage with a short flight and a sharp sound. I don't think that I have ever read the word "alpha" used with respect to parrots, but she is definitely the alpha female in our flock, the alpha bird. She has taught me a lot about how attitude can overcome size and force. Stanee has big attitude. Don't let her slender build, small size and soft trill fool you.

Stanee Steps Up: One Giant Step for a Bird

We had known Stanee for about six months before we bought her. To me she was the "other conure," the one that was not Benji. She was the sour to the Benji sweet, the tough to Benji's soft. Angie had told me that Stanee was nice, but I thought she was just being kind. Angie is often quicker than I am in seeing the good in humans and in other animals. She often sees the positives in people I see as negative. Stanee was the last remaining of the five parrots at the pet store we had known and come to have a relationship with: Benji of sweet and sad memory, Quigley of current craziness, Gump, always the "other" Quaker parrot but a good one, and Squeaky, the beautiful Rosella whom we had seen turn from more humble crimson shades to her eventual startlingly bright red, and who occasionally would charm us with her singing (the cause for us calling her Squeaky). She was tempting, but she was not quite for us. I can't say why that was.

But Stanee was the one that no pet store staff member or customer (except for Angie) took to. This was because of her biting. Stanee, like almost every other green-cheeked conure I have ever met, likes to bite fingernails. The woman who had bought Squeaky had approached Stanee first, but when Stanee bit her, the woman moved up (literally given cage position) to the more obviously gentle (and more dramatically coloured) bird. Stanee then had to compete for adoption with the baby Amazons, Lime and Kiwi—with their newly won trust, since we had been involved with their feeding (as human perches), their slow-moving, bowing-strangely formal politeness, and their general baby bird charm.

But the relationship between Stanee and her future owners was about to change. The last two times we had gone to the store together to see her, she didn't seem to be biting so much. I noticed that she partially closed her eyes when she bit my fingernails. A new idea struck me. Was that eye-closing a mark of pleasure in contact between us rather than the aggressive move I had previously thought it was? Perhaps she was just relating to me the only way she knew how. She was definitely excited to see us when we appeared in front of her cage. I remember that when she was behind a glass wall (because of a bird theft that had recently taken place), she would try her hardest to tell us where she was. I ignored her to go to Lime, while Angie would call to her. Stanee responded by moving quickly about her cage so that she would be hard not to see. She got my attention as well.

The last time we had seen Stanee before the day of the epic change in the relationship between man and bird, I had put my thumb and forefinger around her beak and stroked it. She was inside and I was outside the cage. I do that now with Sam, our bite-prone Senegal. Stanee seemed to like that then (though not often since). And she started softly working on my fingernails, as Benji and Quigley did, a good sign of affection as I was beginning to learn.

Now, for the first time ever with Stanee, I put my right hand into her cage. She didn't attack it as I thought she would. She put one talon on my finger and went for my fingernails as usual, but softly, softly. It gave me confidence that she was beginning to accept me. Sometimes she would bite, and yes, it hurt a bit, but the intent to hurt seemed not to be there. I wasn't going to give up on her.

I persisted. I kept saying "step up," not a command that always worked, even with Quigley. Then Stanee stepped up. I couldn't believe it. Those who have not experienced parrots do not know the glorious feeling you get when a bird first steps up on your finger, a tremendous statement of trust and affection. It is similar to when I used to feed chickadees with sunflower seeds in open hands in the wooded area behind Humber College in northwest Toronto, but so much more as it is very personal, not just an attempt to get food. When a parrot steps up onto your finger, you have earned the trust of an intelligent and social animal. A gift has been presented to you. Treat it with the thankfulness that such a gift deserves.

I took Stanee out of the cage and stroked her head. Her heart was beating fast, driving rhythms of fear and excitement throughout her small feathered body. If I could have felt my own heart, it might have been doing the human equivalent. I walked with her, as I had once walked with Benji, and showed off our mutual accomplishment to the people in the store. Stanee and I both earned this together.

I brought her back, and Angie repeated this conure/human ritual of step up. Stanee complied. Both of us were near tears. I wonder if parrots can cry. I suspect that Stanee would be too tough for tears.

There was another part to the story that I did not know at the time. The day before, Angie had said to Stanee, "If you want to come home with us, you will have to be nice to the man with the big beard." Stanee seems to have followed Angie's instructions to the letter, or at least to the talons. She certainly had been nice to the man with the big beard. She continues to be, years later.

Bringing Stanee into Our House

When we only had Quigley, he was kept in a cage on a shelf high up on one of the walls of Angie's office. When we brought Stanee into our house for the first time, we thought that it would be best to keep the two birds in separate rooms for a while. The theory was that this would allow them to slowly get used to each other's presence without confrontation. That is what we were told to do by the people in the pet store.

We brought Stanee into the bedroom, the room next to Angie's office. Quigley made an inquiring sound and Stanee quickly responded. Then there were multiple communications sent back and forth between the two. I'll bet that if we had some kind of parrot translating device we would have heard phrases such as "So, you're here too" and "I know you." We should have realized that the two already knew each other fairly well through being neighbours in the pet store. The two cages were put into Angie's office. They wouldn't have it any other way.

Parrot Tools: A Sign of Avian Intelligence

Early anthropologists used to say, with typical scientific human arrogance, that humans were the only animals that used tools. It was even used as a kind of non-genetic marker of the genus Homo, starting off with *Homo habilis* (or "handy man"), separating it from the supposedly tool-less Australopithecines. We (my first two degrees are in anthropology) do not look at things that way any longer. Starting with Jane Goodall's classic study of chimpanzees, with their stick specially prepared for putting into a termite hill and pulling out a kind of termite-kabob, and continuing on to the cracking of especially hard oil-palm nuts with anvil and hammer stones, she demonstrated to us that chimpanzees definitely make and use tools. Studies of other primates, especially bonobos (which used to be called pygmy chimps), orangutans and gorillas have followed suit.

What about birds? There are intriguing videos of New Caledonia crows being very ingenious with tools in experiments set up to show their intelligence. Corvids (the family of birds that includes crows) are smart and loud. That's I think why our parrots love them. They can speak in ways that parrots like. The blue jays are especial favourites of theirs, as the indoor and the outdoor birds speak back and forth to each other.

Now, can parrots use tools? The answer is an easy "yes." For instance, Lambert et al. (2015) studied New Zealand ground parrots breaking seashells with stones to obtain calcium, which is necessary for laying eggs with strong shells. And parrots have a distinct advantage in tool use, as mentioned in the first chapter, with their zygodactyl feet—they have two forward and two backward facing toes—instead of the usual bird pattern of three toes forward and one backward.

My favourite example of parrot tool use comes not surprisingly from Stanee. Parrot owners know that a quick way to a parrot's heart is a scritch on the back of the neck. Parrots love it, and when humans are permitted to scritch them in this way, it is great to see the favoured parrot fluff up its head and neck feathers like a baby bird. Juno, Lime, Louis, Quigley, Poccopeck, and on rare occasions Sam allow me to do that, and both human and bird get a lot out of it. Benji and

Louis both did and do the side-scritch "selfie" when I do that. And, of course, it is what mates and preening buddies do for each other. But what about parrots that have no preening buddies or mates, and who don't quite trust their humans enough for that kind of intimate contact? What do they do for back-of-the-neck scritch?

Stanee developed her own answer to that question. Stanee from the very beginning loved straws. She still does. She will play with them while the other birds ignore them. In the first weeks that we had her, she could often be seen playing with straws, familiarizing herself with them. Then one day she turned a straw into a tool. I walked into the old parrot room and there she was with a straw in her right talon, scratching the back of her neck. While she and Quigley were close, they weren't close enough for mutual preening. She only did this a few times in my sight. I wish now that I had gotten Angie to take a picture of her doing this.

In Joanna Burger's *The Parrot Who Owns Me*, she had a similar experience with her red-lored Amazon Tiko (the lore is the area between the nostrils and the eyes). He would first test feathers for their strength and length, and then scritch the back of his neck with the most appropriate one. In both cases the birds did not actually construct the tool, as primates do. They chose objects that they had become familiar with that could do the job. I sometimes do that too, when I have a fix-it problem and go to my toolbox. It must be a problem that can be fixed with a hammer, saw, screwdriver or wrench.

Stanee's straw scritching did not last long. Shortly afterwards we got Louis, and he would preen her, so she didn't need the straw any more. Still, she was a tool-choosing and tool-using parrot.

Hers is not the only example within our flock. Not long afterward we got Lime, our Amazon. She learned to eat yogurt with a spoon and rice with a fork. But, of course, she had seen us eat that way, and we handed her the spoon and the fork to do her eating. This is perhaps not quite the feat that Stanee's straw-scritching is, but it still shows intelligence and tool use. Lime does have the advantage of large talons, so she can manipulate larger objects than Stanee can. Lime still occasionally eats yogurt that way. And many mornings she gets a spoonful of peanut butter. It helps to keep her from shrieking, at least for a little while.Since initially writing these last few paragraphs, I have seen several videos on the Internet of green-cheeked conures scratching the back of their necks with corn cobs. As that is their choice, not part of some human-set test, I tend to think of this as a good indication of just how smart green cheeks are. I hope they never get access to power tools. Parrots are destructive enough as it is.

And for a good example of parrot tool use there is the building of nests out of sticks. But that topic is to be saved for the Quaker chapter coming up next.

Will Stanee Stay on My Shoulder?

One weekend early in our at-home relationship with Stanee, I was spending a lot of time reading about Birute Galdikas and orangutans, part of the research necessary for my physical anthropology textbook. I loved her close connection with the big apes. I kept worrying about Stanee not wanting to stay on my shoulder, and whether we would ever have a closer connection. She would fly off after a few seconds on my hand or scamper to the back of the cage and put her head down for a compromise scritch. She no longer does that. I tried to convince myself that she liked that scritch, but I was not sure whether or not that was self-deception on my part. Then, I walked into the room with my thick bush jacket on and saw her on the perch. Somehow, I thought that she was Quigley, and put my arm out for a step up. She stepped up and then stayed on my arm, then my shoulder for several minutes. I don't know why. Maybe the distance created by the thick cloth made it feel safer for her.

Stanee was much closer to Angie at this time. She would fly to Angie and land on her head. She would even sometimes land on one of Angie's shoulders, the same shoulder as Quigley, but she would not even fly to me.

Stanee often flies to my shoulder now when other birds do it first, particularly Louis and Sam, the two main men in her life. But sometimes, when I am cleaning up the cages, she will fly onto my back. For a while I think it is Louis, but soon learn that it is her. I am beginning to expect it.

Infants bond like parrots. I think of our niece Eva and her "stranger stage" during her first year. We had been close, then she cried whenever I approached her close up. I competed with one of her aunts to see which one of us would get a positive response first. It was a similar frustration to some of the early months with our green cheek, but Stanee is worth the effort, just as Eva was and continues to be.

One Day Months Later

This morning I had another Benji moment. And comparison exaggerates it. He never hesitated to step up to my hand and sit on my shoulder—Stanee almost never steps up onto my hand. Benji frequently trilled, and—you guessed it—Stanee almost never did.

The three days' honeymoon with Benji is an unfair comparison for any bird. Even Quigley, whose feisty ways have fought their way into the fortress of my heart (like the alliteration?), sometimes suffers in comparison. He sometimes doesn't step up, and often bites. It is like comparing a first love (Benji was the first parrot in my heart), forever young, with no long life experience to sully comparisons, with a long-term, real-life spouse.

Patience serves me well; patience and new moments that cannot be compared. Feeding Stanee apple slices was a path to our bonding. She even trilled a few times before grabbing a slice with her beak. One slice for Stanee, one for Daddy, and then one for Quigley. We are both, actually all three of us, happy in the experience.

That evening, I went to Stanee with some papaya in my hand. She stood on my hand and ate it and harassed my ring finger for about four minutes. Little things mean a lot.

Stanee's Voice

Although Stanee "doesn't talk" in the speaking-English sense, she communicates very well in parrot. The first sound I ever heard her make, and this was when we first had her at home, was a trill. A conure trill is a sound of great beauty. I can remember her being on the window sill in Angie's room and trilling in happiness at the sunny day outside. None of our other birds makes a sound anything like a Stanee full trill. She doesn't use it much now, but it is all the more appreciated for its rarity.

Along with Louis (to be formally introduced shortly), she can do the "conure alarm" fairly well when she is acting out her role as sentinel. This alarm has often warned us that there is a cat in the front yard. She has also used it when something big and strange enters the aviary, like a vacuum cleaner, a new mop or broom, or my crutches, when I was forced by a ruptured Achilles tendon to walk on them for three months. The crutches disturbed her a lot. It was hard to get her to step up when I approached her to take her to her cage at night, but then that was true of the other birds as well. She has a number of soft sounds that she uses, like the one she made once when she was stuck in Sam's bucket (a story I tell in a later chapter) and found it difficult to get out. She doesn't often call for help.

And she has another sound too, a complaining sound. Like the trill, it is unique to conures in my experience, although I don't think that I have ever heard Louis make this sound. He complains in a different way. She complained twice tonight. The first time, she was on my right shoulder, Sam was on my right leg. Son Sam was probably the main reason why mother Stanee flew over to me. Quigley was on my left leg. Quigley flew over and got between Stanee and Sam, and between Stanee and the preening of the right side of my head that she was doing. She made her complaint-sound; a disgruntled grunt, you might call it, though it is a series of repeated sounds, like her trill. The second time was my fault. I brought in a small round plate with cooked frozen corn niblets on it. She flew toward it, then Tikkifinn did. I held it for a while as they both chowed down. Then I went to put it on the low table. Unfortunately, in so doing I accidently dumped Stanee onto the table. Her complaint was heard. Message received, girl. I won't do that again.

Early Interaction within Our Two Parrot-Flock

After trial runs (or flights) in which she flew on top of Quigley's cage and got attacked like an umpire by an irate baseball manager, not to mention having her toes severely threatened, Stanee then flew *into* Quigley's cage. I wasn't there to see it, but I could hear harsh words in parrot uttered by Quigley. He is good at getting his feelings across. Stanee apparently huddled in a corner, uncharacteristically cowering, until she was removed.

Later Quigley returned the favour. He went inside Stanee's cage, ate her food and drank her water, and, although it wasn't reported, I bet that a well-placed poop would not have been considered inappropriate.

Later than same day, while I was there, Stanee flew into Quigley's cage again and instantly went deep inside. It took me several tries before I could get her out. I guess that the cage on the other side of the room tempted her into a lapse of memory. The seeds are always tastier on the other side.

Stanee wasn't very forceful in her first few months with Quigley. Typical of the time was the following incident. Quigley climbed into her cage. Then Stanee got on the top of his cage and watched Quigley as he ate Stanee's food and rang Stanee's bell. Then Quigley went up on the top of the cage to challenge Stanee. Stanee did not force him back or away as she would in later years. She simply made her way back into her cage. She wouldn't be that passive now.

Mother Parrot

As other parrots entered our flock Stanee took on the role of the mother parrot to the newcomers. I believe that she was a sexually mature adult when we brought her home. To our knowledge, she had been in the pet store for a least a year or two. Her first child was Louis, whom we used to call our "special needs parrot" before we got Sam, who has a lot more special needs. When we first got Louis, he couldn't land well because of some condition of his legs, so he was always breaking his flight feathers when he crash-landed. He used to do this quite often, his determination trumping his poor skill set. Stanee was there in a parrot's heartbeat, on the floor whenever and wherever he crashed.

I can still tell purely by sound that it is Louis flying, even years later, because there is a lower pitch to the sound of his flying, as though he can't get his wings to flap fast enough, and certainly not as fast as the others do. When we first got him, he used to hang from his talons on a suspended rope and flap his wings as quickly as he could. He built up his flying ability that way. I wonder how much he was aware of what he was doing with his flying practice sessions. He may have been clumsy at first, but he certainly was never stupid.

We initially interpreted Stanee's interaction with Louis as her being a good, protective mate. Now we think it is because she has assumed the role of mother parrot to the flock. When we acquired Misha (or he acquired us)—he was a Meyer's parrot, and we renamed him from the pet store's somewhat obvious "Mike"—his wings had been clipped not long before so that he could coast well, but still landed on the floor when he flew. Whenever he did that, there was Stanee there in a red-tailed flash, making sure he was not there alone.

When we first got Tika, our first cockatiel, she could helicopter in place for a short while, but had insufficient lift to do more than land softly. Initially Stanee

MOTHER PARROT:
Left, Stanee;
below, Stanee and
Finn together.

played mother yet again, not just in accompanying our novice pilot to the floor, but in protecting Tika from the others, and making sure we knew where her new child was. One day I left Tika on top of our Amazon's cage while I got some fruit for the flock. When I returned to the parrot room, I could not find Tika. I could hear her cockatiel sounds, but could not see her. My next move was to look for Stanee. She was on the back of the couch, a place she didn't often visit. Down below her was Tika. I knew that the mother parrot would be close by, taking care of one of the members of her diverse brood.

I have learned from instances such as this to use Stanee as a guide to where another parrot might be hidden away. I watch where she looks when I utter another bird's name, usually Sam, as he is the bird who hides away or gets lost the most often. I also watch where she flies and sometimes where she looks. That has helped me find the "lost" parrot on more than one occasion.

A Mother's Tough Love

Sam was safely secluded in his hut. It is hard plastic, charcoal-gray in colour, and it has the vertical grooves of a tree stump. It is one of his favourite hideaway places. Stanee thought that he should end his seclusion and be out in the open with the others, so she squirmed her way into the hut, went to the back, turned around and proceeded to push him out, evicting him from the hut. "You need to get out more, son." Sam made no attempt at childish rebellion. Stanee's mission was accomplished.

Early in 2015 I saw Sam go over to her and poke his beak near her face, asking for a regurgitation breakfast. She side-kicked him, gently but forcefully, with the message clear. She did that two or three times to be sure he knew what she was saying. When the message was received, he flew away. Even a good mother needs to assert her independence sometimes.

A Mother's Warning

Another part of Stanee's maternal role is issuing warning sounds. She will shout warnings to the others, and to the humans nearby, that there is a cat in the front yard. She did so today. She kept issuing the warning, but I (foolishly) thought that she was just being a noisemaker. Even when I told her to shush, she kept at it. So I looked out into the front yard, and, sure enough, there was a big fluffy cat lurking the underbrush. Job well done, girl. After so many instances like this, I should trust her word.

I have read that what she is doing is called "sentinel behaviour," and that it is something the conures of the *Pyrrhura* genus are known to engage in.

Stanee and Laying Eggs

It is a few years now since Stanee took on her role as mother parrot to Sam. She takes it seriously, as the near baldness on Sam's head-feathers would attest. I am glad to see that he now preens her as well. What I find interesting—the biologist in me is most fascinated by this—is that she has never laid eggs, yet she certainly is of age to do so. Green cheeks reach sexual maturity at two. Rose-crowned conures do as well, as Louis demonstrates periodically as he has sex with a wreath. We have had Stanee for over six years. When she was younger, she would get broody periodically, at which time she would get more aggressive in her interactions with us, more prone to biting. She would also hide away in dark places. Once it was in the deep pocket of a coat that was hanging in the living room (before the aviary was constructed). Another time it was a drawer.

Once we "lost" Stanee for a little more than a day. We were very concerned, but could not bring to mind a moment when she could have escaped out the door to the outside world, or the one to the kitchen. Then I saw the top of a pillow in the living room move. At first I thought that I was imagining it, but when I saw it a second time, I knew neither my eyes nor my brain were fooling me. I called Angie. We went over to the pillow and pulled off the cover. Stanee burst out into flight. As a member of a prey species, she is hard-wired to be quiet when it is dark. You never know when a nocturnal predator might strike, even inside a 1950s-era bungalow in a small town in southern Ontario.

And now back to her role as mother parrot. She still has never laid any eggs, and no longer gets broody-moody as she did when she was younger, before Sam showed up on the scene. My hypothesis is that she believes that she has a child that she has to take care of—Sam, of course—and that this somehow has affected her hormones, preventing her from laying eggs. Now, if I were to do an experiment (which I would never do—I am curious but not uncaring), I would remove Sam from the room for a month and see whether she would lay any eggs. I suspect she would. But she would be really secretive and grumpy before she did.

And if she did lay eggs would they be fertile? She and Louis used to have loud sex. Louis is enthusiastic in all things, and does sex like he does running around under a newspaper, with all the energy he has. I can't remember whether that stopped when Sam showed up, I just know that it hasn't happened in years, to my knowledge. Now, as a rose-crowned conure he is a *Pyrrhura rhodocephala* ('red-head'), and as a green-cheeked conure she is a *Pyrrhura molinae*, so both are of the same genus. To my way of thinking they could produce fertile eggs, just as *Canis lupis* (wolves) and *Canus latrans* (coyotes) can produce fertile young, which are now sometimes referred to as the eastern coyote or "coy-wolves," and in the scientific literature are sometimes referred to as *Canis latrans var* (i.e., a sub-species or "race" of coyote). So, if Sam ever stops being Stanee's child, she may actually lay fertile eggs. But I don't know whether either will ever take place.

A Big Fight

Yesterday both Stanee and I "lost it." I was taking Lime to her cage as Amber, a neighbour girl who is helping us now with the parrots, cleaned the aviary.

Stanee waged a full scale attack on Lime, going at her over and over again in Lime's cage. I yelled at Stanee with an intensity and volume that I had never used with her before. Stanee had never been that aggressive with Lime. Never before had I been that angry with our female conure.

That night, I went into the aviary to watch the hockey game. Stanee flew immediately to my right shoulder and stayed there for a longer-than-usual time. I left twice to wash some dishes. Both times Stanee flew to my shoulder. To show her that I forgave her, I repeatedly gave her my left thumbnail to pry. When I put her in her cage, she did not give me the little bite that she sometimes does when she steps up.

The next morning a bigger surprise was in order. I took Lime from the cage first, and put her up high on an aviary wall perch. I then went to the cage shared by Stanee and Sam, holding a slice of apple out for Sam to get a taste of morning. Stanee invariably comes out and drives Lime from her perch. This morning she didn't. Later, when I came back in to eat my cereal, Stanee did not make any moves toward Lime. Unfortunately, the next day things were back to normal. Stanee drove Lime off her perch as soon as she left her cage.

A few days later I learned that I was wrong to blame Stanee. She was taking the lead from my own anger with Lime, taking my side and protecting me (in her mind). I yelled at Lime for screeching (I am aware of the irony here) and put her in her cage. Stanee followed her in, and attacked Lime. The fault was clearly mine. Sorry, Stanee. Sorry, Lime.

Now I take care that even if I am angry with Lime when I take her to her cage to stop her screeching, I do so with what I hope looks like calm to Stanee. Several times, she has perceived my anger and in her role as police officer of the flock, she feels she needs to punish the offender.

The Relationship with Stanee Continues to Grow

Despite a few altercations such as this, the relationship that Stanee and I share is certainly changing. She now often is the first bird to fly to my shoulder when I enter the aviary. She was never really a shoulder bird for me before. Her preening skills are still a little rough for my tender human skin. Perhaps she has a hard time transitioning from preening feathers to preening skin (nose and cheek). I am pretty sure that she is not deliberately inflicting pain. I enjoy it when she is perched on the back of the chair and preens the back of my head. It is probably done with the same amount of force, but the surface is tougher there, long hair and skull. It can't be pinched. Fingernail prying is still her favourite contact game with me.

I feel that she wants more of my company than before. One night, as I was getting ready to change the water dishes, she flew to the back of my left shoulder and started preening the back of my head. What added a particularly special touch was the fact that she trilled when she was doing it, at least for the first three preens. I hope to experience that more often in the future. A relationship with a parrot never stays the same. That is not true just with Stanee but with all of the birds. It is one of the aspects in which they are unique pets, in my experience. For me, when you form a close relationship with a dog or cat it stays basically the same.

During the next two days Stanee did the same thing. She flew, sometimes along with Louis, sometimes on her own to the back of my neck, preening me and trilling. I have the feeling we are getting closer. She attacked Lime when I was taking her to her cage. I feel that there might be some jealousy here together with that growing closeness. My birdie girls are never boring....

Louis: The Rose-Crowned Conure

Louis is a textbook star, with a picture in a textbook that I wrote, *Introduction to Physical Anthropology* (Steckley 2011). He's right there on page 83, in the right top corner. I was discussing the notion of taxonomy, and how in some senses you can look at birds as reptiles. (Our Sam often reminds me of a T. Rex, and not just in appearance.) Louis' classification is as follows, using what is called a cladistic system of taxonomy:

DOMAIN:	*Eukarya* [i.e., His cells have nuclei.]
KINGDOM:	*Animalia* [i.e., He is an animal, rather than a plant.]
PHYLUM:	*Chordata* [i.e., He has a backbone.]
CLASS:	*Sauropsidia* [i.e., He has a lizard as an ancestor]
SUBCLASS:	*Neornithes* [i.e., He is a bird.]
SUPERORDER:	*Neognathae* [i.e., He can fly.]
ORDER:	*Psittaciformes* [i.e., He is a parrot.]
FAMILY:	*Psittacidae* [i.e., He is more closely related to all our other birds than he is to his buddy Gus, our cockatiel.]
SUBFAMILY:	*Psittacinae* or Neotropical [i.e., He is not a member of the same subfamily as Sam the Senegal from Africa, who is an *Arinae* or Afrotropical bird.]
TRIBE:	*Arini* [i.e., He is not a member of the same tribe as Lime the Amazon, whose heritage is Central, not South American.]
GENUS:	*Pyrrhura* [i.e., He is not a member of the same genus as the Quakers and Juno the Parrotlet.]
SPECIES:	*rhodocephala* [i.e., He has a red head and is of a different species from Stanee who has and is a green cheek.]

My favourite name for rose-crowned conures is the French one: *conure tete-de-feu* ("conure head of fire"). Louis is often fired up with enthusiasm: for food, for preening and for running underneath papers. The name suits him to a tail.

Being Stanee's Sidekick

When we first got Louis, he was a needy boy. He needed a lot of contact, whether it was a few sheets of newspaper placed on top of him so he could run around emitting strange sounds of joy, or whether it was preening. He loves to be preened. When he flies onto my head when I am in the aviary reading or watching sports, I can preen him for great lengths of time, and he returns the favour.

His neediness might relate to the fact that he is physically flawed. He was slow to learn to fly, and when he tried to land he would crash. His legs are malformed, perhaps, at least in part, because when the pet store people tried to pick him up, he resisted and his legs got unnaturally stretched out. He still, years later, is not a great flier. As I mentioned earlier, I can always tell that he is the one flying towards me, even when I can't see him. The low pitch of his flapping and its rather non-rhythmical beat (like a helicopter with one blade a little bent) gives him away. As you read in the first chapter, he also has serious problems flying while wet.

For the first few months that we had him, he often sidled up to Stanee in an obvious move to be preened by her. She had an interesting response when she felt that he was being too pushy and too needy early in their relationship. She gave him a side-kick with a talon that would make a karate *sensei* proud. And it worked quite efficiently with both Louis and Quigley, and, as we have seen, with son Sam as well. She may be a green cheek, but I think that she is also a black-belt karate parrot. Don't mess with Stanee. She has more weapons than your average parrot. I haven't seen the side-kick for a while. Perhaps the birdie boys have learned to be more careful.

Louis is still big on contact. That is probably one of the main reasons why he has more friends than any other parrot we have. He preens Stanee, Tikkifinn, Poccopeck, and sometimes Gus, and is preened by all three of them (I discuss preening in detail in the final chapter). When I am in the aviary, watching hockey, baseball or football, or just reading, he is the bird most likely to fly to me. I preen him and he preens the top of my head. Put me in the list of his preening friends and fans.

Preened by Louis

I don't meditate. The lack of motion would drive me crazy. I don't relax easily. Usually it takes intense activity before I will slow down. I was a head-banger as a child. As a teenager and well into my twenties, I used to run miles every day when I first got up. This is why being preened by Louis is such a different experience for me. Usually he stands on my head and preens, with tongue and beak, the border areas of baldness and hair, like a deer in a field by the woods. But sometimes, some nights when he stands on my right shoulder when I am reading in the aviary, he will preen around my right eye. I hate having things near my eyes. I could never wear contacts, and the idea of laser surgery horrifies me. But Louis, when he preens around my eye, his left eye close to mine with its conure-distinctive black circled with white, I encourage and very much am relaxed by his touch and presence. I see his big but soft curved beak as it comes within eyelash reach, but it does nothing but calm me down. If I had a heart monitor on, I know I would be able to hear my heart slow down. If I had a brain chemistry monitor on, set to make sounds when endorphins are generated, it would be shouting. Reading is one of my favourite things, but I will stop for a long eye preen. If they poured it into a glass, or rolled it up and lit it, Louis's preening would be addictive. Who knows what it could lead to?

Louis

All of our birds are therapy birds, achieving that result by very different means. But Louis has a way of calming me down that never fails to amaze me. He did so again tonight as I write this. Wired for a number of different reasons, good and bad, I sat down to watch a little Blue Jays baseball in the aviary. Louis flew to me, and for at least 20 minutes solid used his beak and tongue on my right temporal region, back and forth, lowering my tension. He knows what he is doing. It is different from a bird-on-bird preen. He must know that he is doing me good. I don't doubt his motives for a second.

Louis as a Timely Friend to the Other Birds

As stated earlier, Louis has more friends than any other parrot in the flock. He is very close to Stanee, Tikkifinn, Gus, and Poccopeck, three different species of parrot. He preens each one of them. But it is not just that he preens them, it is *when* he does it that is important to note. Here is one example. Gus, our male cockatiel, had been bullied twice off his spot on the circular perch by the window, to the left of his girlfriend Lime's bicycle-tire perch. First it was Lime who did the bullying, but this was only because she herself had been driven off the bicycle tire by Stanee and Sam. A short time later I returned him to the circular perch, as Lime had flown off to another perch. Then Stanee flew over and bullied Gus off the perch. She has never, to my knowledge mothered him, although she did with Tika, our female cockatiel. The same is true with Juno. Maybe Sam requires all her mothering attention.

Being driven off his perch, Gus had to escape to a spot on top of Quigley's cage, not a favoured destination for him, as Quigley often defends it as Quaker territory. Gus was quite visibly upset. His cockatiel crest was pointed straight up to the sky.

I didn't repeat my mistake from the first time. I put him on top of the semi-circular thick rope perch on the aviary wall, one of his favourite places, and not a location to which the others generally liked to fly. I then returned to my nightly activity of dumping out the dirty water in the water bowls, washing the bowls and refilling them. I was just about to go out the aviary door when I noticed that Louis had flown over to that perch, on a slightly higher position than Gus was on. He then proceeded to preen Gus for about a minute, a relatively long preen for the two of them.

To me, this shows that Louis has what we would call in human psychology empathy. He hadn't preened Gus at any other time that night. He had witnessed what had happened to Gus, and knew that Gus was upset. A cockatiel crest can always tell you the bird's mood. No wonder you have so many friends, Louis

Louis the Patient

Louis has a problem with his beak. His upper and lower mandibles do not meet exactly, so they do not hone each other, wear them down so that they stay the same size. So his beak becomes too long for him to eat without difficulty. We tried several means of cutting or wearing it down, but we didn't like the result. Louis didn't either. So now we take him on a one hour drive to the Companion Hospital run by the University of Guelph, which runs the veterinary college. They give him drugs and cut his beak down nicely. On the drive back, when he is still slightly stoned, he enjoys riding on Angie's shoulder and 'checking out the view.' He is very popular at the Companion Hospital. He received a Christmas card from the staff there.

We are lucky that we took him there. One time, the vets discovered that there was a lump that significantly diminished his air sacs, making breathing somewhat difficult. It turned out that he had the double problem of high cholesterol and fatty liver. We now use a needle-less syringe to inject two drugs into his mouth. Angie does the injecting, and I hold him gently. He didn't like it as first, but now he gets a pine nut every time he goes through his procedure. And, there are no longer any sunflower seeds in the diet of any of our birds.

Chapter Three
Quakers

There Is Something about a Quaker

Although we love all of our parrots, there is something special about Quaker parrots as a species. Here is one reason why. One day I was depressed. Nothing happening in my life caused it. My brain was just producing depression for no apparent reason, the same way it more often produces happiness. Contributing, perhaps, was the fact it was a foggy, rainy Monday in December. For whatever reason, the feeling was there and I had to deal with it.

Quigley, our green male Quaker parrot, helped me out of my slump. Three consecutive times when I walked into the aviary, feeling glum, Quigley flew straight to my shoulder. The first two times he soon began preening the side of my head. He doesn't often come to my shoulder. Weeks had gone by without my receiving this kind of gift from my feathered friend.

Was he seeking attention for himself? I don't think so. Angie had spent quality time with him during the day, so he wasn't starving for human affection. I believe that he sensed that I was feeling down, and he came to me to turn that around. He has empathy. Quakers are intensely social. Wait until you read about their nests. I believe that for such a species, a sense of empathy increases the chances of survival of the group and the individual members of the flock.

Angie and I have often said that Quakers are the "perfect parrot." They are affectionate. They are attracted to human laughter and can imitate it with a full belly laugh. Their ability to copy human speech and singing charms humans easily. In Brooklyn, where they fly wild and free, they have worked their magic on reputedly tough New Yorkers. There is even a parrot park there, provided for the Quakers. Tours called "safaris" are regularly run for tourists.

It should come as no surprise to you that this chapter on Quakers is the longest chapter in the entire book.

Quaker Parrots: An Introduction

Quaker parrots bear many names. Their scientific name is *Myiopsitta monachus*. They are generally believed to be the only ones of their genus. Their species name comes from a Greek (and, derived from the Greek, Latin) term meaning "solitary" or "one," the words from which the English word "monk" was derived. Perhaps the monk-like gray colour of their chests, which contrasts with the background of green, blue or yellow feathers on the rest of their body, first gave them that name, and also resulted in them sometimes being called "monk parrots" or "monk parakeets." The name certainly didn't come from their having a solitary nature, as they are intensely social birds. They even live in condominium nests , which I discuss below.

I dislike the name parakeet and never use it to refer to any of our parrots. I do so for several reasons. One, it is not really a scientific term, as it is applied to the little guys in Australia, the budgies and the cockatiels, as well as to very distantly related small to medium birds on other continents. The name crosses several genera. Secondly, it seems to diminish the birds somewhat. To me it seems to imply that they are not really parrots like the big guys (cockatoos, African greys, Amazons and macaws). They are "only" parakeets. It reminds me of another similar term I don't use—"lesser apes" to refer to gibbons. (You can read more about gibbons in my book *Gibbons: The Invisible Apes* [Rock's Mills Press, 2015]). The exact origin of the name "parakeet" is disputed, said to come from Old French, Italian or Spanish with different meanings. I suspect there is a diminutive suffix somewhere in its past.

The name "Quaker," which when I mention my birds people often assume is derived from the Christian religious sect, in fact comes from the habit of the young ones to quake when they want food. It involves a bobbing motion that even adults resort to later in life when they are excited about something. Our Tikkifinn does that when she has something important to communicate.

This quaking is very appealing to susceptible humans. On a number of occasions Angie and I have had to walk away very deliberately from quaking young ones in a pet store. Not to do so would escalate the number of parrots in our house into the double digits.

Other names for Quakers include grey-chested parakeet and Montevideo parakeet, the latter after the capital city of Uruguay, which, along with Argentina and Paraguay, is the traditional wild home of the Quaker parrot. Their French name is *perruche souris*, or "mouse parrot," no doubt because of their grey chest. This meaning is also embedded in their genus name *Myiopsitta*.

William Thomas Greene, in his 1884 book, *Parrots in Captivity*, wrote about Félix de Azara (1746–1821). Azara was a Spanish military officer who became a credible and critical naturalist, and who described the birds of Paraguay around the end of the eighteenth century. As quoted in Greene, he referred to

Quaker parrots as "Young widows, because no Parrots show such an amount of smart and coquettish ways as these." "It must be confessed, [that] is a little hard on the ladies," Greene added. But I think (human) ladies should be honoured to be compared to Quaker parrots.

Quaker parrots are very close biologically to conures. Indeed, they formerly belonged to the same genus. Perhaps this explains in part why Quakers and conures seem to get along so well in our aviary. One of the first differences you note between the two is that while conures are slim, Quakers are stocky. One explanation for the difference is the climate that each is built for. Conures are jungle birds, Quakers live in Argentina, which has moderate climate in most areas, snow in the south. They have the same basic build as the now-extinct Carolinian Parakeet, which lived in much of North America, even a little south of the Great Lakes. And there are wild flocks now in New York city, Chicago and other places not known for their warm temperatures.

The Politics of Quaker Parrots

In their wonderful book for young adult readers, *Tango in America*, Steve Baldwin and Alison Evants-Fragele refer to Quakers as "the world's most persecuted parrot." This is an accurate statement considering the way they are viewed in some American states and in European countries where wild Quakers are found (e.g., Britain and Spain). However, whether that persecution is justified is a whole other matter. I firmly believe that the so-called "danger" they pose to human society is minimal and generally exaggerated for the purposes of justifying harsh restrictions. In Florida with the largest population of wild Quakers in the United States—an estimated 100,000—they don't seem to be causing any significant problems.

There are 11 American states in which you cannot own a Quaker parrot: California, Colorado, Georgia, Hawaii, Kansas, Kentucky, New Jersey, Pennsylvania, Rhode Island, Tennessee, and Wyoming. In at least three of those states, Kentucky, New Jersey and Rhode Island, there are small wild populations. Owning Quaker parrots is permitted in Ohio, but only if they have their wings clipped. The good news is that New Hampshire changed its law in 2011, so positive change can happen.

The ownership ban is largely based on what appear to me to be ill-informed, scientifically unsubstantiated ideas, including the fear they will breeding in large numbers if they go feral and become an agricultural pest. There is also a concern that if their population does reach such high numbers, then they will out-compete local birds. Feral cats are a far greater problem for birds, but nobody has banned cats (nor should they), even though domestic and feral cats kill at estimated 200 million birds every year in North America.

Electrical companies seem to play a significant role in the banning of Quaker parrots, as nest building sometimes occurs high atop utility poles. There are strategies employed in some jurisdictions (including in the city of New York) that seem to be fairly effective in avoiding that problem. Setting up poles just for parrot nesting helps, as is sometimes done for ospreys or fish eagles.

One reason for Quakers' sometimes bad reputation is what was written about them by none other than Charles Darwin in *The Voyage of the Beagle* (1839): "A small green parrot (*Conurus murinus*) [a long discarded name for Quaker parrots], with a grey breast, appears to prefer the tall trees on the islands to any other situation for its building place. A number of nests are placed so close together as to form one great mass of sticks. These parrots always live in flocks and commit great ravages on the corn fields. I was told that near Colonia [a town in Uruguay] 2500 were killed in the course of one year."

Clearly the Quakers were then being persecuted by a growing (human) immigrant population, who did not have generations of living with the species to learn and appreciate their ways. Perhaps they scapegoated the birds for the problems they had while growing crops in unfamiliar soil and under unfamiliar weather conditions.

Over 50 years later, in a period of even greater human immigration, in *Argentine Ornithology: A Descriptive Catalogue of the Birds of the Argentine Republic*, volume 2 (1889), Phillip L. Scluler and William H. Hudson wrote about Quaker parrots' declining numbers in Buenos Aires. Though they still survived in significant numbers, young Quakers were killed by the hundreds, and some people even ate them, something which seems to me a strategy of desperation practiced by struggling immigrants. As the writers pointed out, the main food of the Quaker parrots studied was the thistle, not the crops grown in the area.

Our First Quaker Parrot: Quigley Enters Our Lives

Angie had early on developed a special feel for one of the two male Quaker parrots at the pet store when we first began to think about having a parrot in our home. We named him Quigley, after my step-mother's cat, and because the name started with the same two letters as Quaker.

When we lost Benji, I pushed for our getting Quigley that very same day. That was imposing a daunting burden on him. He had a lot of emptiness to fill. It took me longer to bond with Quigley, as I hadn't interacted with him much in the store. But he soon came to charm me with his amazing capacity to climb. I hadn't previously thought of parrots, or any other kind of birds, as agile climbers. When he finally learned to climb all the way up to the top of the cage, Angie celebrated the achievement by exclaiming "Top of the world!" (like James Cagney at the climax of the movie *White Heat*). His strutting around at the top of the cage showed that he was proud of what he was doing, and welcomed the praise. So birds can feel pride, a new thought to my evolving mammal-centric mind. We would later often see this highly visual sense of pride exhibited in his accomplishments building, and in his ability to carry sticks of significant weight and size while flying.

I remember playing the Dave Brubeck Trio for Quigley and his appreciating the sweet sounds of Paul Desmond's sax playing in "Take Five." He even imitated a few notes with his whistling. I wish I had recorded them. So much of parrots' bird brains (not an insult in my use of the term) is dedicated to sound. Strangely, Quigley did not seem to like Charlie Parker, known to his many fans as the Bird Man. A little too wild for Quigley perhaps, with his preference for the softer sounds of quiet, cool jazz, with a clearer progression of notes, easier to imitate.

Quigley's Song

But Quigley would learn to sing a song. Angie took the song "I Love You, a Bushel and a Peck" from the 1950 Broadway play, *Guys and Dolls*, and wrote a Quaker parrot version of it. The opening words of Angie's version are:

> I love you
> a wiggle and a peck
> a wiggle and a peck
> and a bite upon the neck.

Quigley picked up on the song quickly, and could sing it almost all the way through. Years later, as part of his frequent nightly ritual of laughing, saying "Good night Quigley," and singing, he still croons the first three lines. Lime, our Amazon, would learn to sing the "doodle, oodle, oodle" part at the end with great enthusiasm and volume, but not when prompted by the opening lines. It would be good if she did so to complete Quigley's beginning, but maybe that is asking too much of a parrot duo.

Quakers appear to be good with songs. One of my South American students told me about one that lived with her family who could sing "La Cucharacha." I can readily visualize the bird dance that would accompany that singing.

Laughter, by the way, is not an unusual parrot trait. Citing an article in *Bird Talk*, Betty Jean Craige (2010) wrote that "all kinds of large parrots laugh, or at least make the sound of laughter on appropriate occasions." Regarding her own bird, Cosmo, a female African grey, she believes (but is frustrated by not being able to prove scientifically) that her bird's sense of humour "depends on an intuition of the absurd" (see also Bittner 2004). She presents examples of Cosmo saying (and then laughing afterwards) "Cosmo wanna go for a walk" (rather than Craige's dogs) and "Cosmo gonna go to work" (rather than Craige, who had herself just announced that she was going to do just that). I don't think that Quigley has a sense of humour as such, but then, I haven't been looking closely for signs of such a sense.

Quigley Learns to Fly

For weeks after we brought Quigley home he combined "wouldn't" and "couldn't" in his inability to fly. He needed Angie or me to get him to step up so that we could help him get back into his cage after he had been exploring the room. He was a star climber, but, partly because of his stocky build and partly because his flight feathers were clipped when he got him, he was reluctant to fly. I don't blame him. Stanee, on the other hand, was a master pilot. She is built more for flight, with her long slim lines and extended tail feathers. This suited their relationship well. Quigley was more aggressive, but, without flight, his aggression had limitations. She could escape him if she wanted with just a flap of her wings.

We decided early on that we would let Quigley's flight feathers grow back in. There were several reasons. One was fitness. We had been told that one cause of premature parrot death was a bird being fat, unfit, with a weak heart. What could be better for a bird's fitness than flying? Certainly not parrot treadmills. Then there are those old lyrics from Oscar Hammerstein II, from "Can't Help Lovin' Dat Man" in the musical *Showboat*: "Fish gotta swim, birds gotta fly...." Flying is what birds do, and enjoy doing. I have seen our birds fly for what seems to me to be the pure joy of it. You take a lot of freedom away, but of course also eliminate a lot of complications and add a lot of control, when you clip a pet bird's wings. We just could not do it. We would lose birds because of this policy of ours, but we have never changed our minds on this subject.

I should point out that we are not extremists in this regard. In her book, Betty Jean Craige (2010) cites a passage in the May 6, 2008 issue of *Bio-Medicine* as an example of such an extreme position. It claimed that "Thousands of pet parrots are developing psychological problems as a direct result from having their God-given right to fly stripped away from them by unknowing pet owners." I would agree with Craige that parrots only have psychological problems when they are in an abusive home, or one in which they denied an intellectually stimulating and active life.

Quigley did eventually learn to fly. But he still likes to climb, and he can do so with a stick grasped firmly in his beak. He also still enjoys the praise he gets for this achievement and others.

An Early Fight between Quigley and his Human Father

Quigley and I had had a fight the night before. He attacked my hand when I put him inside the cottage cage. It was smaller than his main cage, and infrequently visited by him, although he did claim it as part of his territory. I got angry and slammed the cage door in his face (not making contact). The next night I began the long journey back to trust between us. I fed him, but he still would attack my foodless hand. By the end of the night he was on my arm, but we were both still pretty tentative about our relationship. I early on had to learn not to blame parrots for not being dogs, all forgiving, always greeting you happily. Parrots are usually glad to see you, but they are not like dogs in always demonstrating that emotion. Some days parrots can give cats a run for the aloof-pet crown. You need to develop patience when dealing with birds. It can be a lot of work, but it is well worth it.

Over the next few days, Quigley and I inched closer together in bird-human friendship, but I still didn't completely trust him when my hand came within biting range of his beak, even when he got up on my shoulder. I suspect—and this was a revelation to me—that he felt the same way. He might have been as tentative with me as I was with him. I needed to remember that.

When a Friend is in Pain

One night Quigley was in pain. He flew to me as soon as I sat down in the chair to watch baseball on television. He tucked himself into the double crook of my elbow and shoulder, not moving much. His right wing was at an odd angle. I at first thought he had injured his wing. I was wrong. It was his right talon that had been hurt. The wing was oddly angled as he was trying to keep his talon raised to avoid any extra pain from putting pressure on it. He remained in pretty much the same position for about 40 minutes, before I put him in his cage and told Angie about his condition. There were moments when he raised his head. I would then preen his head, and there were no objections from Quigley, even when I was breaking pin feathers. Head-preening was an art I was still learning, and something I had never tried with him before.

Stanee and Louis, who had been on my left shoulder and head respectively, came down to see how he was. Stanee, who hadn't, as far as I knew, preened him in years, did some top-of-the-head preening, which was as awkward as her preening often is with me. Sometimes he complained, and she seemed almost ready to fight back. Louis preened him, again awkwardly, a few times lower down the neck. To the best of my knowledge, Louis had never preened Quigley before. I certainly had never seen it happen. Louis can read both human and parrot emotions well.

I felt close to Quigley and enjoyed the act of petting him with long strokes, as I would a dog lying on my bed. I appreciated that he did not put on any show of faking that he wasn't hurt to mask vulnerability, as a tough dog or a wilder bird might have done. He was clear in what he wanted. I would have done it all night if I could have and had he permitted me. When he moved with both legs, pushing his way upwards, there was a clear limp. I felt his leg, and he didn't object, so I knew it was his talon that was giving him grief. It was hard to know who might have done it to him. There had been something of a loud squabble about half-an-hour before I went into the aviary. It had not been a sharp bite that disabled him, as there was no blood. It was more that the talon had been crushed. Angie would find the exact spot the next day.

I passed him on to Angie, who continued the care. His trust touched me, as it had once before after he had blood drawn and let me hold him. When I went to bed, I was worried about what I would see early the next day. That is a recurring theme whenever one of them is hurt or sick. I have seen three dead parrots, and each image creates horror in that imaginative mind of mine.

Quigley's Dilemma: A Parrot Love Triangle

When Quigley and Stanee were our only parrots, they were always in each other's company. We called them the terrorists because they were an amazingly destructive duo. Together one morning they brought a room-long wooden curtain-rod cover crashing down. Nothing wooden was safe from the terrible two.

Then came Louis, our rose-crowned conure. It was love at first sight for Stanee. In less than a week they became a mated pair, and from then on until Tikkifinn joined us they would share a cage. Now Tikkifinn and Louis share a cage.

Poor Quigley! Exuberant Louis took Stanee away from him. Now, she wasn't always with Louis. She still had time for Quigley, but in his opinion not enough.

Then came Finn, a female blue Quaker parrot and therefore a prospective mate for Quigley. They took a while to get to know each other. Eventually Quigley would preen her and she would sometimes—rarely—preen him.

But then came Quigley's dilemma. When there was a fight between his two girlfriends, who should he side with? Initially, he sided with Stanee. Gradually, however, he became indecisive as to where his greatest loyalties lay. He clearly didn't know exactly what to do. Sometimes he would walk back and forth squawking between them. "Why can't we all get along?"

His next response was to fight on the side of the female bird in whose territory the conflict was taking place. Quakers have a profound sense of territory. If the fight was on the long wooden perch hanging in front of the window, he sided with Stanee. That was her territory. If the fight took place on the back of the couch, Finn's territory, he was more likely to side with her. That was also the location where he often preened her. This solution lasted for a while, but unfortunately for poor Quigley, Finn never really became his mate. And Stanee preferred Louis's company.

There is one way in which Quigley, years later, still shows his undying devotion to his first love. It happens almost every night. I put the parrots into their cages in a particular order. It begins with Sam (who might already be in his cage for harassing Angie during her cleaning-up), and then Stanee. As soon as Stanee is put to cage, Quigley flies to his own cage and goes inside. She is safe now. His work is done. He does not have to silently, invisibly, protect her anymore, at least for today.

There is another interpretation of this behaviour, of course. It is at least theoretically possible that he perceives that it is beddy-bird time, so he just goes with the bird flow. I could experiment with him, of course. That is, I could start the process with other birds and see what he does. But I won't. That is too manipulative for me, something my science-mind dreams up, but my humanities-mind rejects. The fact that he usually does not begin his flight to his cage when Sam is put to cage suggests that my first interpretation is correct.

Regurgitation and First Love

It is not often that you can call regurgitation a beautiful thing, certainly not so far as the nose is concerned. But what I once saw was beautiful, no doubt about it. Quigley just regurgi-fed his first love, Stanee, three times. And she was quite willing to receive his heart-felt offerings. They were both together on the perch attached to the mesh on the door to the aviary, one of Quigley's favourite perches. After the awwwww-inspiring incident, they both flew down to the central feeding station. Quigley, filled with his success, chased Sam away from the spot. A little later Stanee flew up to the high mesh perch with Louis, and Quigley went into his cage to build. The moment was shared and then it passed. I'm glad that I was there to witness it. I have since seen it take place several times. It never fails to generate a smile.

Quaker Sounds

One of Quigley's favourite articulations, one that he uses to start a night-time series of sounds, is a full-bellied laugh. I can't really say that he learned this from either Angie or me, as neither of us quite laugh like that. And yet, when we do laugh in his presence, it triggers his more fulsome, more enthusiastic laughing. Do Quakers always exaggerate their laugh? I have read enough accounts by Quaker owners to suggest that it commonly occurs.

While Quigley continues to make this sound, there is another that he hasn't made in a long time—years, in fact. This is laughing (or making another loud sound) and amplifying it by putting his head into a cup or glass while he is doing so. That was great fun for him for a while, but not recently. But now I wonder whether there has been a glass or cup placed in the aviary recently. Perhaps absence of opportunity is a factor. This is an experiment almost worth trying.

I seem to recall that Finn did the same thing a few times. It isn't just a Quaker trick. The famous Alex, the African grey, did this too. Brains wired for sound like playing with sound.

And then there is the mumbling complaint sound made by the Quaker parrot. Quigley was the first I heard making this sound, and now Tikkifinn has picked it up. It sounds like an old man muttering about how things used to be a lot better than they are now, or, to quote George Costanza in *Seinfeld*, "like an old man returning soup in a deli." Tikkifinn engages in this when she feels that I have trespassed on her out-of-cage territory. She moves her head and whole body from side to side as she engages in this sound.

Quigley Likes to Make Things Fall

Quigley likes to make things fall. He is like a cat in that way. There's one thing he tips over just about every day. In the aviary, we have what we call the central feeding station. It is in reality an old cage on top of a stand. In the middle, there is a dog dish filled with seeds, pellets and other types of dry food. Every day we place in the feeding station a metal plate with thin apple slices on it as well as a plastic relish dish with small pieces of other fruit (e.g., banana slices, pomegranate seeds, orange slices, black berries and/or raspberries) and vegetables (e.g., peas, lima beans, corn kernels and/or broccoli sprigs). And almost every day, by late afternoon or evening, Quigley tips over the metal plate with the remaining and by then browning apple slices. It makes a loud crashing sound. I have not seen another bird do this, although initially I suspected Stanee of being the perpetrator—with no visual evidence, just dark suspicion. This is purely an act of Quigley.

Does he do this to notify us that there is nothing good left to eat on the metal dish? Is he like a dog nosing a dog dish into full sight of the dog-feeding human? Or can it be that he just likes the sound?

My first inclination was the sound hypothesis. However, this is not the only item that Quigley pushes off the top of a cage. The other articles are sticks. There are lots of small sticks in the aviary. They are there for the Quakers to play, fly and build with. During the time in the late afternoon to early evening when I change the papers in the parrots' cages, I pick up the sticks on the floor of the room and the bottoms of the cages, and put them back on top of the cages. By the time that I put the parrots to cage at night, they are all on the floor or the bottom of the cage again. Why?

Well, I know who one of the culprits is, because I have seen him. It's Quigley. But it's not just him this time. Sometimes I find sticks in the bottom of the cage where Tikkifinn and Louis share a home. As Quigley never enters that cage, I blame Tikkifinn. I have never seen Louis pick up or drop a stick, but I have observed her do both. Why do Quakers do this? Quakers are known to break small sticks off trees, letting them fall to the ground after they have done so. Is this part of that ancestral behaviour? And can that be linked to Quigley's dish dropping?

I have no hard and fast answers to these questions. I still like the sound hypothesis for the metal plate, but I'm still not sure about the sticks.

Quigley Reaches Out

Quigley and I have had an uneven relationship. Angie is his favourite, but sometimes he wants his dad. We went a long time before I could safely touch him. Sometimes he can give me a real bite. Much of our touching has involved him cleaning parrot-bite scabs (sometimes from his own bites) from my hands and arms.

I wonder whether he has a name for me in his language. There is a low sound he makes when I am in the aviary. When he makes it he tends to be in one of the positions—the top of his cage, on the perch outside, or on the roof above Stanee and Sam's cage—where he usually preens my head. He doesn't utter it when he is in one of the places he considers his territory to claim and defend. Am I projecting the idea that he is trying to say "John"? I am not sure. But I do feel that it is his name for me.

Our relationship seemed to become closer when a blood sample was taken from him. That day, I held him in my hand and stroked his back as I would a dog. He had come to me, and I made him feel safe. Increasingly, when I make my night visit to the parrots, he flies over to me, usually when Louis is on top of my head. He preens me, a little more roughly than Louis does, but I appreciate it. If I stand still when Quigley is on the slanted roof above Stanee and Sam's upper apartment of the double cage, he will preen my right eye.

One night not too long after the blood work, he came over to me and wanted to be preened. I am not sure how I knew that; perhaps it was his body language. Preen I did, stroking his back as I had been doing the last few months, but more intensely. I gave him a human version of the parrot preen. I brought my second finger and thumbs together behind his neck, scratching his neck. He baby-birded for me, the feathers around his head rising to the occasion. I had rarely done that to him before. He even made the yawn of delight and the side-scratch (Benji-scritch) of happiness. Never before had he made either of those two gestures while I was preening him. I even stroked his beak, and he did the beak-clacking gesture, pressing his beak against my palm and making the sound. I have no idea how he does that, and I have never heard another bird make that sound. It is unique to Quakers. Quigley stayed on my shoulder for about 40 minutes, longer than ever before. Our time together only ended when I had to get up to change the water. Later, when I returned from changing one water dish, he preened the area around my right eye as I stood beside the double cage.

Like a Magic Spell

There are times with Quaker parrots that are like magic spells. One day I was going to clean out Lime's cage when Stanee appeared on the left front corner. I gave her my thumbnail to pry, her favourite form of contact with me. Quigley came over as he views the left side of the top of Lime's cage as his own territory. They fought a bit. The reinforcements Louis and Tikkifinn came to support Stanee,. I put my hand to the left of him so that he could step up onto my arm. He did and I cuddled and petted him for about five minutes. He made Quaker small talk, very pleased and happy with the situation. I like to think that the time was magic for both of us. At the end, he started to make small attacking moves and I knew that the magic time had ended.

Our Finn

We were instantly charmed when we first saw her, a bird touched by the sky: a blue Quaker. There was never any question concerning whether we would bring her home. Although she never became the complete mate for Quigley we thought that she might be, she did preen him, and she learned from him how to build and how to sing "Wiggle and a Peck." She also learned the following questions and answers from Angie:

How does the doggy go? Woof, woof, woof.
How does the ducky go? Quack, quack, quack.

That became her little party piece. But instead of answering the questions, she would ask them, expecting us to give the appropriate answer. This was more difficult than it sounds, as her "doggy" and her "ducky" sounded almost identical to the human ear (well, my aging human ear). Still, it was lots of fun to play that with her. Quigley only ever gives the answer when we question him. He does a good quack.

Finn was also a great preener not only of Quigley but of her humans. She preened more softly than Quigley did, and did a more complete job of it.

I think if you had asked both Angie and I who our favourite parrot was (always an unfair question), Finn would have been our answer.

I wrote a poem about her:

Finn

Blue Bird
Across
Estimated millions of years
We share senses as if family,
Feathered cousin
And one of those relatives
Who lost her fur
A long time past,
And yet we speak
And sometimes understand
Like explorers who suddenly
Know where they are
And sometimes misunderstand
Like friends
Who are fast to forgive
And eager to return
To the body language
Of long term companions
Who can't afford the loss.

Do you love me, do you Quaker Girl?

This next section is very hard to write. I used to sing to Finn the Beach Boys song "Surfer Girl," with the words subtly changed to describe my relationship to her. When that song comes on the radio now when I am driving, I change the station as fast as I can. It hurts too much to hear it.

It was a Sunday in June, 2013. We had just come back from a visit in a nearby park with the dogs. The birds were excited that we had returned from a long absence. Finn especially was excited and had flown into the kitchen to visit with Angie. I was rushing back and forth opening and closing the door to the aviary.

Finn wanted to go back out so she tried to fly through the door just as I was shutting it. The door hit her. She bled and flopped. I picked her up, and my shirt got covered with her blood. I brought her to Angie cupped in my hand. We both were crying. As it was a Sunday night, we took her to an after-hours animal clinic, about half an hour's drive. They were kind and caring, saying they couldn't do anything, but gave us a number to call in Guelph, where there was an animal-care centre associated with the University of Guelph's veterinary school. Angie drove, I held Finn. Periodically she would move, but only spasmodically. Our hopes weren't high, but they still existed.

When we got there, once again we were met with kindness and caring. As we waited while they examined her, we spoke to each other about the unspeakable. They brought her back, a tube keeping her alive. We were told that they could keep her alive, but one of her eyes was ruined, and there were no guarantees.

We spoke the unspeakable. They injected her with a quiet death. We cried.

That night, coming back home, we tried to take some small solace in the birds we still had. But there was a huge spiritual hole in the home. I wanted to quickly go out and get another parrot, as we had when Benji, Misha and Tika had left us—not a replacement, that was impossible, but someone to fill part of the huge hole in our hearts. Unsaid was the idea that she had been the favourite of both of us. But I didn't say anything; my heart was filled with a guilt that I felt gave me no right to say what we should do.

Late that night, Angie said out loud what I had wished for but didn't dare ask, that we should get another female blue Quaker parrot.

Now, as I write this, I have a picture that Angie drew of Finn. I asked for it a week or so before she died. It shared my office at work, and now that I am retired it is behind my laptop computer at home. In a small way I still have her company, even with the massive hole in my heart and soul.

I don't usually like to look at the pictures of those I have lost, my mother and my nephew, Gordon Dias, being the sole exceptions, but I can look at this picture now not just with pain but with some sense of my good fortune in learning from this small soul.

Her ashes are in a box in the closet in our bedroom. Angie will be cremated with them.

It took three wonderful birds, Tikkifinn, Juno, and Poccopeck, to perform an unenviable and admirable job in putting charming bird substance in the hole that never can be completely filled. I have no favourite birds now. I am afraid to do that. Tika was my favourite, followed by Finn. I don't believe in curses, but I enjoy all the birds now as equally as I can manage. Stanee certainly is benefitting from that (as am I from her). I still can't bear to hear the song

"Surfer Girl." Maybe I never will.

Just a little phrase sometimes reminds me of Finn. One night we didn't have any peanuts to give Sam and Lime, who expect that after they are put to cage, so I gave them some Nutri-Berries, which are known in this house as "baubles." I asked Lime whether she wanted a bauble. It put me in mind of Finn repeatedly saying "a bauble" when one was being offered. The thought shot straight to my heart, and it hurt.

Tikkifinn

She came into our lives with a big role to play, in a way as Quigley had to do when we lost Benji. There was, however, the big difference that we already knew and liked Quigley before we took him home with us. Tikkifinn was an unknown, similar to but different from someone we loved.

That morning Angie arranged to meet with the owner of a six-month old female named Tikki, who lived about 40 minutes' drive away. I don't want to say it was love at first sight, because we didn't know the blue bird yet, and she evoked painful memories. But we were certainly charmed when we first saw her. When we opened the cage door, she flew away into the tall-ceilinged rooms of the house. But parrots teach you patience—it's either that or deal with perpetual frustration. It was her bad landing skills that betrayed her. Landing seems to be the last flying skill to be learned by most parrots. Eventually she landed clumsily on a tall plant and Angie was able to catch her and hold her gently. I think that the blue bird then known as Tikki was a little out of breath, as I could see her chest bounding. She was afraid, and in largely unfamiliar territory. She didn't know us, and I suspected at the time that she had never bonded with a human being.

After we said that we would buy her, and gave the young woman the money, Tikki's owner walked us to the door. At no time did she demonstrate any kind of recognition of the personhood of Tikki. We both wondered how anyone could give her up so easily without even saying goodbye. Tikki appeared to have been playing the role of feathered decorative piece in a carefully controlled life. In a way, she was a lot like the tall plants that ornamented the room. I wonder how long those plants will live.

When we were driving home, Tikki filled our car with potential for future companionship and fun. That potential would soon be fulfilled. She was still scared when we put her in the carrying cage to take to the car, but she was also very curious about the new situation that surrounded her. When we were in the car, driving back home, she would often look out to see what was going on, especially when we stopped.

She made baby parrot noises that we had never heard before. I knew that a big challenge for us would be to recognize her uniqueness, and not to think of her mostly in terms of what Finn had been or done. Her making different sounds helped. And we would continue to learn of her uniqueness.

Then there was the matter of what we would call her. We had first thought to call her Finn, like my Aunt Nell with her all budgies called Richard, but that didn't seem to work. That would be putting an unfair emotional burden on her and on us. We soon tacked her previous name, Tikki, onto the name, making it similar to the name of another bird we had loved and lost and who is discussed in the chapter on cockatiels. She would be called Tikkifinn.

The first days with her are something of a blur now. We had bought her cage, and she was comfortable there. She soon would fly out of the cage to a second cage suspended by the window in the small room where Angie and I watch television and Angie operates her office. She soon learned that our human hands inside her cage were not a threat, an important lesson for a Quaker, a notably cage-aggressive species. Within a few days we could touch her on the beak, even though she would move to the back of her cage when we did so.

We played parrot-touching games with "beaks" and "toes," but the beak was always the main focus. After I touched her beak, I would lay down my finger, just in case she would step up, but no luck. A couple of years later, still no luck in that regard. She usually pushes the finger away, a gentle, 'No thanks.' But that doesn't mean that it won't ever happen.

While she was in quarantine in that room, Tikkifinn was responding not just to us, but to the parrot sounds just down the hall. I don't think that it is just our imagination that she responded most to Quigley, our male Quaker parrot. He spoke the same language and she knew it. She would listen when he spoke, and return in kind. She still does.

We could sometimes touch her on her chest, and Angie was able to cuddle her in her hand. I haven't been permitted that much yet.

A few days after Tikkifinn came home with us, we developed a game. I would go "deedle, deedle" followed by a "boop," when I touched Tikkifinn's beak. She raised her head up and pushed her head and beak forward when I did that. She soon anticipated the game with a subtle eagerness. She used her Quaker whisper-voice to copy the deedles in the game. Now it is how we often greet one another. We both look forward to it and enjoy it. She sometimes stretches up as far as she can reach (even though the stretching isn't strictly necessary). And she sometimes bobs her head up and down, a Quaker sign of joy. She is definitely participating actively.

One day I went over to deedle-deedle-boop her and she had a piece of food in her beak. She shifted it to her talon when she saw me coming so that she could play the game without losing her food. When we finished playing, she put the food back into her beak again. Smart bird, that Tikkifinn.

We still tried to teach her commands Finn had known, but with no real luck. We have to remember that she is her own bird, and not another. She puts her own verbal signature on what she says, as Finn did in learning Quigley commands. She will interact with us as she sees fit.

We had introduced her to Quigley first. We were hoping they would bond.

First time in the aviary, she was on Angie's shoulder beside Louis. She preened Louis, full preen, and he was very happy. No one had ever done this to her, but she must have seen it. Good girl. Unsurprisingly, , getting her out of the aviary was difficult

Tikkifinn and Louis spent their first day together on the same side of the aviary wall. She preened him and both were happy.

The second day with the two of them on the same side, we came home and heard the rhythmical ringing of a bell. Tikkifinn was having sex with her parrot toy, which has a bell on the end. I had heard it first thing that morning and had no idea what it was. Should I be feeling dirty at this point for being a sound voyeur?

There is some question in our minds whether Tikkifinn is a girl or a boy. Stanee does not usually get along well with other birdie-girls. But Tikkifinn and Stanee get along much better than we would have thought. We don't believe in having blood samples taken from your bird just to see what sex it is. That seems like bird abuse. We will just have to wait and see. There's no hurry. The way she fights Poccopeck, a later arrival to the flock, for Louis' attention suggests that she is a female

We had to go away for a few days after getting this far with Tikkifinn. That may be unfortunate as she still has yet to step up for either of us. She will sometimes land on the back of the chair in the parrot room where I sit when I am watching television or reading. She will only do this when Louis is on top of my head, preening my baldness with his magical beak. I have tried to make her step up from there, but she only flies away. Some nights when I put Tikkifinn and Louis in their shared cage (which used to be the cage that Louis shared with Stanee), I try to get her to step up to my finger after I have put Louis into the cage, with no positive results. I then offer her a long stick. She either steps up on it or flies off, and then into the cage door opening.

One day, maybe, a change will come.

Tikkifinn's Vigil

Quigley was showing clear signs of being ill or injured. He was breathing heavily (his beak was open and his tongue was moving) and he had his wings tucked in tight. Angie had him on her shoulder for a few hours in her office, and he made few calls in reply to the anxious calls from the aviary as to where he was. We were worried about him. When Angie put him back in his cage, she decided to shut the cage door so he would not be disturbed by the others or driven from his cage. He was in his cage for a couple of hours as we ate dinner and watched television. But he was not alone.

In the small confined space between the top of the caged-in area and the ceiling of the cage, Tikkifinn was standing (or, more accurately, crouching) vigil. When I went into the aviary to do my usual parrot inventory, I could not find Tikkifinn, until Angie suggested that I look there. And there she was, in a position that cannot have been all that comfortable, doing her version of blue Quaker whisper-speak. The way that I see it, she was worried about him. It could be simply because he was locked into his cage while the others were allowed to fly free, and she thought that was cause for concern, or because she correctly read the signs of his physical distress. I believe that it was a combination of the two. Whatever the balance of causes, I felt very proud of her for caring. She really does like him. She only left her vigil once I had put Louis into their shared cage, and she knew that it was time to join him there. My respect for her, ever growing, went up a few more notches. She is a special bird.

Quigley was better the next day. He flew from his cage when it was opened to his favourite perch on the aviary wall. Then he flew to the opening of Sam's cage. He was back.

Quakers as Compulsive Builders

A website about Quaker parrots asks the question, "How do you know that you were a Quaker parrot in a past life?" One of the responses is: "You are a compulsive builder." Seeing that compulsiveness emerge in our Quigley was a lesson in the ability of birds to build. Quakers build their nests almost exclusively with sticks, which makes them unusual in the bird world. They build condominiums or apartment buildings of nests that are described as being as big as a small car and weighing 400 pounds! These large-scale buildings—I can't really call them "nests"—can hold as many as 12 mated pairs, sometimes including other species, even non-parrots such as yellow-billed teals (a South American duck) and a small bird of prey, the spot-winged falconet. The odd possum can find its way into the higher chambers of the condo. Even though nesting pairs share the building, it should be noted that they fiercely protect their own personal apartment or nest within it. For pet Quakers, this tendency manifests itself in the fact they are quite cage-aggressive until they are convinced to be otherwise. These large construction jobs are one reason why electrical utilities are very much opposed to the presence of Quakers in the United States.

In writing about Quakers, W.T. Greene (1884c) identified their nest-building instinct as one of their most curious characteristics. Most of his discussion of Quakers related to that singular ability. He even used a quotation from his "esteemed correspondent," a Mrs. Cassirer, to put the following words into the beak of the species. It is a curiously nineteenth-century sort of passage: "I, though a Parrot, find that as I live in bogs and marshes, the trunks of trees and branches are apt to be damp, and my young to be drowned by a sudden rising of the waters, therefore I will build on trees, and since I am good tempered and sociable, I will join my sisters for our common protection from enemies...."

Angie used to wash and then dry in the oven sticks for Quigley to build with. Corners of his cage were interwoven with patterns whose ultimate nature was known only to Quigley. He would fly by me, stick in beak, sometimes quite long, and show off with pride his latest piece of building material. Sometimes he would seem dissatisfied with what he constructed and would rebuild, more or less from scratch. For a while he stopped nest building. I wondered at the time whether he stopped building because he had no opportunity for a mate. But now it seems that he had another focus at the time.

It means a lot to see and say that Quigley is building again. I do not know whether he actually stopped building when Finn died, but that is how my mind pictures it. I have observed that he does not drive anyone out of his cage anymore, and to me that is a bad sign in a Quaker. Finn and Tikkifinn are clear examples of never surrendering space that is claimed as territory. So seeing him build again is a very good sign of his strength of spirit. He has been somewhat obsessively adjusting the sticks in his cage, and he is even bringing sticks to the cage, an even better sign that his Quaker spirit is reviving.

Finn the Builder

Of course, when I think of Quaker building, one beautiful sight, now sad, comes quickly to mind. Finn and her Dairy Queen Blizzard spoons fly only too swiftly into my imagination. There was a great sale on these frozen desserts one month; I think it was late winter or early spring. We had them almost every night. The Dairy Queen is only a short waddle away from our home. (To locals who want to know where we live, I just say, "Behind the Dairy Queen.") Finn interwove bright red plastic Blizzard spoons in the upper corners of her cage. She was so proud of what she had made. After eating the Blizzard, we would give the red spoon to her, she would fly it into her cage, and then weave her magic pattern in front of our eyes. Her pride made it beautiful to us.

One of the saddest sights was coming back after we had Finn put down and seeing her empty cage, with the red spoons recalling happy times no longer to be experienced. The next day I threw them all out. I wanted to cast that scene from my heart. We didn't order any more Blizzards for a long time, either. It wasn't a diet; just a way to avoid seeing red spoons in the house.

Master Builder

It is hard for the human mind, and certainly hard for this human's mind, to wrap itself around the idea that Quaker parrots can construct nests out of sticks primarily using their beaks, and only secondarily their talons. Quigley showed me, yet again, that he is a master builder. He took a huge stick roughly twice his length (including his tail), crept down the outside of his cage, and stuffed it into his cage, while not losing his grip (physically or emotionally). The stick got stuck for a second or three in a container of seeds hooked into the top of the cage. I felt like reaching in to help him but I didn't have to; it was well-handled by the beak master. He moved the stick to the upper corner where his wooden nest was and wedged it in. He didn't like that position so he withdrew it and put it back in. I would have been satisfied with the way that it was, but I am not a master builder. He wedged it in and then shook it to see whether it might

Above, Quigley the builder; below, Quigley and Angie

come loose. It did not. I cheered him all the way and he certainly deserved the cheers.

Minutes later, I heard the crash of a stick on the floor and thought that I might have been a bit hasty in calling Quigley a master builder. But it was Tikkifinn who had dropped the stick, from her position atop his cage. Quigley went over to the offending object, scrutinized it a bit and rearranged it several times on the floor, passing it down his beak a few times, from end to centre, then flew it into his cage.

Meanwhile, Tikkifinn, who had clearly been watching Quigley when he had put the first stick in, had selected a much smaller stick to grasp with her beak. She stood on the cage door as she moved her beak to the centre of the stick, as she had seen Quigley do, and then shook it, possibly imitating Quigley's way of checking whether the stick was secure. Eventually she dropped it, not really knowing what to do with it in the next stage. Meanwhile, Quigley had completed his second project.

Tikkifinn and Building

We wondered when we first got Tikkifinn whether she would ever be a builder. We know full well that we have to love her for what she is, not what we have lost. But it would be a beautiful thing if she ever took up building. We needn't have worried. She is a Quaker after all.

Tikkifinn claimed two upper spaces on the cabinet as her territory. There is a parrot piñata of a donkey that reaches into the rightmost one, and when Gus tries to play with the back end of it while standing on the top of Lime's cage, that upsets Tikkifinn. Being territorial is typical of Quakers. How else could they maintain the bird condos they are famous for building? But then Tikkifinn showed another typical Quaker trait: building. There is a big stick in one of those spaces, of the kind often used to induce Sam our bite-prone parrot to step up. Tikkifinn started to lift and lower it with her beak, as if she were lifting weights. Was that the beginning of her building impulses clicking in? To test this hypothesis I put some smaller sticks in the space, the kind that Quigley often uses for building. The experiment began.

The first results were not what I expected. She expressed territoriality; that's for sure. She dumped the sticks on the floor. But then something else happened. I watched Tikkifinn lift one stick and adjust, lift and adjust, changing the angle many times, giving it a quarter-turn or making a 45-degree adjustment. She looked as though she was fine tuning (or Tikkifinn-tuning) her work, making it just right. The stick rattled and rattled as she worked. She was very engaged in the entire process. It absorbed all of her attention. I doubt if she had the same sense of a purpose that Quigley would have if he were the one picking up the stick. She seemed just to have an undefined feeling that she should be picking sticks up and making them right. Then, content somehow, Tikkifinn decided to fly away, her work apparently done for the time being.

Is this some kind of builder's boot camp, with the object being to familiarize yourself with the materials before you do anything substantial or purposeful with them? I can't remember Quigley ever going through such a stage, but it is possible that he did. With him, we were watching a bird-builder for the first time. We had no clear sense of where he was going with things. It was only when his built nest began to appear that we really understood what it was that he was trying to do. With Tikkifinn at this point, there had only been a few days' activity. We would have to see where it goes—and we did. Later, Tikkifinn turned the stick around by 90 degrees, so it went into the full depth of the cage rather than length-wise.

Then Angie put up a cage front with a stick wedged up into it. We would soon see what Tikkifinn would do with this opportunity. First, she defended it as I tried to get her to go to cage at night. But I was still hoping for some building. It might be a fair question to ask why I feel that way. Is it because I want her to become more like Finn? Or is it because I want to see the bird learn and develop? I am a teacher, after all, and I love it when people learn.

The next day, Tikkifinn is still lifting and dropping, lifting and dropping, and stuffs the stick in the front of her cabinet territory. She still defends it fiercely, but is willing, eventually, to step up on a stick—the first time for this.

The next day, I hear for long periods of time the construction sounds of Tikkifinn in her cage-away-from-cage. She clearly has learned to love the process. I wondered when the results would come, and how she would do it.

The first result is a slanted stick with one end against the side wall and the other wedged between two wires of the partial cage-front. It's a start.

Weeks later, on a cold November early evening, I come home and go into the aviary. I greet Tikkifinn in her cage and she gives her raspy reply. As I do a little cleaning, she flies over to the aviary wall. I pick up a chopstick and give it to her. Mere minutes later, she has wedged it into the aviary wall. As I go to congratulate her on this feat, I notice that she had already wedged a long twig into the mesh of the wall, something I hadn't noticed before. Our Tikkifinn is now a builder. Even though she takes the chopstick out and tries to see whether it can balance on a toy, and eventually drops it, I am no less proud of her. I know what she had to do to learn this, and that increases my respect for her.

Later in the evening, she took a chopstick out of Quigley's cage and tried to wedge it into the aviary wall. She was partially successful but it didn't stay long. She tried several more times and dropped the stick each time. I decided to give her a break and lay the stick across the food container in her cage. Within a few minutes she was in her cage and had angled the stick into a precarious position. She has persistence!

Finally, success: Tikkifinn wedged several small sticks into the mesh of the aviary, just above the wooden part of the wall. I didn't see her do it, but I know it was her doing. Angie didn't do it, and Quigley would never build outside of his cage. Never underestimate the power of Quaker persistence. Building is in their blood. They just vary in the time it takes for them to get the job done.

Months later, Tikkifinn wedged a stick between the bars of the cage-like aviary wall at one end and one of the toys hanging from the wall on the other. She did this no less than three times to high praise from me. I am beginning to think that it is not the perfection of the product that makes her do and re-do, but the success of the *process* that she likes, that keeps her working.

Tikkfinn's building advanced by leaps and bounds (or should that be climbs and flights)?. Eventually she has more than 15 sticks wedged into the mesh of the aviary, and she frequently adjusts them, even removing them and putting them back in again. She is so busy at this that she may have inspired Quigley, who hasn't been doing any building but then decided to put one new stick into his complicated nest. It is a good sign. Has he been inspired by the blue female? Time will tell.

For several days, the aviary reverberated to the sound of Tikkifinn continuously tightening and shaking a stick that is wedged in the webbing of the aviary. She seemed obsessive in what she was doing with no result apparent to the human eye and mind. And then she demonstrated some tremendous beak-to-eye coordination. She flew to the central feeding station and picked up a particularly heavy stick by the end. What dazzled me was the fact that she proceeded to slide the stick down until her beak was at the approximate centre and the stick was perfectly balanced.

Tikkifinn's Gender: You Decide!

I returned to the aviary one day after washing one of the water dishes. I heard a scrambling noise on the top of Lime's cage and some slight conure sounds coming from the area. Out from under the newspaper emerged Stanee and Louis. They were playing the old game of running around under the newspaper. It was Louis's favourite game, something that I think he preferred even to food. I hadn't seen or heard them do that in a while. You know when it's happening as Louis emits happy sounds of pure joy, as he runs back and forth in the semi-dark, accompanied by the sound of fast-rustling paper. Stanee plays along with him, but remains in a lady-like silence. She is the mother of the flock, after all.

I left again, to take another water dish out to be cleaned and refilled. Then I heard a squawking from the aviary. It sounded rather crow-like, like a black bird who is fed up with all that is going on. When I re-entered the compound, I saw that it was Tikkifinn that was disturbed. I addressed the problem not with a behaviorist carrot or a therapy stick, but just by talking to the bird, as you would with any friend who was bothered about something and complaining. Tikkifinn quieted down, but still walked about, dispersing much of her considerable remaining energy.

What Tikkifinn did next is what is most interesting, and the main subject of this particular narrative. Her head bobbed up and down in the pre-regurgitate motion. She looked like she was trying to feed Stanee. Is Tikkifinn actually a male parrot? I need more evidence.

Tikkifinn's Gender Story Continues

We still call Tikkifinn a female, and now a little bit of evidence emerges to support that. She flew over to her right space, and shortly afterwards Louis came for a visit. Tikkifinn bobbed up and down in the classic regurgitation-and-feed maneuver. She was about to feed him, but it never came to be. I'm not sure why. He moved close, she backed away. These actions repeated themselves again, and then he flew away. But I still think that she would have fed him. I don't think that is a thing that a guy does for a guy, unless it is parent to child. He is older than her, even though he often seems like a perpetual child (kind of the same way that I often am!). I don't think that Tikkifinn thinks of Louis as her child, but as an almost-mate. We continue to try to figure out the "she-ness" or "he-ness" of our Tikkifinn. Of course, eggs would be a good, clear indicator!

Deedle, Deedle, Boop

"Deedle, deedle, boop" is a human-and-parrot dance. I approach Tikkifinn, and she starts her motion in anticipation of the dance. Often at first she moves like an old-style boxer, bobbing and weaving, lunging and jousting, and then finger and beak meet. The first few moves are aggressive on her part. Then we begin to set up a kind of two-person rhythm. I say the words "deedle, deedle" and we come together with the "boop" in anticipated timing. Usually I lead and we both reach to the other at the same time after the two deedles. Sometimes I just hold my finger and go "boop" when she pushes her beak forward, moving for both of us. Sometimes she stretches on tippy-talons reaching as high as she can to touch-boop my stationary finger. Sometimes I will do two down and up strokes and she will bob her head twice in unison. Sometimes I go side to side and she does as well, easily copying my movements. It is a dance of human and parrot, with both partners enjoying the moves (but only one potentially getting bit).

Moving like a Boxer

As mentioned earlier, sometimes Tikkifinn "boops" like a boxer. This is particularly true when I cross the borders of her other-than-cage territory. She will feint below my finger, then she brings her beak up quickly for a sharp "boop" to the soft pad of my index finger as if it is a punching bag. She will lift her wings up slightly just as a boxer does his or her elbows. And the sounds she makes are like those, I just realized, of someone being hit by a boxing glove. She dances like Muhammad Ali did as I approach her. And a couple of times I have learned that she can sting like a bee. She once hit me on the head with a bang that startled me. I considered myself stung.

Tikkifinn: From Attack to Deedle Boop

Tikkifinn, when she is on a particular rope perch on the aviary wall, attacks the curve of the rope in front of her several times as I approach, calling for a deedle boop. Eventually she will boop, but not before she shows me how powerfully she can attack. "I could hurt you, but I have chosen, this time, just to play fight."

On one occasion, Stanee had flown into Tikkifinn's territory in the mesh of the aviary, and Tikkifinn was very upset as a result. She let out Blue Quaker intruder alert sounds, giving Stanee her message loud and clear. After Stanee wisely flew away, I approached. I put the back of my hand in a fist about an inch away from the ledge that Tikkifinn was standing on. She almost bit me a few times and settled into a simple push with her beak. Once she came to realize that I did not mean to trespass on her precious space, the push became gentler. She almost rested her head against my hand. Quigley uses that push as well, as a clear alternative to a bite. It expresses the fact that there is a potential territory violation that can be more gently resolved with a beak push rather than through a bite. I wonder how often that might be used in the wild, when Quakers have many neighbours, and don't really want to attack them with open beak when they feel that others are crowding a little too close. It is a warning, not an attack.

Two Landings: Tikkifinn Stories

It may seem like a small thing, but it was big to me. Tikkifinn landed twice on my shoulder. Once she landed when the conures did, her finding her place on my left shoulder. And she stayed and was happy to remain where she was. We even did a little diddle-boop with my nose touching her beak, something of an act of trust on my part. We did this a few times and she seemed to act as if it were no new thing. Then all three flew off in unison. Not long afterward she and Louis flew back. She stayed for a while but was destined to leave. What happened? Admittedly I was standing up behind the plastic chair and not sitting in it, so there was no safe back-of-the-chair to secure her landing. It was on my shoulder or nothing. I'm glad she chose the first option. Our relationship moves very slowly ahead, but it progresses. You celebrate small things with Tikkifinn—her "stepping up" onto a stick, not a hand, and the small raspy response when I say her name. One day in December 2014, she landed on my head, and then, after she had flown away, swooped down again with Stanee, this time onto my left arm. She was excited to be there, stretching and calling. Stanee pinch-bit my arm, but I didn't want to drive her off because of Tikkifinn. Eventually, I tried to get Stanee off and both birds flew off.

Two months later Tikkifinn landed on my shoulder. I was watching the hockey game (the Leafs won!) with Louis sitting on my head, preening the top. I heard a flutter of wings and a Quaker landed on my left shoulder. I thought it was Quigley. I greeted the bird with a hello, but did not move my hands towards the Quaker body that was in the periphery of my vision. Tikkifinn is a kind of blue that can be interpreted, by me, as green in the right or wrong light. I often mistake the two Quakers. I'm not colour-blind—I just have a mind that can readily over-ride my senses. It's not hallucination, just powerful misplaced interpretation. Shortly afterwards, the blue-green parrot flew off my shoulder. It was only when I looked back at the mesh of the aviary wall that I saw who it was. That was the first time Tikkifinn had ever flown to my shoulder, after many times landing on the top of the chair behind me. I wish I had known it was her. I hope that it is an indication of times to come. There are memories in my heart of a blue Quaker on my shoulder, one that I could preen and who would preen me. This is the stuff that my parrot dreams are made of.

More Landings

I was sitting in the aviary reading, a much favoured way to relax, when Tikkifinn flew to my left knee. Louis was on my shoulder, so it was not a total surprise that she would be in the area. We played a long game of deedle, deedle, boop, and then I returned to my book. She flew back to the back of the chair. But it did not end there. She flew back to my knee. More deedle, deedle, boop, and then, somewhat regretfully, I returned to my book, she to the back of the chair. Much to my delight and surprise it still did not end there. She flew back to my knee again for yet more deedle, deedle, boop. We both enjoy the game, and I don't think that I am being overly optimistic in saying that I feel that we are getting closer.

Tikkifinn is quite articulate, not in human words that we can follow, but both in the sounds she makes herself and in those made by other birds. Recently she has been imitating Sam's "okay" sound. When she utters it, she makes that patented Quaker move with the head, turning her head to face left as she moves her head in a rightward direction. It is a song and a dance.

Yesterday as I write this, Angie sang the song "Wiggle and a Peck" to Tikkifinn, and in her own, always distinctive way, our blue girl picked up the word "wiggle" and repeated it. It means a lot to Angie and me to have her sing it. Tikkifinn loves to sing and to articulate her repertoire of sounds. We would both love it if this became a regular part of her repertoire.

Tikkifinn: Two Years Plus with Us

What can I say about life with Tikkifinn after more than two years of her living with us? She still very rarely ever steps up for Angie or for me. She complains loudly when Angie cleans around where she has done her building in the mesh, and still lands behind me, on the ledge of the chair, rather than on my shoulder. That she does only when the conures and Sam, and sometimes Quigley, are on or are very near me. I have never been permitted to preen her, and she has never preened me, nor is she ever likely to. She entered our lives as a kind of younger sister of an over-achieving older sister. You try not to compare, but it is very easy to slip into that kind of thinking. Still, I can truly say that I am very close to Tikkifinn. She is a lot of fun to play with, and her articulations are a joy to hear whenever she gets going on them at full speed. And when I am having my breakfast of Cheerios, she gets one when she is standing on her perch beside her mesh building. Sometimes she will come to the back of the chair to quietly wait for me to discover that she is there and reward her flight with food.

Territoriality and the Quaker Parrot

Quaker parrots are very territorial, despite the fact they live in parrot apartment complexes (or perhaps because of it). For example, they are cage-territorial. To be sure, Quigley is not as much this way as he once was. He makes warning noises when he is in his cage and I reach in to change the water in his bowl or the papers at the bottom of the cage. But he doesn't bite. I can nod my head down for a preen, but sometimes it is rougher than normal when he preens me in that position.

He is, however, very protective of the left side of the roof of Lime's cage. That is his territory, although he does not build there. He will drive the others away, especially Sam, and has had a number of battles there. Angie and I have to be careful what we do there for fear of a Quigley attack.

Finn was more cage-territorial than that—so much so that after a short period during which she shared a cage with Quigley, it was clear that she was gradually trying to evict him from their common dwelling. We eventually moved him.

She made a distinctive sound when she felt that the integrity of her territory was being threatened. I knew when I heard it that there was someone, usually Lime, on the outside of her cage. I think that Lime sometimes did this just to tease her.

Tikkifinn makes the same sound now. Perhaps it is unique to female Blue Quakers, as I have never heard Quigley make the sound. Tikkifinn uses it when she feels that someone (e.g., Quigley, Lime or Angie) is trespassing on her nesting ground on the mesh wall of the aviary, where she regularly perches and where she carries out her building. I know when Angie is cleaning there because I hear the sound. Tikkifinn does let Louis into her space. After all they share a cage. And, of course, Stanee is permitted there too. No one denies Stanee. But it is only on very rare occasions that you see Quigley there. I don't remember seeing Sam there, either.

This is curious as Tikkifinn likes to hang out on the door of Quigley's cage. And, in company with Louis, and sometimes Stanee, she sometimes ducks (or is that "Quakers") down to squeeze herself into the crawl space between the ceiling of Quigley's cage and the root layer above it. When Angie brings the vacuum cleaner in and turns it on, Tikkifinn often takes refuge there until the loud monster has finished its growling. It is too big for even a Quaker to challenge.

Tikkifinn is Making Her Move

There was a time for several weeks that I noticed signs that Tikkifinn was making a move on Lime's cage. It is much bigger than the bottom half of the big cage that Tikkifinn shares with Louis, so it is prime cage territory. At first, I saw sticks in Lime's cage. I didn't put a lot of thought into why that might be. I should have. My sociological senses should have been tingling like crazy. A Quaker is making a statement. Then, one day, when I replaced the newspapers at the bottom of Lime's cage, Tikkifinn took great offence at what I was doing. She even lightly bit my arm as I hauled the dirty old papers out, and I had to get her to step up onto the big stick to get her out. It wasn't easy. Stanee seems to be giving her full approval of Tikkifinn's move, as she went in there with her, and came back after I got her to step up on the stick too. It is unlikely that this is a sign that Tikkifinn is reaching sexual maturity, as Quaker parrots generally reach that stage between 12 and 18 months, and we had had her for more than two years at that point.

After I left the room and came back, she had returned to the cage, and there was a stick lying on the paper. She stood on the lower ledge just beneath the door, pronouncing her right to be there, challenging anyone to tell her she did not belong there. Stanee visited with no challenge, and Louis came down to set himself beside her.

When Angie went to wash off the door, Tikkifinn made the well-known (at least in our household) sound of a female Quaker sounding her intruder alert. It became something of a war of wills between the two females. It was close, but Angie won.

Tikkifinn spent most of the evening on the ledge. She was high up on an aviary wall perch when it was time for beddy-bird. Louis had already been put in their cage. She flew first in the direction of Lime's cage, then shifted direction to the one she shared with Louis.

The next morning, by about ten o'clock, she was back in Lime's cage, eating off the cage floor. There was a second stick there. Later in the day two more would follow.

The day after that, Tikkifinn put five sticks into the cage. At about ten at night, just before being asked to go to her own cage shared with Louis, she was declaring to the world as only a Quaker can that Lime's cage was her place, walking back and forth on the floor of Lime's cage like a town crier strutting down Main Street.

The next morning I heard a clang and went to see what was going on. One of the bigger sticks is leaning against Lime's water bowl, which is situated high in the cage. I suspect that Tikkifinn shoved it in from outside the cage. Then I watch her as she climbs across the cage to the open door, bringing in a thin stick with her. She places it on the floor of the cage, to adjust and readjust its position somewhat obsessively, as she does with sticks on the aviary wall. By 4:30 p.m., the time when the papers in the cages are changed, there were seven sticks in the cage. She is not staking her claim, she's sticking it. But then that night, she was back in her own shared cage before it was beddy-bird time.

Three days later it was ten sticks.

One interpretation is this. The next night Tikkifinn had sex with Rita the wreath in Quigley's cage. Perhaps she is feeling hormonal now, and this behaviour will end with a decrease in hormones. For the next few days she drove Quigley out of his cage, so that she could have access to Rita.

I wonder how often this happens in the wild with Quaker parrots and their condos for 12 couples. I suspect it does happen not infrequently, when a bird, possibly most often a female, decides that someone else's territory looks better than her own.

A week later, and Tikkifinn had ended her claim to Lime's cage. There were no more sticks being put there, and she didn't defend it with words and attacks when I come to change the paper. Some months later Tikkifinn went through the same routine with Gus' cage.

Poccopeck: Responding to the Call

As much as anything else, it was the call that did it.

We had been going to oue favourite parrot-acquiring pet store for some two months visiting the young light blue Quaker baby when she started calling us when we went to leave. As soon as we were out of sight, we would hear the call. The sound was both charming and saddening at the same time, a sign that she was alone, and wanted company. It was her very own two note tune. None of our other Quakers had made the exact same sound. We knew what it was about. It wasn't just our imaginations that were saying that she was reaching

Poccopeck

out to us. She was calling us back.

The inevitable happened and we brought her home, putting her in a different room for a few weeks. It wasn't long before we would hear her use the same call to respond to the inquiring notes from the other birds. "I am here. I am here." she seems to be saying. Within the first week one of the flock (probably Sam the Senegal) had learned how to imitate her call.

In the store they had been calling her Pocco. We added the -peck, because when Angie sang her "I love you, a wiggle and a peck", she would almost invariably repeat the 'peck', sometimes the 'wig' of wiggle. We started calling her 'Peck', but that didn't seem like enough, so we combined the two parts, like we did with Tikkifinn. This turned out to be a difficult name to say right. It took a while.

The same was true of her response to 'step-up'. It was hard at first to get her to trust us consistently. She had to be tricked into it at first, but now she responds right away. She was on my left forearm, wrist and hand when I was typing this.

Of course she evokes memories of Finn, more than does Tikkifinn. She has the same bright spirit; she could be called the energizer parrot. She has even taken a few baths in the sink, as Finn did. She probably came from the same breeder.

Miss Peck, as we sometimes call her, competes with Tikkifinn for Louis's attention. She has her cage outside of the aviary. When we let her out of her cage, she often goes to the aviary mesh wall. If Tikkifinn is with Louis, then there is a highly vocalized battle between the two female Quakers, with poor Louis having to play the part of peacemaker parrot. Similar loud bouts take place when Miss Peck is allowed into the aviary. If it is quiet in there when they are both inside, there is a good chance that Tikkifinn has retreated to the cage that she shares with Louis, occasionally making grumpy Quaker sounds. Young Poccopeck is a force of nature. Sometimes, however, the room is quiet because Stanee has exercised her alpha bird privilege and is preening and being preened by Louis. Neither of the two female Quakers has ever in our viewing mounted a serious challenge to Stanee. That would be foolish.

Chapter Four
Amazons

Amazons and Destructiveness: Lime Did What?

Konrad Lorenz (1903–1989) was a pioneering scientist in devising ways of getting inside the mind of a bird, doing so amazingly well with graylag geese, ducks, jackdaws and cockatoos. It should be no surprise, then, to find the following wise words in his ground-breaking work, *King Solomon's Ring* (1952): "The capacity of an animal to cause damage is proportional to its intelligence." If so, Lime and her fellow Amazons must be very, very intelligent birds—as indeed they are.

I was working on a new book, *Learning from the Past: Five Cases of Aboriginal Justice* (2013), an all-the-time-I-could-grab-while-not-teaching job of writing. I was doing my writing in the aviary, my favourite part of the house in which to hang out. The keys of my laptop clicked away as though they belonged to another species of bird. I left the room; I don't remember why or for exactly how long—certainly over an hour. I only know that I returned to a horrible sight, a sight more frightening to a writer than a rejection letter or book signings at which virtually nobody shows up. Just about every key on my laptop was stripped off!

Now, I had already lost a few keys before this. The first gave me a great opportunity for a one-liner. I had lost the "O" key, so I went to Staples and asked one of the young women who worked there if I could "buy a vowel." She didn't understand the joke, not being a *Wheel of Fortune* fan, but after I explained my plight told me that you can't replace the keys on laptops (obviously a design flaw for an Amazon owner).

This time nothing could be done. I had to buy a new laptop. Worse was the fact that Lime had also crunched my computer flash-drive like it was a peanut. Although I hadn't seen what had happened, Lime was the obvious culprit. She had the biggest beak in the house. She liked to crunch peanuts. She liked to play with computers. She had once created a computer folder (yes, a folder, not a file) called, I think, "mmmmmmmmmmm8jk," or something like that. I still don't know how she did it. And for once her beak is shut.

The crushed flash-drive and I travelled from place to place to see whether it could be fixed, with no luck. The data could not be retrieved. The stick contained the most up-to-date versions of two chapters of my book. The previous versions were fortunately on the hard drive of another computer, but the work of the last week was lost. I didn't take my frustration out on Lime. I couldn't stay angry with her. But after that, I did my keyboarding in another room. Lime sits on my shoulder or my head, sometimes for an hour or more when I am writing, but she is no longer allowed near the computer. There are some distinct hazards for a writer who wants to inform people about parrots. The parrots can interfere with the writing process—and the writing processor.

Amazons

Amazons, genus *Amazona*, are relatively large parrots. They measure over a foot in length and up to a pound in weight. I typically describe Lime as being the size of a hawk. Their traditional home "in the wild" extends from southeastern Mexico to northern regions of South America. Despite the name, most do not live anywhere near the Amazon River, nor are they a race of female warriors, although with our female Amazon, Lime, I sometimes wonder. I would not want to face a row of female Amazons bearing attitude and sharp beaks as weapons.

At the conclusion of her excellent book, *The Parrot Who Owns Me: The Story of a Relationship* (2002), ornithologist Joanna Burger reflected on parrots generally. However, I suspect she was largely influenced by the fact that most of her direct interaction with parrots was with Sam and Tiko, two male *Amazon autumnalis* or red-lored Amazons (because of to the red band across the front of the face). Tiko was the bird she rightfully claimed "owned" her. As Burger said, "THERE IS NO SUCH THING AS OWNING A PARROT. You can't have a parrot as a pet. A dog, certainly, a cat maybe, but a parrot never. Quite the contrary; you are the pet, and parrots vary in their ability to make good masters. Be warned—being owned by a parrot is not for the faint of heart."

I have only known three Amazons, two of them quite well—Koko, the pet store Amazon, and Lime. The third is the fictional Captain Flint (see chapter one). Still, I find Burger's words to be accurate. Owning an Amazon, or being owned by them, is definitely not for the faint of heart, and especially not for those keen on controlling their birds, or those who like a quiet, tidy household.

The species known as the yellow-headed Amazon parrot or double-yellow-headed Amazon (I don't think there is any difference between the two) is a trouble-maker, even in the eyes of those who like to draw up neat systems of taxonomies. I will avoid a long discussion on the subject of parrot taxonomy as it is both boring and not yet completely settled when it comes to Lime and her species-mates. Let's just say that they are often referred to as *Amazona oratrix*, a name that aptly describes them. The species name, *oratrix*, relates to their being speakers (the Latin term being cognate with the words "oral" and "orator"). Interestingly, in "law-speak" the word refers to a female plaintiff or complainant in equity pleading. That description certainly suits Lime. When she is picked on by the little birds, or when I am writing and she wants to be on my shoulder, she is definitely a plaintiff or complainant loudly pleading her case. Amazons belong to the tribe known as *Androglossia* ("human speaking"), which tells you that they have a great capacity for human-like speech. Be careful what you say in front of or even near an Amazon. They are very clear in the human words that they repeat. And ours has a fondness for words spoken with emotion. She would never learn to say "pretty bird," unless I make it sound like it is spoken in anger: "Damn you, pretty bird!"

Amazons have been pets of prominent Europeans for centuries. Christopher Columbus brought a few from the Caribbean back to Queen Isabella of Spain. (I wonder who ended up ruling in that household.) On the Internet I have come across a 300-year-old picture of an English aristocrat woman with her Amazon parrot. Maybe she loved the bird's beautiful singing voice, which is sometimes referred to (and that includes by me) as operatic. Their ability to speak would encourage aristocrats to have them as pets as well—so long as the birds kept refined company and didn't repeat the foul words spoken by the servants, much less those spoken by the master of the house when he spilled hot tea on his lap, by the mistress of the house when the master dropped and broke her fine china cup, or by the pirates who brought them across the Atlantic.

There would appear to be a special British connection with yellow-headed Amazons. Beginning in the sixteenth century, English pirates found safe haven in coves in yellow-headed Amazon territory, while waiting to attack Spanish ships. A British settlement was founded in what is now Belize, one of the species' native habitats. In 1638, Belize became part of the British Empire as the colony of British Honduras, finally achieving independence in 1964. Unfortunately (I am showing my distinct Amazon-centric bias here), the national bird for Belize is the toucan. These large-beaked birds are not parrots, and, as far as I know, do not talk, except on Froot Loops commercials and in Disney movies. There is no accounting for people's taste. Maybe in Belize they wanted a less talkative species as the national bird. Perhaps, as a member of the British Commonwealth, they didn't want the Queen visiting and being sworn at by their national bird.

Yellow-headed Amazons live in the wild in Mexico and the northern areas of Central America, including the aforementioned Belize. At least since 1984, feral yellow-headed Amazons have also been seen near the Wilhelminia Zoo in Stuttgart, Germany (because of their love of Wagner as an operatic composer, perhaps?), and in parts of southern California (they are blonds, after all).

Their numbers in the wild declined by as much as 90% between the mid-1970s and 1994, when the figure was estimated at about 7,000 birds. Since then the rate of decline has eased somewhat but the numbers are still troubling. The causes of the decline include deforestation, the illicit smuggling of Amazons for the foreign and domestic pet trade, persecution for allegedly destroying crops (you wonder whether there is any evidence), and fishermen hunting them for food. To obtain young ones for trade, the nesting trees are cut down, destroying habitat and probably a couple of the three to four hatchlings as well (see http://www.birdlife.org for more information).

A number of famous and strong-minded actresses have had Amazons as companions. Elizabeth Taylor had a yellow-naped Amazon named Alvin for 10 years. Actress and conservationist Stephanie Powers has had a male yellow-nape named Papuga for decades (she says it is the longest relationship she has ever had with a male). Another actress, Elizabeth Hurley, has a male blue-fronted Amazon called Ping Pong. Interestingly, in all three cases the relationship is between a female human and a male Amazon; I'll return to the topic of gender relationships between parrots and people in chapter eight.

Lime Enters Our Lives

One day when we went to the pet store, the same store that had supplied us with Benji, Stanee, Louis and Quigley, we were invited into a separate room to see something special: the hand-feeding of two baby yellow-headed Amazons, Kiwi and Lime. Not only did we watch the feeding, but—a good marketing move, this!—we were invited to participate in the feeding of the Amazon chicks. Angie got Kiwi and I got Lime. I can picture Lime still, years later, walking up my arm slowly, in a way I might call formal, cautious step by cautious step as if on a tightrope. Mind you, I learned a little bit about her sneaky nature in that first encounter. As she walked she took large, careful strides up my arm, to stand on my shoulder. Then she carefully, deliberately reached over with her beak to grab my glasses, a certain sign of the saucy bird to come. I soon learned to take my glasses off when I was in the store.

Later on when we went to the pet store, I would go straight to Lime's cage. We were bonding. I was struck by the almost aristocratic elegance of the way that she moved, like she was being introduced at a fancy dress ball, followed by a dramatic entrance down the broad stairway to the main ballroom. It was at this time that Lime and I developed our first shared bird-human communication. One day I stood in front of her cage and moved my body side-to-side without moving my feet. It wasn't long before she did that too, in reply. Eventually that became a form of greeting between us. Today, whenever she is in her cage, and wants my attention (and for me to let her out, if she has been punished by cage incarceration) she moves side to side. She must know that I cannot resist that. I return the motion and let her out.

One day when we came in, we heard that one of the Amazons had been stolen. For a very brief moment of dread I thought that it was Lime, but it was Kiwi. Yellow-headed Amazons are expensive birds, fetching around $2,000 each, one reason why sleazy breeders/sellers of birds and smugglers are attracted to them as sources of quick and plentiful cash. This theft would affect our purchase of Stanee, but that is a story told in an earlier chapter. I felt sorry for the owners, for Kiwi, for Lime and for Angie, as Kiwi was Angie's Amazon friend, not mine.

Then a pattern developed. I would walk into the pet store, speak with the owner or some member of the staff, and I would hear a loud and long "hello" in the distance. Lime knew I was the one speaking. The owner and staff members assured me that Lime did this for no one else but me. I realize that that would be a good sales technique, but I firmly believe that it was true, as her behaviour at home would later show. Then I would rush back to her cage and we would greet each other with side-to-side body language and verbally communicate back and forth, glad to see each other again.

I am not the sort of person who idles away his time. I work hard and set limited and specific periods aside for not working. I do not go window-shopping, not even in the music store nearby where they have drums. So, when I drove back home from work at the college, I would typically plan what I would do when I got home. Would I mark, organize my writing, or take the dogs for a walk? But now, as I drove up Highway 50, I would think, "Should I visit with Lime?" The workaholic demon that has long been one of my inner voices, that is constantly telling me to work, work, work, was hard to hear for once. As soon as I got to Bolton, I would turn right, park in front of the pet store and visit with Lime. I would tell myself, as a form of justification, "She needs to be properly socialized so that someone will want to buy her and she can have a home." Then I would hear the loud, old woman's voice (my great Aunt Hazel Macmillan came to mind) call out a loud "hello," and I would be glad I came. Our time together would fly, although Lime at that time could not.

After a couple of these visits I began to seriously wonder whether we should buy Lime. It was, I thought, a completely outrageous thing to do. She cost around $2,000, an amount I had never spent on anything that wasn't a car (and I had bought some cars for less than that), a set of books for my research, or drums. And Amazons live as long as we do, and she was, in Amazon terms, just a toddler. She would have to be in my will, and maybe the wills of my sons, or other future owners. It wasn't "practical," "rational" or "sensible to buy Lime.

But another voice would speak—actually other *voices*, if you include the loud "hello" that greeted my entrance to the pet store, Lime's ears picking up what her eyes did not yet see. I knew that Lime and I had bonded, and that I wanted to have her at home with us. And my sixtieth birthday was coming up. I believe in trying to do something a little crazy when a significant birthday happens. When I turned 30, I wore for my birthday a ten-dollar tuxedo, the only tuxedo I ever wore in my life. When I was 40, I had my left ear pierced, and for several months I wore what I now realize were completely outrageous ear rings, including ones that hung down to my left shoulder. So Angie decided, because she knew of my close bond with Lime, that my bird friend should be my present of presents. I have never seriously regretted Lime's entering our home, although I still sometimes wonder, "What the hell was I thinking?" And when Lime has been put into her cage for bad behaviour, she knows that she can get her way with me by moving side to side. It always works.

The Simple Elegance of Amazons

A friend once told me that there were some fledgling Amazons in a humane society north of us that were being put up for adoption. It upset me that I could do nothing about it. When I hear about human tragedy, it does not usually pull at my heartstrings in the same way. I get angry at the oppression lying behind most human tragedies, but often remain relatively untouched by individual stories. Not so with parrots. I look up at Lime today and she shows that look of simple elegance that she first charmed me with, like a polite Edwardian child, a girl waiting by the gym wall for her first junior-high dance, an old man standing proud because he wants to show that he can still stand with his back straight. It completely wins me over every time. She is on a perch over the big cage. She does not come to me as I reach for her, but it is as though she is showing or , teaching me something I can't quite grasp. If I had wealth and time away from my other demands, I would take care of every Amazon fledgling I ever heard about. Lime may be a brat at times; she may give me the occasional nasty bite. She is a child of her emotions, and sometimes I am, too. But when she displays her basic elegance, I can't look away or turn my heart in another direction.

The Sweet Smell of Lime

In *Raising Susan*, author Bill Burns reports that Cecil Hyndman felt connected to Susan, the golden eagle, through what he could smell when the two were close together. I was glad to read about that, as smell is part of my connection with Lime. I don't smell the others to the same degree as I smell her. Is that something she presents, or is it just that she smells more than they do? I suspect that it is part of her digestion. Is she trying to regurgitate for me, but is holding it back, waiting for some unknown sign from me? I hope that I never inadvertently give her any such sign. I will eat leftovers and take second helpings, but not that kind.

One of the first things I noticed about Lime was I thought that she smelled good. I never really thought of birds as having a smell before. If asked, I might have said that they smelled like old down pillows or comforters. They don't have sweat glands; and they certainly do not use under-wing deodorants. They cool down by panting, like dogs do, and by lifting their wings. In fact, evolutionary biologists have suggested that cooling was the initial function of feathers and wings, although this claim has recently been challenged. And birds can cool off through their relatively featherless legs and featherless feet.

What I notice now is that when Lime is on my shoulder and preening my moustache, her breath smells sweet. I have read that birds inhale with the two holes that constitute their nose openings. I imagine that Lime's sometimes sweet breath comes out of her mouth. The other birds, Louis, Stanee, Poccopeck and Quigley, do not have that smell when they preen my face. Then I had another thought, one I don't particularly like but am able to live with. Maybe it's the "sweet" smell of regurgitation. The primary function of bird regurgitation is feeding the little ones, but it is also a sign of deep parrot affection (see chapter eight). Parrots are known to show their love for their owners in that fashion. "I love you, smell my breath." One reason that I think that the smell might be thought of as "sweet" is because my younger son's Vietnamese wife has spoken of a dessert "delicacy" essentially made up of "bird barf" (my terminology). Maybe Lime is showing her appreciation for her dad with a little *aire regurgitaire*.

Right-Shoulder Bird

Lime is my number-one shoulder bird. She began to take on that role whenever I visited the pet store. I remember someone at the store saying that allowing her to perch there would make her think that she was in control, the old, out-dated behaviorist view emerging in his words of warning. —No, she *likes* being there and I like her being there. And we both think that we are in control. Sometimes I am right. Sometimes, perhaps more often, she is right. Parrots, like other birds, like to choose the highest perch on which to stand. Human heads and shoulders make good parrot perches. That is, as long as the humans don't mind too much the inevitable fecal result of long periods of parrot shouldering.

Lime prefers to be on my right shoulder. I put her on my left shoulder this morning, and she made her way carefully behind my head to get to my right shoulder. I am wondering why that is. Is it because the right shoulder is the one I usually place her on, so she feels more comfortable there? When I think about it, most of the birds seem to prefer my right shoulder, except for Stanee. She often lands on my head or my back and makes her way to the left. Is this because I have rarely got her to step up for any other reason than to take her to her cage bird-on-hand, so that she has relatively little experience being placed on my right shoulder? These are the types of things that a parrot sociologist thinks about.

Lime and the Other Birds (and a Dog)

Lime is not popular with the other birds. Stanee polices and bullies her. Quigley preened her a few times in her early days with us, but hasn't in years. But the small males adore her. First, there was Gus, our male cockatiel, who calls

Lime

to her when she is outside of the aviary and on my shoulder. You will read about that amazing relationship in chapter six, which deals with cockatiels and other cockatoos. She doesn't seem to do much to encourage him, but in typical male cockatiel fashion, he is not easily deterred. More recently, an even smaller male, Juno, our parrotlet, has developed a fascination for her. When he is allowed in the aviary, he is never more than a few flaps of his wings away from her.

Tonight, as I write this, Lime showed strong persistence in dealing with the other birds. She went to the central feeding station, loaded with new food, five times. The first four times she was chased away by Stanee, who was then joined by her allies, Sam and Tikkifinn. In the initial two situations Lime had been with her one ally, Gus, who left shortly after she was chased away. The next two times she was alone when Stanee (the bully) picked on her and made her leave. But Lime was not to be denied. The fifth time she went to the feeding station and was not driven away. Great going, girl—I'm a fan.

Like Wolves and Ravens

It is not just a coincidence anymore. Our dachshund Trudy and Lime have come together like wolves and ravens. Only in this case the wolf-dachshund is the scavenger, and the birds are the providers of food. I will be sitting at my computer writing or researching when I hear the sound of flapping Amazon wings. Lime lands on the plastic basket that holds the wooden spoons. I know what to do next. I have forgotten to lock the aviary door and Trudy has broken in, determined to munch on the seeds, vegetables and other delectables that have fallen onto the aviary floor. Lime must be quick off the mark, because the door, when opened by Trudy, is never fully open, and she must fly fast before it closes to the point she can't get out. She is more the raven than Trudy is the wolf, but they both gain from the relationship. Among other things, it adds new meaning to the phrase "bird feeder." And Trudy is certain ravenous (both "raven" and "ravenous" come from a Latin root word that means "to seize").

Greetings from Amazonia

Most parrot jokes that I have heard relate to a parrot swearing at an inappropriate time, in front of an inappropriate person (a priest, minister or rabbi, or a particularly religious aristocratic woman) at an inappropriate time. I hear them a lot because people know I have parrots, and there seem to be only a few things that these people (unlike parrots) can think of saying. "Do they talk?" "Yes, and sometimes I understand." But you've read this rant in an earlier chapter. With respect to these jokes, a general rule of thumb is that you should not believe a supposedly true story about a swearing parrot and a famous person, because chances are there's no truth to it. I've checked. They are urban legends. I highly doubt whether American President Andrew Jackson's pet parrot ever swore at his funeral (unless it wasn't allowed to feed at the buffet). And a more-than-100-year-old macaw named Charlie, still alive in a zoo in Britain, probably wasn't once owned by Winston Churchill, and wasn't trained by him to say 'F--- Hitler.' Churchill did, however, have a budgie called Toby, who was given a lot of freedom. On the other hand, Queen Victoria's eclectus parrot (*Eclectus roratus*), Lorey (featured in two pictures painted by famous British artist Sir Edwin Landseer in the 1830s), a member of a species native to northeastern Australia and island chains in the region may have actually said "God save the Queen" as is rumoured. However, despite a satirical cartoon published in 1841, Lorey did *not* declare, when asked what Victoria's next child would be, that it would be a burden on her and on John Bull (the British public).

That being said, Lime, the yellow-headed Amazon, does occasionally say "f---ing dogs," after hearing the phrase only once. And she has made up her own word, "f---ado," which she calls to me when I don't respond to her when she is in the aviary and I am not. This is no doubt a sign of intelligence, but not one that you want children to hear.

Amazon parrots, and I suspect all parrots, choose what they want to say and not to say—rather like humans in that regard. But if you say something with emotion, Lime will pick it up after hearing it only once or a few times. Take, for example, her question "What's going on?" articulated at full Amazon volume (11 out of 10 on the parrot scale, and only out-shouted by the cockatoo and macaw, who rate a 12) when the other birds (usually the Quakers) are squawking about something.

From her days in the pet store, "hello" has been her loud greeting for me (and anyone who knocks at our front door), with an expected reply in kind. Her "hello, booboo," "hello, ho-ho" or 'hello, lady' is shared between us at certain times. For example, when I used to come home from work (I am retired) I would get it, and it was always accompanied by the "mad" (in both senses of crazy and angry) Amazon look. It is also articulated when she has been whistling for me for a long time and I finally, *finally* come into the aviary to take her with me to where I am writing. She is also liable to give me a "hello" or "hello, ho-ho" when she escapes from the aviary and lands in the kitchen, where the suspended plastic container of large wooden and metal spoons is located. Again, the mad Amazon look accompanies it: spread tail feathers, uplifted head feathers and a constriction of the pupils of her eyes. It seems to be some form of recognition that she is in trouble with dad. Fortunately, it is not long before she returns to normal.

Lime uses another greeting, which she uttered one time when I really needed it. It had been a day of stressful driving—accidents both ways on Highway 401, which crosses Toronto like a slow-moving river. What better way to be greeted when I came home that night than to hear Lime say to me, head feathers up and expanded: "Hi, Lime, Whatcha doing?"

I Love You ... But by a Different Name

Lime can always come with surprises for me. This morning as I had her on my shoulder, she did her whisper-speak, her ghost talking, something she used to do more often. At first I did not hear any specific words. Then I heard those three little words, "I love you." I was touched, especially as she repeated them several times. Then I noticed that there was at least one more word after the first three. That word was "Quigley." She was saying "I love you, Quigley," repeating the soft words that Angie often says to the little guy. I think that she caught the right emotion. It is something you say to someone close to you. I am no less moved that in saying those words to me, she used someone else's name. You did intend it for me, didn't you, girl? So far she has only spoken these words on the one occasion, but I hope I will hear them again— possibly not followed by the word "Quigley" at the tail end!

Whistle Communication

Lime's whistle communication involves a two-note (a long A down to a short F sharp) or three-note sequence (the long A followed by two short notes, A and then F sharp). She uses these when I am not where she thinks I should be: either in the aviary or at my computer writing. She does so when I am shovelling snow, walking up the path behind our high cedar hedge, or getting out of my car after a long time away. Indoors, she uses the whistle call when I go to the bathroom or am in bed trying to have an old man's afternoon nap. I find it nearly impossible to resist her call (or is it a summons?), even when I am very tired. It seems to me that she is demanding a response. Her whistle is a form of contact call, like those Canada geese use in flight to locate each other. Once I return her call, we whistle back and forth for a few minutes, and, usually, I get up to see her.

Lime's One-Way Conversations

In her quieter, more reflective moments, when she is talking as a way of telling me that she is in the aviary and wants to hear from me, Lime copies human speech in a different way than the others. She picks up sentence intonation well, placing word-like units in these sentences as if they are part of her casual remarks about life in general.

John and Lime Sing a Duet

I have heard Lime sing many a time, her melodies taking her wherever she wants to go musically. At the end of many verses of nonsense words is the word "Lime." One day, however, we sang together. I had just received new speakers for my laptop as a birthday present, and was eager to try them out. So I found Great Big Sea's version of "We'll Rant and We'll Roar like True Newfoundlanders" on YouTube. The song is a favourite of mine, which I once sang a capella at a reception for teachers from Indonesia. They had regaled us with songs from their country, and someone had to represent Canada. There were three deans in attendance, so I felt I had to perform well, or at least with due energy. I managed the latter.

When Great Big Sea started singing, I sang along with them. Lime was on my shoulder. She fluffed up her head feathers and joined in as well. Admittedly, she sang to her own tune, and added no words to the piece, but that was more than made up for by her enthusiasm. We both thoroughly enjoyed the experience.

Lime Recognizes a Worried Tone

Lime also calls out "Louis?" with the correct questioning tone whenever we are looking for a bird we can't find and call its name. She learned this trick when Louis got stuck in the pedal-operated waste paper basket and we didn't find him until more than an hour of steady searching. Now she calls out "Louis?" any time she hears us say another bird's name in a worried-sounding way.

Often when we go into the aviary we find ourselves looking for Sam. He is the one most likely to be hidden away behind the cabinet, or in some other forbidden and forbidding location. It isn't unusual for either Angie or me to say "Sam," calling his name while looking for him, although we don't expect that he would ever answer back in any way that we would recognize.

Lime then responds by saying "Louis?" in pretty much the exact same tone, with perhaps a little more worried emphasis. Of course, her doing so doesn't help calm us down when we are looking for Sam, and she gets a "Shut up, Lime" from the both of us.

Just now, I had to go out to move my car so that Angie could get her car out. When I came back less than five minutes later, one of the parrot waste paper baskets was turned over, the contents spread out in an avalanche of paper, seeds and parrot poo. I yelled at the dogs with some anger. Lime picked up on my tone and said one of the fiercest "hellos" that I have ever heard. She is good at recognizing and using human emotional tones, the best in the flock. Be careful what you say, an Amazon is listening!

Parrot Alarm System

I heard bumping and crashing sounds beside and perhaps behind the house. Our son Rob said that he saw two cats fighting. I'm used to the more usual squalling sound cats make. This was different, as was Lime's response. She let off a scream that was unique in my experience of her. It was a definite alarm. She was very upset about something. She came quickly to my shoulder when I returned to the aviary. She is on my shoulder now as I type this. She is quiet (for her), letting out little under-her-breath sounds, responding to the sounds the others are making in the aviary, particularly one of the Quakers, who themselves are great ones for warning when something strange is happening. She also makes these soft parrot-growling remarks without being prompted by the others. She stares straight ahead, not looking over at me as she usually does at least briefly when she is on my shoulder, and is backing and ducking (parroting?) away from my hand as I go to touch her head. She is definitely upset. There is some comfort to her in being on my shoulder. I bet she won't fly away. But she does not want to be disturbed either. She is on full alert.

Asking the Question

When the other birds set off their alarm systems—usually it is one or both of the conures or the Quakers—and every bird is loudly commenting on the situation, Lime's contribution is an equally loud "What's going on? What's going on?" It provides another example of how human words or phrases spoken with strong emotions are those most likely to be learned and repeated by Amazons, Lime in particular.

Lime Introduces a Screech

Lime has introduced an incredibly annoying and disturbing screech, followed by foul language to get attention. I don't know which word is best to describe the initial sound, "screech" or "shriek." We really need to socialize this out of her repertoire. She is creative—we have to give her that. She is always finding new ways of getting attention. We tried yelling back at her, mostly with a very loud "No!" but that only cuts an outburst short rather than stopping future ones. The best strategy so far involves a spoonful of peanut butter. Once she has uttered a cry, I go into the aviary and hand the spoon to her. She takes it in her left talon, and is immediately quiet. As long as it works, we'll stick with this strategy. If she returns to shrieking, I chase her around the aviary, wildly waving a newspaper in my hand. She flies back and forth across the room until I can hear her breathing heavily when she stops.

Lime's Clucking

I have read that people shouldn't engage in "courtship behaviour" with birds. The problem is that Lime cannot read, so, as you will see later on, she does cluck and shake sometimes when she is on my head, and she is feeling hormonal. I assure you that I do not do anything to encourage such behaviour. I have never bought her flowers or written poetry for her, and I wouldn't want her near a candle.

However, sometimes when she is on my shoulder Lime starts to shake as though she has swallowed something that is blocking her breathing passages. Then she "clucks," sounding just like a hen that has been disturbed. Her head even retracts a bit, much like a clucking chicken. She used to do this a lot; the behaviour stopped for a while, but now it's back. It seems to happen most in late winter and early spring, perhaps a point in the year that can be linked hormonally with Amazon reproduction. Typically, she flies onto my bald head and the behavior starts. I reckon, as so does Angie, that this is a sexual expression, and she thinks she is my mate. It must be difficult for birds in captivity, not having a proper mate with whom to express those biological urges. I love you too, girl, just not in that way.

By the summer the clucking and shaking have completely vanished, but I feel certain that it will return the same time next year. In *Life with Ben: A Story of Friendship and Feathers* (2010), Jessica Hagedorn notes that her vet explained that springtime was the mating season for Amazons, and once Ben's hormone levels fell, the strange behaviour that she was noticing would diminish. It did. Joanna Burger, with her male Amazon Tiko, experienced clucking as well, as she described in *The Parrot Who Owns Me*, and there are YouTube videos of Amazons and other relatively large birds clucking when they are in season.

Preening, Lime and John
Lime-Sur-Tete: An Early Coming Together

For the last half an hour Lime has been on my head, tail to the front, her head to the back. She occasionally makes contented sounds, and preens my head as Louis does. This is new for her, part of our growing closeness. My posture is also improving.

Why does she like being on my bald head? Parrots, like many smart birds (I'm thinking crows and blue jays), like to be on the highest perch they can find. It is where they are comfortable. I think that by being on my head, Lime (like Louis, Poccopeck and sometimes Quigley) is demonstrating her great comfort with me. I take it as a compliment, not as a symbol of dominance. I like it.

John Preens Lime

It took a very long time for Lime to permit me to preen her in the back of her neck. Such permission had only been given previously to me by Benji, Tikka, Louis and Quigley. This began with an unusual exception to the no preen rule between John and Lime. When I stand outside the aviary mesh, and put my fingers through to where she is on the other side, she will typically bow her head down so that I can preen her with two fingers. Maybe she does not completely trust me when my hands are free: too many incidents of "tickle parrot, tickle parrot." She only trusts my fingers. This permission lasts for only a short period of time, but I like it, and I know she does too. We often do this.

Preening as Peace Making

Lime has been perched on my shoulder or in the crook of my right arm, left talon on elbow, right talon on forearm, facing me, for well over two hours now. This could be the longest that she has ever done that. It's the day after one of our fights. This may also be the first time I have ever seriously preened her; I can't remember. I have been breaking the nail-like casings or keratin sheaths of her pin feathers on her head and neck, and she lets me do that. I am not so good with the white tufts of down, and she is not pleased when I try that. I will stick with the pin feathers. I know why they call them that now, as I have several times jabbed myself with one. She even tucked her head into my shoulder when I preened her. I am pretty sure that that is a first for us. She fluffed up a bit several times after I had crushed the sheath of a pinfeather between my thumb and second finger nails. And, in return, she preened my mouth, making sure that the toothpaste that was left around my mouth, something that Angie often comments on, is no longer there. I try not to bring to mind the time that Lime bit and numbed my lip.

Preening seems to have changed our relationship. She sometimes rests her head against mine when she is on my shoulder. I often now can simply pet her as I would a dog , and she does not move her head or go to lightly bite me as she would have done before. Mutual preening has brought us closer together.

I am discovering with Lime how difficult it is to properly preen a bird, which involves breaking the sheath of the pin feathers in a way that Lime likes. If my fingers go too low on the pin feather, or pull it, it must hurt, as I immediately get a squawk and an almost certain bite in return. There is a fine art to it. I have since read that when pin feathers begin their cycle of growth, they can also be called blood feathers, as there are veins throughout. The veins gradually withdraw. I wish that I had read that earlier. I've also learned that parrots' beaks have veins running through them, so they can feel it when you touch them there, much more so than a human can feel someone touching the surfaces of their fingernails or toenails.

Mind you, it is easier for birds to preen birds than it is for humans to preen birds, as they get to put their faces right into the feathers of the other bird and come face-to-feather, eyes-to-sheathes with the pin feathers. I have to part the feathers with fingers that are very far from my eyes and try to break the keratin sheath without pulling on it. As a result, I have to go by feel rather than by sight. But I am learning and I have to respect Lime's patience with me. After all, I'm only human—possibly the best use for that phrase I've ever found.

Self-Preening Calms Lime Down

Lime had been put in her cage so Angie could clean the aviary without fearing an attack. Angie was just letting Lime out when the little birds attacked Lime. Lime became very distressed by this, her fluffed-up feathers a sure sign. Angie called for me to come get Lime, who definitely looked upset as she stepped up. I carried Lime back to my office. She was still fluffed-up standing on my shoulder, so I put her on my head. That did the trick. She began a long, extended self-preen. Soon it looked like it was snowing on my sweatshirt, or that I suffered from a severe case of dandruff. She continued to preen herself did this for about an hour. When I returned her to the aviary, she was a much happier bird than when she had left. I was happier too, except for the birdie dandruff all over me.

Preening and Trust

I have always hated objects coming near my eyes—eye-drops, for instance. This is a major reason why, although I have worn glasses since I was 15, I have never worn contact lenses and in fact am totally "grossed out" by the very thought of them. As I am now an old man in my sixties, I have my eyes checked every year for glaucoma. I am normally a good patient when it comes to injections, blood withdrawals and other physical indignities. But with the glaucoma test I flinch several times in anticipation of the puff of air attacking me.

In stark contrast to this is my love of having Lime preen my right eye. I see her large, often destructive beak slowly approach my eye socket, right next to my nose. I feel no apprehension. In fact, I feel the very opposite. When Lime preens my right eye, it calms me down. From the beginning it was a matter of building trust for me, rather like the team-building game where you let yourself fall freely backward into someone else's waiting arms. I had a very hard time with that game and I can well imagine that Lime felt the same way when I first began preening her.

Lime and Her Talented Talons
Lime and Spoons

Lime has talented talons when it comes to grabbing things. Early on, we taught her how to eat yogurt with a small spoon, and she repeated that trick several times during her first year with us. Today as I write this, she was being very loud, swearing, singing and generally trying to get my attention. Angie suggested that I give her a spoon with peanut butter on it. I did, and she was instantly quiet, holding the spoon in her left talon. She demonstrated her dexterity by flying to another perch and landing without dislodging the spoon. And she kept quiet.

She regularly receives a spoon with peanut butter on it in the morning. As you read earlier, I will admit that the primary purpose of doing so is to keep her quiet. I am amazed by how well she handles the spoon. If she grabs it upside down, she can quickly turn it over, using beak and talon. When she picks it up too close to one end, again she grabs it with her beak, moves it, and takes a new talon-grasp in a better place. Those talons are hands. To tell a bad joke, she is "talonted."

Her Talons Rise

Lime's talons rise as her right foot slowly lifts up. It looks like the reverse version of those old grasping devices in glass enclosures that I encountered in fairs and exhibitions as a child. (A similar contraption figures in one of the *Toy Story* movies—remember "the claw"?) You slowly moved the claw down to try to grab a toy or, better yet, the grand prize, a table lighter—that must surely be a collectors' item by now! When I mention a table lighter to young people today, I expect looks of complete bafflement.

As Lime lifts her right foot up she fluffs up too, baby-birding her face. She slowly, methodically, dreamily strokes her lower face. It is then that she reminds me of the young bird—never little; somehow I imagine her emerging from a huge, adult Amazon-size egg, feathers fully fledged—that she was when we first reached out to bond with each other.

This behavior always attracts me to her, but when I reach out the moment is lost, though the bond is intensified. We play together, her biting the hand that her talons have sought out to gain support. I wonder sometimes whether she acts like this only when I am around, or whether she also does so when I'm not. I think it is the former, but that might be difficult to prove. Somehow I don't think that I could hide anywhere near the aviary without her being aware of my presence. She can see, hear, and, I suspect, smell me as well.

Battles Between Bird and Human

Lime and I sometimes have our quarrels. Today, for instance, she flew off my shoulder to the large spoons and her spot in the kitchen. Quigley was perched on Angie's shoulder. Lime flew over to Angie's other shoulder, and there was a fight. Angie said that Quigley started it. I went over to remove Lime from Angie's shoulder, but I should have been more careful. I've been bitten doing this before, and that is what happened this time, too: Lime bit me as hard as she has ever done before, the lower part of my right thumb quickly beginning to bleed. I'd already had a bad day writing and was feeling mildly depressed, so my temper flared. I grabbed ahold of Lime and marched her to the aviary. I hate getting that angry at a bird or a dog or a cat. And Lime has a special place in my heart, so it hurt doubly.

I knew that at some point Lime and I had to make up, as I calmed down and felt guilty for being angry. I looked into the aviary a few times, and she looked back, but I didn't make a move. Then, when I was in the bathroom, I heard her two-note whistle, the one that sounds like she is right in the room with me. That can be a heartmelter, as it is intended to be. So I went over to the aviary and got her to step up. Her tail was a bit spread, her crest a bit fluffed, and there was a slight constriction of the pupils. This indicated to me that she still was feeling some emotions that she hadn't completely dealt with yet. We both were powering down and wanted to spend time with each other, but both of us had to be careful with the other.

I brought her over to where I was working on some historical research. I got to pat her longer than ever before. We went beak to beak (called "billing" when two birds do it, as in the English phrase "bill and coo"), with her beak fitting into the curve of my nose down to my mouth. Wait! Is that a kind of courtship behaviour that I should be avoiding? She tried to get food from my lip, but did so gently. She even preened me a bit. We had made up. It seemed to be something that we both needed, and both received. We will fight in the future, but I know that we will always make up.

Lime and I Make Up

I just sat down to watch the hockey game, Lime flew to the top of my head, and everything was fine. Then Stanee flew to my right shoulder, which made Lime jealous. Unfortunately, never having won a battle with Stanee (to my knowledge), Lime took her jealous anger out on me, and gave me a nasty bite. I nodded her off my head and then expressed my anger at her with a towel, chasing her around the room. Then I sat down. Lime looked at me, cocking her head and making soft noises. I couldn't resist that for very long, so I stood up and walked over to her cage, where she was on the top outer perch. She made a point of very, very softly putting pressure with her beak on my finger, really nothing like a bite at all. We were making up.

Lime is Angry with Me Again

Tonight Lime is angry with me again. I came home from the college at about 9:30, after leaving home before seven o'clock this morning, a long day for me. She stared at me from a distance as I swept into the aviary to gather up, clean and refill the water dishes. When I went over to her to put her in her cage for the night she was a little fluffed-up and bit me twice, hard. She then flew from her bicycle-tire perch to one of the perches on the aviary wall, threatening to bite each time my hand approached her. I was tired, and not the most patient person on earth. I wanted to go to bed myself. We battled and I grabbed her hard. I tried to stroke her beak once she was inside, but she was not in a mood for such pleasantries. Clearly she was angry with me, and the only reason I can think of was my long absence from her. I had some explaining to do.

The next morning she did not fly to my head as she often does when I am sitting on the plastic chair and eating my cereal. She wasn't ready to make up with me, even for food. I played with her a bit before I left for work. Her heart wasn't in it, and I moved my hands quickly so not to get bitten. When I got home after work, I had to spend some serious time with her before we were able to make up.

Another Fight

Months had passed since our major last conflict when Lime and I had another fight. It was the second morning in a row that she bit me hard, slightly drawing blood on my thumb. I was instantly angry and gave her a smack with my left hand. Later, after I had breakfast with the birds, I went over to her on her favourite perch to make up with her. She bit me hard again, and I retaliated again. This had become serious.

Later yet, I came back with a peace offering of a spoonful of peanut butter. But on this occasion she was having none of it. This was the first time that had ever happened in our years together. I left the aviary unhappily, returning to my writing.

I came back about 20 minutes later, to offer Lime a step up and time on daddy's shoulder. Again, she refused—another first. Okay, a serious fight means serious making up. I kept offering her my hand, and after about five minutes, she accepted my peace-offering, and she and I then enjoyed some shoulder time. I gave her a section of orange, something I know that she likes. My hair is sticky with juice.

Later that same morning she gave out the now-familiar screech. I went into the aviary, and got her to step up onto my shoulder. She spent about half-an-hour there, and when I had to get her off so I could go outside, she was reluctant to leave.

That evening, she escaped from the aviary and perched on my shoulder. She listened carefully when I said "No bites."

The next morning I was extra careful, and there was indeed no biting. But she again refused the spoonful of peanut butter, after months of having it every morning. Just when you think that you have figured them out.... This behavior would last for more than a week.

During the last few days when she has screeched, I have come over to get her to step up, and she has refused the offer, instead climbing up the mesh of the aviary. Later on, maybe the second or third try, she makes herself available. She seems to be playing hard-to-get.

Lime Has Me Confused

These days Lime really has me confused. It began after our big fight, when it took a lot to coax her into accepting her spoonful of peanut butter and to step up. For the last few days it has been difficult for me to get her to accept the peanut butter. Sometimes if I'm patient she accepts it, but sometimes she does not, no matter how patient I am.

It's the same with refusing to step up. Instead, she climbs up the aviary mesh wall until she is out of reach except for a beak skritch. One morning she whistled me into the aviary. I expected that she would step up, but no, she didn't. No matter how I tried to coax her, she was not having it. I don't have the slightest idea why she is doing this. She has me baffled. And the bafflement increased later that same day. Twice she called me to the aviary, and both times she readily stepped up. The first time she stayed on my head, quiet and unmoving, for a little over an hour. I finally had to take her back to the aviary as I needed to take the garbage out.

The next morning, it one refusal and then one acceptance. I really don't understand it. I continue to need to learn about and from her.

The Attack

And then there was the week when we experienced the downside of having an Amazon in the house....

Lime attacked Angie, whose left eye still looks like someone punched her out. (I'm sure that when some people see Angie and me together, they are giving me a dirty look and don't buy the idea that a bird did it.) Because of the attack, Angie is afraid to be in the aviary with Lime, and I don't blame her. So I've had to put Lime in her cage whenever Angie wants to clean up in there or spend time with the other parrots, particularly Quigley. Still, I feel bad doing it.

The Happy (Chapter) Ending

But I don't want to end this chapter on a negative note, so here is the happy ending.

The Old Side-to-Side

Lime had been in her cage for quite some time. I put her there because Angie was spending time in the aviary, first interacting with the parrots and then performing her cleaning regimen. It was a while after Angie left before I remembered that Lime was still in her cage.

I went into the aviary to release her, and she looked at me and did her old side-to-side routine, just like when she had been a very young bird in the pet store. I think it had been over a year since she last did that. She must know that I cannot resist that move. I released her from her cage with a tear in my eye.

Here's Looking at You, Kid

For the last few minutes Lime has had her beak in my eye; not in my eyeball, but right beside it, mere millimetres away, her upper mandible not moving, the lower mandible moving as her tongue slides up and down between my nose and my eyeball. (Both parts of her beak can move, so they are both mandibles.) She is feeling close to me right now; I can smell it on her breath. I sometimes wonder how she detects my emotional closeness. However she does it, I am sure that she knows what I am feeling. We are back together again. And despite all the stories I have told of the two of us quarrelling, close is our usual state.

Chapter Five
The Africans

Sammy: A Senegal's Story
by Angelika Steckley

Sammy came from jail, where he'd been confined to a large enough cage, but was never allowed out into the exercise compound. He was surrounded by other prison mates, some who shared cages with their own kind and others who, like him, were in solitary confinement. He lived in lights-out conditions for most of the day, and was fed a diet of seeds and water, the "bread and water" that simply kept him alive. He had to fight for his safety and, through rigorous practice, became a to-be-feared biter. The extent of the inmates' communication was mostly screaming for attention from the jail-keeper.

Sammy was an innocent soul, incarcerated for being a Senegal parrot. When we first spoke with him, he offered a plaintive "Hellllo?" We ended his sentence by paying $450, granting him freedom under our care. At home with us, he lives in an always-clean perch-furnished cage, which is supplied with fresh water, healthful foods, gravel and toys. We had to wean him off seeds, the only food he knew. He now enjoys a varied diet of fruit, vegetables, pellets and nuts. His favourite food is the pistachio. After two months of sharing a loving home, he sometimes resorted to biting, especially if he misunderstood our intentions when we approached him. Quickly, he apologizedwith his usual "Hellllo?"

After a few days with me, Sammy found a wonderful look-out perch on my shoulder from which he observed life as a free spirit. He surprised himself when he suddenly took flight and gave a little "chirp" when he landed on a shelf. Sammy quickly grew to trust me and after a week, he looked *forward to our cuddle time. Whenever he seemed fearful, feathers tucked closely to his body, I would calm him gently, saying, "It's OK." He even caught on to the word "ya" that my husband and I use in our chats. During his talk-times he invents variations on the theme "It's OK." With pride, he fluffs up and tries out different phrases like "OK? OK?", "It's OK? Ya, Ya. Ya. OK. OK," and "It's OK? It's OK? OK."*

When we first brought Sammy home, I'd prepare him for gentle petting by saying, "Scritch." The word meant I wanted to please him, not hurt him. Soon after my offer of "Scritch," he lowered his head in delightful anticipation. One day, while perched on my shoulder, happily watching me tap the keyboard as I worked, he produced a strange sort of hiccup sound: "Eh-hhhh." I stopped typing and turned my head to check on him. His pupils were dilating and contracting wildly. I asked, "Are you OK?" He cocked his head, and seemed content. I continued typing. After a few seconds, he repeated the murmur, "Eh-hhh," almost a choking-like utterance. He wanted a scritch.

[The author intrudes: To me the sound seems like Sam imitating a dog's bark. However you describe it, the meaning is clear: he wants physical attention. For me it means "Stroke my beak."]

African Parrots

Africa is home to many different parrot species that range from the diminutive, deeply monogamous lovebirds (genus *Agapornis*, from the Greek words *agape* "love" and *ornis* "bird") to the best-known face of African parrotkind, the much larger African Grey, ably represented by the very vocal Alex in *Alex and Me* and the *Alex Studies* by Irene Pepperberg. This chapter is about neither of those two types of bird, although I have met both and would have no objections to having a pair of the former and one of the latter in our aviary—though we would definitely have to expand it! However, this chapter is about Meyer's parrots and Senegals, specifically one of each.

Meyer's Parrots and Misha

Meyer's parrots, bearing the scientific name of *Poicephalus meyeri*, are subtly beautiful African birds. They are named after German physician and naturalist Bernhard Meyer (1767–1836). They live in the wild in the east-central part of Africa, from Ethiopia straight south to South Africa. Their numbers are still considerable in most of the countries in which they live, particularly the southern country of Botswana.

Misha Memories

I can't write much about Misha because we did not have him long, and he was much more Angie's parrot than he was mine. He never stepped up onto my hand as he did with Angie. She even got to cuddle him, a gift not many parrots offer. What I do remember about him was that he went to bed (cage) at the same time every night, religiously following the store hours he had become used to before he moved in with us. I liked to watch him when he played with small wooden vines that we would provide for him. It was fun to see him systematically destroy them. He was entirely engaged in the process of destruction, as parrots can sometimes be.

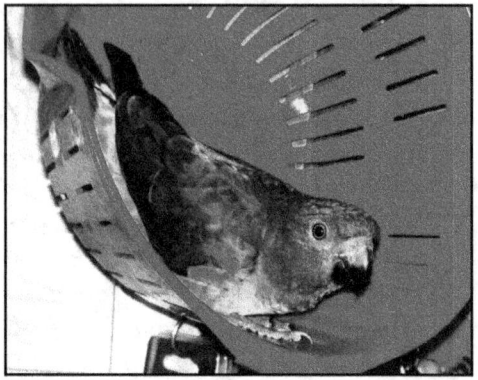

Misha

I wish I could have gotten to know Misha better. We lost him when he flew out our front door one cold day in December. A delivery van came to our house, and the driver foolishly opened the door even though there was a big sign on it telling people not to do that. Angie was busy helping our neighbours with a tree that they had just cut down. I was at work at the college when I received Angie's frantic call that Misha had flown out the front door. The drive back home from work was not a pleasant one. I was conjuring up too many pictures in my mind of a lost and freezing parrot.

I remember looking for Misha, scanning the trees and the skies around the neighbourhood. There is a line of well-groomed bushes near our place, the result of a factory owner's dedication to nature. I looked very carefully through those bushes. Every bird I saw looked like Misha for a microsecond. I crossed the small highway that runs north and south through our town. There was a pigeon highlighted against the darkening sky by the lights near the Canadian Tire store. For a few agonizing minutes I thought that it might be Misha. For weeks afterward—months, really—I sought Misha on every walk that I took with the dogs. I whistled to the sky in ways that I hope would attract him. I would repeat those whistles even louder close to home.

About two years after we lost Misha, a distraught young woman came to our house. She was looking for her parrot that had flown away. She knew that we were "parrot people." It is hard not to notice that, what with the volume some of our birds achieve, particularly Lime, and with no curtains on the aviary window (for reasons that, now knowing about the destructiveness of parrots, will find obvious). More sympathetic to her plight we could not have been. Both Angie and I searched for that parrot; every walk I took I looked up, hoping to see her bird. I re-lived in a small way our own loss of Misha.

We acquired Sam because we were looking for a Misha-type. We could not find a Meyer's parrot but instead got a Senegal, an African parrot that belongs to the same genus. There is a strong resemblance.

I still wonder when I walk by the nearby bushes whether Misha will appear, still imagine that a bird will come flying out of the bushes and land on my shoulder (as Misha actually never did when he lived with us). That dream lives on years later. It combines with my daytime fantasy that a parrot I have never met before will fly towards me and land on my shoulder, knowing me to be a "parrot person." I know people to whom that has happened.

Senegals

A blogger named "Mona" posted the following Senegal story, which tells you something about the species. The context for the story was a parrot show put on by a local bird club. A would-be bird trainer was trying to demonstrate the value of clicker-training, a benighted behaviorist strategy for which I have no sympathy:

> The Senegal upstaged the demonstration of how to use a clicker as a bridge for behavior training. The purpose of the clicker is to signal to the bird that they have correctly performed a specific behavior and a reward is forthcoming. This little guy turned the tables on the demonstration and made the clicking noise himself. I was charmed by this demonstration of who was directing whom. Some behaviorists term this "begging" behavior but I later learned that it was a demonstration of how well these little birds mimic and how quickly they figure out just exactly what they need to do to get their favorite person's undivided attention.
>
> That day, I made a mental note that my next bird would be a Senegal ('Mona', "Senegals as Pets", November 17, 2009; taken from an article in *Pet and Aviary Birds Magazine*, February/March 2004).

I am in complete agreement with Mona. And I love how the Senegal outsmarted the trainer.

As I mentioned, Senegals (*Poicephalus senegalus*) belong to the same genus as do Meyer's parrots. There are several etymologies for the genus name *Poicephalus*. All agree on the obvious translation of "cephalus" from the original Greek word for "head." It is the "poi" part that is contested, with various meanings given: "made of," "different" (as in "different from the body"), and "green" or "grassy." The definition that makes most sense to me is that suggested by Dr. James Mejeur of the National Aviary in Pittsburgh, who says "poi" comes originally from "phaios," meaning "grey" or "dusky," with later scholars sloppily changing the spelling to "poi," which is close to "poia," meaning "grassy" (www.moonsgarden.com/12_5dbfa03576668b01_1.htm). Supporting this definition is the fact that of the 10 different species in the genus, eight have a dusky grey or brown head.

It is Senegals' dark grey heads that lend them their name both in French (*perroquet à tête noire*, or "parakeet with a black head") and in German. The German name is *Mohrenkopf-Papagei*, the first word literally meaning "Moor's head," a reference to the old name for the dark-skinned people of northern Africa. Today this German word is also used to refer to two chocolate-glazed treats, one a chocolate-covered marshmallow, another a cream cake. The second part of the name is from a word for parrot in ancient Persian, a name something like *babagha*. It was then borrowed into Arabic, then into the Germanic languages, including the English word "popinjay," which first referred just to parrots, then to flashy, extravagant, flamboyant self-presenters, a term that fit our Senegal Sam, and probably many other Senegals as well. Not reflected in the species' name is the fact that, when seen from the side, their bright yellow eyes make them (especially Sam) look like they are descended directly from *Tyrannosaurus rex*. As my favourite description of this feature puts it, "Their yellow iris gives them a somewhat intense gaze, but don't let that fool you into thinking it is possessed" (www.birdchannel.com/bird-species/profiles/poicephalus.aspx).

As their name suggests, Senegals are native to West Africa. Another prominent Senegal feature is the V-shaped orange belly and chest that to my hockey-focused mind makes them look like they are wearing old Vancouver Canucks' uniforms, the really bright ones.

Senegals are one of the relatively few parrots whose sex can be visually identified. You can tell whether they are male or female by their under-tail covert feathers. It is easy to remember which feathers are the coverts as they are the ones that *cover* the others. They streamline the air flow to aid in flight. Females and immature Senegals have mostly green under-tail coverts. In physically mature males they are yellow.

Our Sam loves dark places. This should not be too surprising as Senegals in the wild nest in holes in trees, especially the palm oil tree. The males defend their nests, as Sam does his own dark places. His sudden lunge is a scary surprise if you are not ready for it.

Senegals migrate within West Africa, and are considered by millet and maize growers to be agricultural pests. As you have read earlier, I never completely trust those kinds of statements, as I know that with Quaker parrots (and I suspect with yellow-headed Amazons too) the destruction they are alleged to wreak is grossly exaggerated. As Bernd Heinrich said of similar negative opinions about ravens, "facts expand in minds when they are not opposed by knowledge." (Heinrich 2006:xvii)

Senegals have long been known in Europe. The Venetian explorer Aloysius Cada Mosto (1432–1488) made written reference to them in 1445. In the second volume of Greene's *Parrots in Captivity*, it is stated that in 1884 they were commonly available "in commerce," and were relatively inexpensive in Britain (Greene 1884b:58-9).

Their status in the wild is threatened, in significant part because they may be the most captured-and-traded parrot in the world. Their bright colours, ability to talk, agility and often-comical nature have made them popular world-wide. In 2012, Steve Boyes, a Meyer's specialist, cited the statistic that over three million Senegals had been traded over the last 30 years. They appear in local African markets and are flown (often illegally) to other places in the world. Their forest habitat is severely threatened by forest degradation caused by charcoal production (for heat and for stoves), logging, and the clearing of fields for agriculture. And their palm-oil nesting trees are much favoured for producing an ingredient used in many products (e.g., margarine), resulting in severe deforestation in a number of regions.

The Story of Sam
The Buying of Sam

After we lost Misha, unable to find another Meyer's, we went online and found a near-relative—a Senegal that might fill at least part of the hole in our hearts left by our loss. Quickly bringing a new parrot into our lives when we have lost one is something we have done more than once. In fact, four of our eight parrots have had the unenviable role of replacing a beloved bird. All have done a beautiful job.

We arranged to meet Sam's owner at his home. The house was nice, but the basement where the parrots were kept was very much as I imagine slave ships to have been below decks. It was deathly dark before the lights went on. The birds were crowded together: conures, cockatiels, cockatoos, macaws and Amazons, one Quaker, and Sam. (And I'm probably missing a few of the sad crowd—in no real sense was it a flock—that we found there.) We wanted to free all of them. But we could only take one. Sam was alone in his cage. There was obvious animosity between owner and bird. They hated and feared each other. We had been tentative about buying him before we got there, but not when we saw how he lived. I don't come from a culture of negotiation; the owner did, but I still talked him down. He could have stood his ground. What he did not know was that there was no way that we were leaving without the little guy. We were to play the role of rescuers.

It was a cash transaction. We drove over in separate cars to a small desolate strip mall on the seedy outskirts of Brampton, Ontario. I went to a bank machine and took out the payment, all in twenties, for our new family member. It probably looked as though a drug deal was taking place. I handed over the cash and we took the bird, which was in a covered travel cage. No one looking on would have known what it was that we were purchasing. Had the cops been nearby, they would have detained us for sure. It would have taken a great deal of careful explaining to make them believe we were buying a bird. "Is parrot some kind of code word for marijuana?" I can well imagine both Sam's and the officer's response, especially if the latter's fingers came within striking range of Sam's sharp black beak.

The first day we had Sam at home we learned what an amazing imitator he was. Several times that day I thought that the microwave had signalled that it was finished its nuking, but it was Sam that had made the sound. He has refined this talent over the years. Not only does he do a perfect imitation of our programming the microwave, but he also makes the sound before the machine does. He hears the microwave door open, and anticipates perfectly what the next sound will be, sometimes following up with his version of the "cooking is done" beeping.

Senegals are well-known among their human owners as birds that imitate mechanical noises amazingly well. The list of their imitative accomplishments includes doorbell chimes, smoke detector alarms and fax modem sounds (Beaudoin n.d.). Their African Grey cousins are able, as duly noted by Betty Jean Craige in regard to her bird Cosmo, to anticipate and imitate the squeaking of cabinet and garage doors as well as mimicking microwave ovens' sounds (Craige 2010: 23).

Senegals can also sound a bit mechanical when they articulate human words. Terry Beaudoin accurately refers to their speech as "almost computer generated" (Beaudoin n.d.). That accurately describes Sam's "good night." It is one of those strange coincidences that one of the early text-to-speech computer devices was known as SAM (software automatic mouth).

What follows is the first story that I wrote about Sam. The One Big Parrot still survives over all the years since this was written. I don't think now that it will ever go away. There is a fear in Sam that haunts him to this day, not surprising for a basement-dwelling bird who lived much of his early life in the dark—and not the comforting nesting darkness of a parrot hut or personal bucket (of which more below).

That One Big Parrot: An Early Story of Sam

Senegal Sam is always looking out for that One Big Parrot. Let me tell you his story. When we first met Sam, he was alone in a cage in a room full of crowded, lonely parrots. He was very afraid of everything—people, sounds, sights—and showed his fear by biting. If I had gone through what he did, I would bite people too.

Sam is a beautiful bird. The top of his head is gray, most of his body green, but there is a big V in his chest that converts the green above to a brilliant orange and yellow below. And then there is his large hooked black beak. He used that weapon a lot when we first got him. He bit a toe off Stanee, our female green-cheeked conure (for which, amazingly, she forgave him soon after, as he was still only a baby in her eyes). He seriously blooded Louis, her rose-crowned mate. He savaged human fingers that came near him. And he was perpetually searching for that One Big Parrot.

How do we know that he is looking for that One Big Parrot? We first saw evidence of this when he walked past a box with a hole for parrots to walk through. He cried out and made himself look as large as he could, fluffing up his feathers and holding up his wings like he was Dracula ready to spring forward and bite an innocent female victim. He made serious clicking noises as he did this. He was very scary looking and sounding—if you didn't laugh to break the mood he appears to be trying to create.

Whenever he passed the box, he made himself big, ready to defend himself against that One Big Parrot. He does the same thing when he lands somewhere new. His body gets big as he clicks out loud, "Watch out, One Big Parrot. There is a very big fearsome Senegal parrot coming. Get out of the dark. I am ready for you. I am big. I am loud. I am Sam."

Sam seems to be true to his species' usual behaviour in his liking for dark places. His favourite spot now is a big black box made of plastic. He perches on the ledge, gets big, gets loud and jumps into the box. We might not seem him for hours, but we know, even if we can't see him, that he is there. The One Big Parrot will not catch him unawares. Sam is vigilant.

Sam learned a lot in the first year that we had him. Stanee decided that she should be his mother parrot and preened him, calming him down. He loves her. Quigley, our first parrot, the mayor of our little Parrotville flock, also stands by him (this would change years later). Sam has calmed down a lot. He bites us less often, although you have to be careful. There are a few bloody incidents with the other parrots, but we feel more comfortable leaving him alone with them without us watching over the whole flock.

But there is still that One Big Parrot. Sam flies. Sam lands. Sam fluffs up huge and clicks loud. Sam is still looking for that One Big Parrot. Anyone can have an imaginary friend. Sam has an imaginary foe, an enemy he needs to defeat before he can be happy and satisfied with himself. I think that the One Big Parrot is fear. Someday, we hope that One Big Parrot will disappear into a black hole somewhere, leaving Sam alone with his bravery and his friends. But so far that day hasn't arrived.

Sam the Child

Sam is still Stanee's child. I saw evidence of that one morning when I was watching the Canadian men's hockey team win gold in the 2014 Olympics. Sam dropped to the floor several times, most of those times going for my foot. Why I don't know—I had my shoes on, not my flip-flops, nor was I barefoot or wearing just my socks. The four times that he went down to the floor, Stanee did too. That's what she did when we got a new bird and it couldn't fly. She is still protecting him, though I'm not sure why. He gets his own food (although she still feeds him with regurgitation). For a while he had his own cage, but that was the first place she went to when she was released from her own cage each morning. There is something about him that, at least for her, gives off bird-child vibes. Maybe it is the fear inside him that she somehow senses, the fear that I can see only when he fluffs up to challenge the One Big Parrot.

Determined Mother and Reluctant Son

Mother and son are standing beside each other on the wooden ledge that meets the mesh. Stanee is trying to preen the top of his head, but Sam is having none of it. The top of his head is nearly feather-bald because of her preening. He is complaining and his wings are spread out to make himself look big and fierce. She ascends up the mesh so that she is ideally positioned for top of the head preening. His wings are still out. He is still complaining, but he accepts that there is really nothing he can do in the face of a tough form of mother's love.

In small ways she is letting him grow up. They are not together as often as they once were. And she does not automatically take his side when Quigley drives him away from a food dish. But she still feels a need to preen him.

Sam Says "Goodnight": An Early Interpretation

When I put out the stick for Sam to step up onto, he often says "goodnight." If he doesn't say it then, he will say it once he is placed into his cage. Sam is one of two birds—Lime is the other—who used to expect to receive a peanut after everyone else was put in his or her cage. When I left the aviary to go fetch the peanuts, he repeated his "goodnight." He kept this up until he received his peanut. Then he was silent, save for the delighted crunching of the peanut. Were his repeated goodnights reminders that the goodnight process was not yet complete when it was peanutless?

I have begun to notice that whenever I am in the aviary "too long"—if I'm watching overtime in hockey or extra innings in baseball and stay beyond the usual ten o'clock closing time—Sam starts saying "goodnight." He is usually in his cage when he says this. I think he is dropping me a hint. Although Sam is usually very direct in his approach, perhaps his goodnights have a variety of meanings related to the proper ending of the day.

By the way, I no longer offer up peanuts to these two birds at night. Too many partially shelled and uneaten peanuts were dropped onto cage floors. But I still think that Sam's goodnight is meant as a bonding communication, whatever the more specific meaning might be in a particular context. Later stories illustrate that.

Sam and Dark Places

Sam is in a dark place (both metaphorical and actual). This is not unusual for him. He has a number of such shadowy sites that suit him, including underneath newspapers in his cage, one reason why changing the paper or water dish can be dangerous if you don't check the papers first. This time the dark place was a hut made specifically for parrots. It looks like a rounded hut carved out of a stump, or a large half-coconut—the sort of place where beachcomber parrots would sip piña coladas on a deck chair (if they could sip) and use straws rather than chew them. But he is inside and hidden, looking out at a threatening world. Whenever I come to visit the birds at night, that is one of the most likely places to find him. The other birds are out somewhere, in small groups or happy and satisfied to be alone, self-preening. Only Sam is hidden in a dark place. I hope that he feels comforted there.

Entering a Dark Place: Before Sam Moved In with Stanee

Sam flies to the door of Stanee's cage, full screech, full threat, wings outstretched when he lands, feathers high. Then he slowly, almost casually, looks around the cage for potentially threatening figures. He waits a bit. Then, as if suddenly struck by the thought, he hops over to Stanee's dish for some food. At night, when I go to put him in his cage for the night, I often find him in that cage, after looking high and low everywhere else. He will be high on the right side, in the dark, a shadowed figure. He is very hard to see when he is there. It is a safe place for him to be at the end of the day, but it's not safe for my hand if I don't know that he is there

We eventually put him in the same cage with Stanee. It has been over a year now, and both seem happy with the situation.

Just Stanee and Me and the Bucket Makes Three

Sam now has a new favourite dark place. It might be said that Senegals are the only creatures for whom the only thing on their bucket list is, in fact, a bucket, especially one filled with paper. Or maybe it is just Sam. He has his own such bucket. It is white and made out of plastic. When I conduct an inventory of the birds in the aviary and I can't see him, I look for him there. It would be easy and probably anthropomorphic to say that he looks "sad" there. Maybe, like Superman, he needs his Fortress of Solitude. Sometimes his bucket has a protector, as Stanee is often perched on the rim. Even Tikkifinn sometimes parks herself there. He is safe in his bucket.

The story of Sam's bucket began this way. After he spent months climbing into a deep white plastic bucket filled with dirty, shat-on papers, we decided that he should have his own white bucket with his name on it, and clean paper inside. No Senegal could ask for more.

Well, maybe he could. We have an identical bucket that we put poopy papers in before throwing them into the garbage outside. Not long after Sam got his new bucket and was sitting inside it, Angie, cleaning the aviary, started dumping dirty papers on top of him. The indignant look he gave her when she realized what she was doing, and took the papers back out of his bucket, was priceless. Sam got back at her about 10 minutes later. He flew over to the dirty-paper bucket, the one that Angie was using, and poached paper from it. Is turnaround really fair play? Sam, the dysfunctional parrot, seems to think that it is.

This bucket confusion happened several times over the next few weeks. We chucked papers into his hideaway and pressed them down. Then we realized Sam was nowhere in sight and an explosion of frantic movement in Sam's bucket would ensue. The lifting-out of papers and apologies were required. I wonder if he sometimes has nightmares of the sky crashing in upon him.

Sam and Stepping Up

Sam is one of only two of our birds who does not step up onto our fingers. The other is Tikkifinn. To be fair to Sam, I can't remember the last time I tried to ask him to step up and offered him anything other than a stick to step up onto. Of course, the main reason I don't ask him to step up onto my finger is the long series of bites that Angie and I have experienced from his beak. Saying this, I still don't think that I have the nerve to ask him. Putting a single finger in his path seems some kind of "bite wish" on my part. Periodically I try it with Tikkifinn, but she uses the Quaker gesture of pushing my hand away with her beak. I am able to give her the benefit of the doubt, but I can't yet imagine trying it with him. If I did and he bit me, it would be my own fault, not his. I also don't put my hand on a hot stove or my fingers between the blades of a whirling fan. Doing things like that is more than tempting fate. It's teasing it, too.

Sam Approaches

Sam flies to the plastic box on the table beside the chair I am sitting on, and looks up to and over at me. He wants to be up on my shoulder, I know that, but he does not try to let me know that beforehand. He seems to believe that stealth is the only way that he can come close to me. He's like a child who has never been around his parents. I ask him to "step up" on a stick I hold out to him, but he doesn't and he won't. Then, a few minutes later, he flies to my left knee.

He wants up, but makes no moves for a few more minutes. Then he clicks, the one language we share. It usually indicates that he wants his beak rubbed. He flies over to my right knee, where the pad of paper I am writing on is resting, and begins to shred it, one of his favourite activities. The shredding gets dangerously close to where I am writing and I flip him off.

He flies back to the plastic box, then to my left knee, clicking again. He then hops over the short space to my right knee and I shift the pad to my left. It is classic Sam to approach in tentative stages.

Stanee flies back over to my left knee, and he clicks again. I stroke his beak, he quietly threatens with an open mouth, but it doesn't seem too serious a threat. I suspected early on, though it took a while to be sure, that Sam likes having his beak stroked. He next moves to my left elbow when I'm not looking, then to my stomach and crawls up to my beard. I feel threatened and flick him off again.

Stanee preens me. Then Quigley chases her off and *he* preens me. Sam watches. Part of him wants to be with me. Part of him wants to bite me. Part of me wants him to visit my shoulder. Part of me wants him to stay away. Sam is in a dark place, but in some sense we are in that place together, and can't find our way out.

Irony and the Senegal

It's ironic that the closest physical contact that Sam and I have had is through his beak, the wreaker of havoc, blood and pain. One night I stroked his beak in between reading sessions. He very much enjoys the touch. He blinks his eyes and pushes his beak forward for a deeper touch. And he stays on my knee, the right one this time, even when I am not stroking his beak. I don't have the nerve, usually, to scritch the top of his head, so this has to be the best way that we relate.

But Sam is fickle. The next day he comes to my knee, but does just about everything he can to keep me from stroking his beak. There is to be no beak stroking tonight. Sam has put his beak down on the matter.

Sam and My Feet

Sam likes to go for my feet. He hits the floor running and chases my feet. Usually he does this when I am barefoot, sock-foot, or wearing clogs, but recently he has begun attacking my shoes. I know that parrots sometimes go after each other's toes. Poor Juno, our parrotlet, has suffered more than once because of that. Maybe Sam is carrying on a Senegal tradition.

It is not surprising that Sam is the only bird in our flock who goes after my toes and footwear. Nor is it unusual that he never learns that I will fight him on this matter. It's not just that he is wild. All of our parrots are, in a sense, wild animals. But he does not know how to learn from his mistakes; he just holds onto his fears from past experiences. He owes that mainly to his abusive past. The fear lives on, although the fear-provoking experiences do not. My rejection of his company probably reinforces the fear, however momentarily.

I have read on several websites that you should not react visibly or emotionally to Senegal biting. According to these "experts," you should respond calmly, letting them know that everything is "cool" (my choice of word). You shouldn't yell at them, flick them across the room, or spray water at them. Such actions, it is claimed, will only make the behavior worse. I beg to differ, and I would love to see one of these parrot whisperers in the aviary with Sam when he bursts out from underneath the paper in someone else's cage, and bites hard. To quote *Seinfeld*, I just can't picture them saying "Serenity now" and being peaceful, at least not without the help of calming drugs. Sam knows when he is bad, and he has learned that from our loud and sometimes wet reaction to him. If I splash him with water several times, he is keen later on to re-establish friendly contact.

Sam and the Man: The Water Torture

It was an epic struggle between man and beast, mammal and bird, human and parrot, bearded and feathered. When I sat down in the aviary to read, Sam started attacking my feet. It wasn't that it hurt, because I had my shoes on. It was merely annoying, not painful. At first I tried shooing (or is that shoeing?) him away with my feet, but that strategy didn't work. I had to fetch a stick for him to grab and for me to fling him away. That worked while I was sitting reading. However, once I started changing the parrots' water dishes, he attacked me again. I had to do something different, something sneaky, something very much like what Sam himself would do in my position if I were the parrot and he the human. I wet my fingers and started aiming little droplets of water onto his head and body. After repeating this a few times, he flew off. Success!

Don't count your chickens before they hatch, or your parrots before they stop a behaviour you don't like. And definitely don't count on your Senegal to give up easily in a war of nerves. He is keen to march on. The next time I came into the aviary he was on the ground again, ready to resume his assault on human pedal extremities. I repeated the cascade of droplets onto his parrot person. He flew away again. I took a dish out and returned. He was back on the floor. This time was different, however. He backed away when I approached him. He had never done that before. Success?

To reinforce the message, I dropped more little specks of water on him. Again, he flew away—four times now. He is determined, but so am I. Fifth time, action repeated. The sixth time I came in, he was not on the floor but up on his cage giving me a Senegal stare, exhibiting his *T. rex* heritage for all to see and fear. I suspect that I have won the battle tonight, but who knows how I will fare if the war continues. Life with Sam is never boring. I am sure he would say the same of me.

As I lay in bed later, I tried to recall what story this set of experiences with Sam reminded me of. The answer did not come to mind right away. And then I thought of the books written by the Scottish vet in Yorkshire, James Herriot, including one in which a dog regularly chased him to a fence. At some point the dog gave up, perhaps because Herriot had pulled some trick on the dog that the dog did not like. Later, when Herriot wondered what had happened to the dog, the farmer told him the dog's spirit had been broken as he would no longer chase after James. That made me wonder, and worry a little bit, about whether I might break Sam's spirit by ending one of his favourite forms of play. I would rather he tried to bite my feet than lose his spirit. Call me sentimental.

Update on the Water Therapy

So here is the new situation. Sam still goes to the floor to attack my feet, but he is not so bold as before. A stern "Sam!" can sometimes stop him mid-attack. And he is learning to expect the drops of water. One drop and he will fly off in a feathered huff. I think that is probably the best that I can expect: a Senegal standoff.

One more comment about this "water therapy." When I am changing the water dishes, I sometimes offer fresh, clean water to Sam. He never fails to take it, usually several times. No other bird, except occasionally Stanee, does this. Water bonds us, and it separates us too.

Sam Changes his Mind

Sam kept looking at me from on top of Lime's cage. I was sitting on the aviary chair trying to relax. Sam made a conversational clicking sequence at me. I knew he wanted to visit with me, and I returned the sequence.

After a while he climbed down the cage door. Instead of flying over to my knee, as I was expecting he would, he swooped down to the floor not far from my right leg. I was wearing my flip-flops. He usually looks upon that footwear choice as an open(-toed) invitation to attack my feet.

Sam walked over to my foot. I issued a few warning calls. He dropped his beak down on the sandal, in a characteristic Sam gesture that resembles one of those metal drinking-bird sculptures dipping down to obtain water. He clearly contemplated attacking my foot, but after some deep thought, and my clicking to him, he started to beak-and-talon climb up my pant leg, until he made it all the way to my right knee. I rewarded his decision with a full beak massage. He had changed his mind for the better.

The next day was different. He attacked my feet three separate times, with the attacks separated by his climbing midway up my shin, then back down again. He even attacked my feet, or really the shoelaces, when I changed into my shoes. There was no changing his mind this time.

Sam and the Water Dishes

Speaking of water, Sam likes to spill it. What happens is this. He is in the cage that he shares with Stanee: the upper level of the big cage. I have taken the water dish out so that I can bring it back with fresh water. Not wanting to disturb him or get bitten, when I return I put the bowl of clean water on top of Quigley's cage, and take the next bowl in the lower level shared by Louis and Tikkifinn out to refill. When I come back, Sam has overturned his bowl. I can't figure out what joy, pleasure, or gain he gets from knocking the bowl over, but it is clear that the action does provide some kind of positive reinforcement (to use behaviorist terminology). Quigley knocks over the apple-slice dish, but never the water dishes. It is another one of the mysteries of the parrot called Sam. Maybe in a past life he was a cat. Maybe he knows that doing this will get him his dad's attention.

A Successful Stay with Sam

As I write this, I just had a successful stay with Sam. Maybe we are developing a new routine together. He was on my leg, and climbed up to my left elbow and stayed there. He was comfortable, and I felt that he wouldn't bite me if he stayed there: win-win. Louis was on my head, and that caused a little jealousy on Sam's part. Tikkifinn flew to the back of the chair for one of her visits. Sam stayed where he was and then offered me his head to preen. Often when he does that it is a trick to ensnare me. This time I felt that he meant the offer sincerely, and he did. I scritched the back of his head and we both enjoyed what was happening. I almost crushed the little pin feathers on the back of his over-scritched feather-balding head, but stopped before I did because I didn't feel complete trust. Still, the experience was good. I hope that we do this again.

Later that same night he attacked my sock-covered toes. One drop of water on the head and he pulled back and flew away. One step forward and one step back with Sam, but at least we have some good experiences.

Sam Apologizes: Another Meaning for 'Good Night'

I was doing my nightly cleaning and refilling of the water dishes. It had been a long day, and I wasn't paying as much attention as I should have. As I put my hand into Stanee's cage, Sam rushed at me and gave me a nasty bite. I got very angry with him, thrust a stick into the cage for him to grab ahold of, and carried him out of the cage. Once he was out I gave the stick a quick flick and Sam went flying. He knew I was not pleased with what he had done.

Not long afterwards it was beddy-bird time. As soon as Sam got onto his step-up stick he said "good night," and I responded in kind. He said it one more time before I put him in his cage, and again when I closed the cage door. Each time I gave him a "good night" back. As I put the others in their cages—Sam is always the first—Sam said "good night" several more times, with me responding each time. After I left the aviary and turned out the lights, I heard two more "good nights," as did Sam in reply.

It took me a little while to figure out what was going on, but I think now that he was apologizing to me, wishing to re-establish friendly contact because that is as important to him as it is to me. In some ways we are two of a kind. The next morning as I sat in the aviary eating my cereal, I gave him a Cheerio before I gave anyone else one. He flew to the chair beside my own chair and made his begging-schmecking noise several times, receiving the desired offering in response each time. Sam might not have many words in his vocabulary—he prefers non-human sounds—but his "good nights" hold a lot of meaning. "Good night, Sam." We are friends again.

A few months later, I was watching a hockey game with Sam spending serious time on my left knee. I stroked his beak often, sometimes even venturing to scritch the top of his head a bit. We click-talk a few times, back and forth. When it came time to put him back in his cage, he gave me more than 10 "good nights," which I responded to. Sam may have been saying that he had a good time with me, and he wanted to comment on that good time.

Yet Another Meaning for "Good Night"

Sam seems to have added new meaning to "good night." Several times now he has said it first thing in the morning, when I am taking Louis out for his medicine, but leaving the other birds in their cages. At first I thought that it related to him wanting some extra sleep, a message of "Go away and come back at a decent hour." But now I believe that I relates more to wanted to catch my attention to let him out of his cage. If it can be said with meaning going into the cage, perhaps, it can be said for the reverse. "Here I am, Let me out."

Losing Sam? Two Scary Events
Sam Wedges Himself into a Slot

I was watching Team Canada edge out Latvia. The parrots heard, but fortunately did not learn to repeat, some choice words of mine when the referee did not rule that Team Canada should have a penalty shot. I was sweeping up the aviary when I saw that Sam was wedged into a slot he had apparently created between two planks. One thing that living with parrots teaches you is that they can be a klutzy as humans are. They are not all grace and coordination. My first impression was that he was dead, that I had somehow killed him by moving the plank forward. I realized in a flash how much I really care for the deeply disturbed little fellow. Seeing one apparently dead bird brought memories of others to mind, as unhappy pictures flew through my mind. But no, he was just stuck there, and when I moved the plank, he quickly flew away. I didn't have time or emotional space to be angry. I was just so relieved that he was alive. He is an important part of my life, but sometimes I need reminders of that fact.

Sam's Disappearance

He had gone. Sam, the master hider, was nowhere to be seen. I received a panic call from Angie while I was at work. She had looked for Sam for two hours, with no luck. There was a chance that like his predecessor, Misha, he had flown out the front door. I drove home from work quickly, thinking of how to find him and even more of how I was going to feel about his disappearance from my life. It is every parrot owner's darkest nightmare. I tried to minimize the possible loss. He was a foolish bird who didn't learn from mistakes but kept repeating them. He was hard to bond with because of the ever-present threat of biting. I even had the "Of all the birds that could disappear, I would prefer that it was him" refrain playing through my head. I lived again through the anxiety of looking for Misha in the skies, in the trees, along every road. I did not want to go through that again. I hoped that Angie would find him in some new hidden, dark place while I was scurrying home.

No such luck. The look on her face when I walked through the door said everything. I looked everywhere in the aviary. I went through the garbage bucket. Angie went through the garbage. No luck. There was a growing resolution that he was gone and we had to accept that fact. I even wanted to change the background picture on my computer. It showed Angie with four of her birdie boys: Quigley, Louis, Gus and, of course, Sam. I wouldn't be able to look at it again without twinges of those thoughts. I hate those parts in movies and television shows when people stare at pictures of those they have lost. I can't do that. It just brings pain. I can never look long at pictures of my mother, who died over 35 years ago.

How could I possibly write the story of Sam's disappearance? What would it take to put that into words? I decided to go get the mail. There was a publisher's cheque in it, but it seemed like a small gain after a big loss. When I got back I looked at Angie. She was smiling; on her shoulder was our little disappearing boy. He had been out of the aviary; that much we had been sure about. But he had been hidden behind the cage-lining-newspaper drawer in a large wooden cabinet beside the aviary's outside wall. When in a last desperate move Angie had pulled the drawer out, she had been greeted with a "Hello" as though the phone had rung and he was answering it, along with some wordless but otherwise meaningful parrot small talk. If she hadn't retrieved him from there, he might have slowly starved to death. There would just be a lot of shredded paper and one dead bird.

I felt a flash of deep emotions, as though the tears I had been holding back would flow out, but then we both burst out in sudden laughter. It was so *Sam* to do what he had done. He was a foolish bird, but we were both very happy he was still with us. The troublemaker was back, and his troubled presence was welcome.

Stanee Didn't Know Where Sam Had Gone

One reason I thought we had lost Sam was because, after some frantic searching, I asked Stanee where Sam was. Doing so had helped me find Sam and Louis several times before. She would keep staring in a particular direction, and I would find the lost boy there, behind or under something. It didn't seem to work this time. She did look over at the cabinet that held the television. I suspect, although I have no real proof, that she may have thought that Sam was there. That's where he usually was when he was lost to us. That's certainly where Angie and looked most carefully and longest when we searched for him this time. If that was what she thought, then we were all mistaken together. She was guessing just as we were. That was unnerving. Stanee didn't know where her child was.

When we couldn't find Sam, Stanee was visibly upset. If you know a parrot well enough, moods can be read not by interpreting words but through body language. She kept to herself. Unfortunately, I wasn't there to see Stanee's reaction when Angie brought Sam back to the aviary. I suspect that in the short parrot play that followed, he was the prodigal son returning home. The next morning, however, I did see her fly double-quick to his cage once I let her out of hers. She made regurgitation movements several times without him even coming near. She wanted to mother him.

We wondered, when we thought that Sam was lost, whether Stanee, no longer able to take care of her foster child, would return to her broody periods. No need to wonder now.

Sam and I: Our Touching Relationship

Sam and I share only one form of safe touch. I stroke his beak, preventing it from becoming an instrument of human pain as I do so. I believe that he likes it. His eyes open and shut, and he does not try to pull away. He does not move, but stands still as I slide my finger up and down his great black beak.

As I mentioned earlier, we verbally communicate through clicks that he sometimes initiates or that I give voice to first. Sometimes he initiates it when he is on my leg or nearby in some other way and I am paying attention to Quigley, Louis, or some other bird. It lets me know that he is around. His expressions of "good night" are also reminders. Right now, after I have left the room for a few minutes, he is making a series of what appear to my ears to be random noises. Are these reminders too, less obvious than the whistling and the hellos of the big bird Lime? Sam, I think that my fear you are always about to bite me limits our connection. But we are still connected, never fear.

Soft-Mouth Sam

We have had some dogs who soft-mouth and "take pretty," and others who just scarf food down. You count your fingers after they're done. Wiikwaas, our border collie, is pretty much a soft-mouth, while Trudy, our dachshund, is much more aggressive. The same is apparently true of parrots, although in the case of our guys in a somewhat strange way. As part of the morning opening of cages, I offer up slices of apple or pear first to Sam, then to Quigley. With Quigley, I have to be careful, as he attacks the slice of apple or pear, sometimes getting finger instead (by mistake?). With Sam, the biting parrot, it is done in a much more graceful way. He moves his mouth slowly, usually taking the first bite with head upside down. He then peeps a happy sound, and takes other bites just as softly, chewing more carefully than Quigley does. I wish that he treated human fingers as gently as he does a slice of apple.

Sam the Schmeck

Sam makes a schmecking noise (a bit like a click, and a bit like a smack) as I hold a piece of apple for him when I open his cage in the morning, usually right after he takes his first bite. Later, when I am having my cereal in the aviary, he often flies to my knee, and I give him a Cheerio. He bites part of it, and drops the rest. Then he "schmecks" for another. This morning, he schmecked for at least six Cheerios, once even uttering a whole sentence of schmecks, telling me that he really, *really* wanted another one. I can't resist when he asks so politely.

Sammy Keeps the Beat

I was watching the Blue Jays build up a big lead, drumming a 4/4 beat with my feet and a snare-type snap with my hands on 1 and 3. Then, out of one of his huts, the one on the floor, he came, my Sammy. He tapped the floor with his beak, three times twice, both times in perfect synch with me. He not only can imitate sounds, he's got rhythm. He came out further and repeated the trick. He's my birdie son, inheriting one of his talents from his drummer dad.

Giving Each Other the Eye: Cat and Bird Face Off

I was approaching the aviary and saw that Brenda, our cat, was at the aviary door, staring through the crack between the door and the makeshift wall, her tail waving back and forth in anticipated pouncing. As I was about to shoo her away, I saw that on the other side of the crack was Sam. He was staring right back at her with his big *Tyrannosaurus rex* eye. He didn't look afraid so much as he was trying to stare her down. There is a lot of fear in Sam, but there is also a lot of courage. He appeared ready to take her on. After I shooed the cat away, I went back to the kitchen. When I returned, the scene was the same, neither backing down. It was a standoff.

Later that same day, I saw the two of them facing off again. I shooed both of them away, but I learned more about what was going on a little later on. When I returned to the aviary, the cat was gone but Sam was there, looking as though he was practicing scary looks. He appeared in front of the crack in the door and then disappeared again. Was he taunting her, or was it just his curiosity? Here was the ever-fearful one taking on a predator. He was not fluffed up, but definitely has a purpose. What it was I cannot be sure. He can be a bird of mystery.

Bitten Yet Again

I hadn't been blooded by Sam in months. I gave him four bites of apple that morning instead of his usual two as he seemed especially hungry. Then, when I came in with my breakfast cereal, I gave him a Cheerio. He came up onto my knee for more Cheerios. Then it went too far. He climbed up my arm to get on my shoulder, and I gave him a Cheerio there. I love having any of the birds on my shoulder, so I neglected Rule #1 with Sam: *Don't let him up on your shoulder.* When I got up to leave, he gave me a painful nip. I wanted to trust him, hope trying to win out over experience. Experience holds a painful truth.

The Sum of Sam: A Tentative Tally of Pros and Cons of Our Senegal

Pros
Saying good night.
Turning his head upside down to take the first bite of his apple slice as I hold it in my hand.
Making a shmecking noise when he sees food that he likes.
His One Big Parrot display.
His imitations of microwaves, stove timers and other birds.
Asking for a scritch while he is on my knee.

Cons
Biting my ear.
Biting my hand.
Biting my toes.
Biting my feet when I wear flip-flops (dorks).
Biting my shoes.
Biting generally.
More biting.

In sum, the pros outweigh the cons. We are keeping Sam. My left knee would feel naked without him, though my ears would remain unpierced. He is one of my treasured birdy boys. My life would be less without him, and not just less stressful.

Chapter Six
Cockatiels and Other Cockatoos

Cockatoos

There are 21 species of cockatoo, and they live in Australasia, which includes Australia, Indonesia, New Guinea, the Philippines and the Solomon Islands.

Cockatoos are very much in-your-face parrots. With the exception of the cockatiel branch, they are large, ranging from 30 to 60 centimetres (12 to 14 inches) in length (when their crests are down), and weighing from 300 to 1,200 grams (two-thirds of a pound to two and two-thirds of a pound). Their large crests are characteristic of the species.

The big cockatoos can be quite loud, and at their most extreme their voices can be quite hard on the ear. That is a major reason why, when we went to the World Parrot Rescue site on Vancouver Island, they kindly provided us with ear plugs. (The macaws there are also very loud.) But cockatoos can also have very sweet and endearing voices, an aspect of what I think of as their seductiveness. When I read that Mozart had a pet starling from 1784 to 1787 and that he wrote down some of the notes it sang, I was glad that he did not have a cockatoo. Heavy metal would have to wait for another two centuries. Wagner might have liked to have had a cockatoo.

Although cockatoos are not usually as brightly coloured as are other parrots, they do have a more subtle beauty that cannot be denied. Most cockatoos are primarily white, with possibly white, red, pink or yellow tinges, and others are black.

Cockatoos are intensely social and can be quite demanding of their owners, or of people visiting them in parrot sanctuaries (I write from personal experience as you will see). They do not like to be ignored. This is one reason, along with their size, longevity (Fred, a sulphur-crested cockatoo at the Bonorong Wildlife Sanctuary in Australia, is said to be at least 100 years old), and loud vocalizations, that they are often found in sanctuaries, abandoned by owners or by relatives of owners who themselves have died or moved to seniors' homes. There are many sad cockatoo stories. But I want to tell you one with a happy ending.

The Tale of Lucky Lou
We Meet Her at the World Parrot Refuge

In the early fall of 2015, we twice visited the World Parrot Refuge (WPR) near Coombs on Vancouver Island (as shown in the above photo). At that time Coombs included among its attractions not just the WPR but mountain goats seen and often photographed on the grass-covered roof of a market/restaurant. For both Angie and me, the cockatoos were the main charmers at the WPR. When we first entered the large one-story building, we encountered several of them in the hallway between the two large enclosures in the building's front section. The first to get to me had only a few feathers on the front part of her body, but a full set on her head and on most of her back and tail. It is very startling to see a parrot without feathers over much of its body. I had seen such birds before, and had had to look away, as they looked part plucked chicken and part lizard—not a pretty sight. But this time it was different. There was something magic about her (when I am attracted to a parrot I often assume it is a female) that I could not avert my eyes from. I started scritching her head after she climbed up and out of her open cage to meet me. And I kept doing so for about 20 minutes, with a short interlude while I scritched another cockatoo that approached me. Cockatoos are difficult to resist even when another cockatoo has your attention first.

I left my friend for a while to interact with other cockatoos in other large rooms at the sanctuary. Although I made other friends, she was my first and my closest. At first, when I returned to her, I was a little nervous, as she was in her cage looking straight at me with an intense stare, and she was shivering, perhaps because of lack of attention. But I couldn't resist her. I reached into her cage to get her to step up. She seemed to warm up and stopped shivering. Her beak opened and shut regularly as a sign of pleasure. Had I been a cockatoo, my mouth would have, too.

After we left, we spoke often of our cockatoo friends, and how we were going to see them again on our way back from our visit to the beautiful seaside town of Ucluelet.

The Revisit

The second time I encountered my best cockatoo friend, I took to calling her "Tatters." I went straight to her, no further into the sanctuary. We only had about 40 minutes before the centre closed, and she was the one that I wanted to see, talk to, and touch.

Other cockatoos tried, quite literally, to grab my attention—one by my shoe, another by my sock. But I belonged to Tatters for the duration of my short stay. She stayed in her cage for the first half of the time I was there. Then, on some impulse, she made her way to the door, up to the top, and then over to my outstretched hand. She then strode straight up my arm to my right shoulder. Not long afterwards, she wanted to shift to my left shoulder, and, with my assistance, she made her way across my chest to the shoulder of choice. She made soft, slight sounds, no clear words. I broke the covering of some of her pin feathers so she might re-feather or re-fledge more quickly. I hoped that between the attention and the pin-feather preening, she would let her feathers grow back (if that were possible), so that her full beauty would return. Even without them, she is still beautiful in ways that I find hard to describe.

There was a short stretch of time in which I scritched another cockatoo who was hanging from the aviary enclosure opposite. For the first and only time, Tatters crested her comb to full disturbed and disturbing stretch.

Cockatoos always seem a little sneaky to me, except for Tatters. One side-stepped up to me with great stealth and then passed barely noticed to my other side to receive a short scritch.

They are very competitive for attention, and that does include Tatters, as evidenced by her reaction when I was paying attention to another.

Tatters did not play coy or falsely shy as the others did. She was more of a "Here I am, feather plucked and all" cockatoo. My connection with her started with pity, moved on to sympathy, and then to a solid bond of human-bird friendship.

As I sat in the airport the next day, I was wearing the same shirt that I'd worn the first time that I met her. I had miscounted the shirts I'd packed for the trip. (I did better with underwear.) I could still sense the faint smell of my favourite non-cockatiel cockatoo, where I held her to my chest when I first met her. It was a faint, musty smell, like a goat with very good hygiene, a gentle scent of *eau de goat*. I missed Tatters as I smelled this. I wanted to hear about her when we are far apart.

I Learn Her Name

It turned out the bird that I called Tatters was likely a female umbrella cockatoo named Lucky Lou. Umbrella cockatoos (*Cacatua alba*) are white-coloured (a translation of the Latin *alba*, as in "albino"), medium-sized cockatoos that live in the wild on small Indonesian islands. They are an endangered species. They are well-known among cockatoo fans as cuddlers, a trait which has given them the nickname "Velcro birds." They stick to you. Both Angie and I experienced that cuddling, which we both found quite endearing. Here is the sad-beginning and happy-ending story of Lucky Lou, beginning with an e-mail sent to me in September 2015 by Wendy Huntbatch, the founder of WPR:

> The bird you saw I believe was Lucky Lou.... This is her story. Lucky Lou was brought to us 20 years ago. She was almost completely featherless. She just shook with fear. It was very sad. She would suddenly stand upright like a human—and without feathers believe me their bodies do look almost the same as ours, then she would start yelling "You are so ugly I hate you—you are a bad bad bird." She would then proceed to hammer her chest with her beak and rip out any feathers or down. It was heartbreaking to see. The owner's son told me that when she started to pluck out her feathers his mother put her in the basement—alone—which of course aggravated the problem. The woman could not let anyone see the bird because it would look as though she had failed. When she would come home from shopping the bird would scream for attention. Her answers were the words that the bird repeated. Honestly—the bird sounded just like the woman.
>
> Well, we just had to change this behaviour in the easiest way possible. As soon as I would see her start to shake and stand upright, I would sing "Happy Birthday to You." Her wings would go down and pretty soon she stopped doing it so regularly. She was surrounded by people and other parrots so she had a much more normal life for a cockatoo. She learned to sing "Happy Birthday" and would repeat it several times a day. Now she will say "happy birthday" to people and sometimes will sing the song all the way through. She is the sweetest bird. Her feathers are the best they have ever looked. When they are as damaged as hers are right down into the follicle, they never grow back properly. We love her the way she looks anyway.
>
> She had a partner—Dinky Doo. He is another Umbrella cockatoo

with a serious plucking problem. However, together they were happy and looking great.

I wish I had known about the "Happy Birthday" song routine. I would have loved to have sung a duet with her. We probably would have run through it several times, maybe with a few others (birds and humans) singing along with us.

The Refuge Closes But Lucky Lou Is Rescued Again

Then came a horrible twist to the story of Lucky Lou and her engaging flockmates. In February 2016, Wendy Huntbatch, the founder of the World Parrot Refuge, died. And by the following spring it became evident that the WPR, said to cost $40,000 a month to maintain, would have to close down, with 450 birds to be re-homed. It had been running for at least some 22 years (Ryan 2016) but closed in July 2016.

But Lucky Lou lived up to her name and landed on her talons. (Not so Dinky Doo, who died.) When homes were being found for the parrots of the WPR, Lucky Lou, along with a female Goffin cockatoo named Coco, were fostered by Danita Morrison. She had worked as a volunteer during the closing-down of the WPR, and fell in love with the two of them. She has dedicated much of her life to their rehabilitation, with medicine (some of it from the Netherlands), a nebulizer and lots of TLC.

On Facebook there is a site called *Lucky Lou and Coco Too* that shows pictures and tells stories about the two of them. I discovered this late in September 2016. You can see in the series of pictures on the site that the two birds are looking healthier. There are more feathers now, and they have gained some weight.

One of the features of this site that is amusing involves tales of Lucky Lou swearing, clearly reflecting her human upbringing in her hideous first home. She told a man delivering mattresses to "F— off," and he thought to himself, "Some old lady is yelling at me!" He parked his truck further away as he waited for foster mom Danita to appear. Lucky Lou has also sworn at a gardener that she could see through a window, and sometimes she swears under her breath.

The two birds are obviously very close. Coco runs to Lucky Lou when she is scared (both birds are flightless because of plucking out flight feathers), going behind her or tucking her almost completely feather-bald head under Lucky Lou's beak, making her look like Lucky Lou's child in such a pose. Lucky Lou even lets her take food from her beak, a sign of complete and utter trust.

There is another sad twist to her story. She had a small tumour, and had to take pain killers. On June 24, 2017, Lucky Lou died, having lived up to her name in her last year of life.

Cockatiels as Cockatoos

And now for the main attraction. Despite their diminutive size, cockatiels are definitely cockatoos, just like the big loud guys. The emotion-altered crest gives that away. Cockatiels, as cockatoos, cannot lie about what they are feeling. A high crest tells you that your bird is filled with feelings. Pay close attention to a cockatoo's crest. It can help you avoid being bitten or, with the big guys, being yelled at.

Cockatiel Background

Cockatiels, which are native to almost all of Australia, differ from all of our other birds in that they belong to the superfamily *Cacatuoidea* (i.e., cockatoo-like), the family *Cacatuidae*, which they share with cockatoos, and the subfamily *Nymphicinae*, which is distinct from that of their much bigger, louder cousins. Since 1832 they have borne the scientific name of *Nymphicus hollandicus* (literally, "Dutch nymph"). And nymphs they truly are, as we have discovered. But why the species name *hollandicus*? And how can it be that Dutch (or at least a Dutch version of a Portuguese word) provided their common name cockatiel, originally something like *kaketielje*, which would seem to be a diminutive (i.e., "little cockatoo") of the word *kaketoe*, meaning "cockatoo"? The answer to both questions stems from the fact that in the seventeenth century the Dutch appear to have been the first Europeans to discover Australia (the Aborigines having discovered the island continent some 60,000 years earlier). The early settlement was called "New Holland in English during the eighteenth century. Maybe the orange patch on the cockatiels' cheek connected with the Dutch—as World Cup fans well know, orange is the Netherlands' national colour, and hence the colour of the jerseys of their soccer players.

The first written account of cockatiels dates from James Cook's voyage to Australia of 1770. The first cockatiel to travel to Europe may have been aboard his ship. By the mid-nineteenth century cockatiels could be found in several countries in Europe.

Cockatiel Classification

Order	Psittaciformes
Superfamily	Cacatuoide
Family	Cacatuidae
Subfamily	Nymphicinae
Genus	Nymphicus
Species	hollandicus

Key Dates in Cockatiel History

1770: James Cook visits Australia and first sees cockatiels.

1845: First captive cockatiels bred in Europe. Within the next 20 years they were being bred in France, Germany and Britain

1910: First breeding pair of cockatiels in the United States.

Unknown: First cockatiels come to Canada (unfortunately I can't find out when this occurred).

1950s: Cockatiels become popular in the United States, particularly in California and Florida.

2010s: The Steckleys have live-in cockatiels (their world will never be the same).

Cockatiels do not on average live as long as do the larger cockatoos. Usually figures of 15 to 20 years are given. They are also not the human talkers that the big guys are. However, as you will read, they are good communicators. Their whistling in particular is a rich form of articulation.

Cockatiel Books

I was surprised to find out how many books about cockatiels have been published. I was not surprised, however, when I found to my dismay that they were all how-to books, with nothing about the fascinating world of interaction between cockatiels and their humans. That's where this section of the book comes in. Like a male cockatiel, it boldly goes where other cockatiel books don't dare to go. I am not writing about what you think they should do and how you should make them do it. Instead, I want to talk about how they are, and maybe even how they make *me* do what they want me to. Cockatiels can be very persuasive. There is nothing like a 'tiel.

I didn't at first like cockatiels. When the pet shop where we've bought most of our birds had a cage full of them, they looked like a bunch of silly little blondes to me, mourning doves with crests, not the beautiful majestic fellow-Aussie cockatoos, who, as you have seen, always find a way to charm me. Maybe in part it was that they were in a crowd, like budgies, so I didn't see them as individuals. Humans don't present themselves well in crowds either. I should have thought of that at the time.

Two birds turned the situation around for me. Here in my home office, there are three pictures of cockatiels beaming down on me with approval. One is simply a picture once attached to some parrot toy. The bird looks like Tika. The other two are beautiful drawings that Angie made of our Gus, and which she gave to me as presents on two successive Christmases. The pictures capture his feisty soul, the big bird within the little body.

The Story of Tika

Tika haunts me still. She was the seventh bird in our flock, and the one who taught me not to judge this species of parrot by its size, relatively inexpensive price in a pet store, and lack of human words. She was the last of a small flock of cockatiels in the cage at the pet store. She and another bird had been the only two left for quite a while, and after the other was sold she was alone, and looked lonely. Some birds can manage alone, but I don't think that cockatiels can. We felt sorry for her, so we thought that we might socialize her by walking her around the store as we had done with the others. We should have known the inevitable result. All of the birds with whom we'd walked around like that we ended up taking home. Once we had, to no one's surprise, decided to add Tika to our flock, too, we taught her to respond to, "One, two, three, Tika." She would peep after her name was spoken.

When Tika came home, Stanee played mother bird yet again, not just in accompanying our novice pilot to the floor, but in protecting Tika from the others. One day I left Tika on top of our Amazon's cage while I got some fruit for the flock. When I returned to the parrot room (formerly known as the living room) Tika was not there. I could hear Tika, but could not find her. I looked for Stanee. She was on the back of the couch, a place she didn't often visit. Down below her was Tika. I knew that the mother parrot would be close by where the child (albeit one of a different species) was hidden.

TIKA

Tika was my shadow bird. She was almost always on my shoulder. She liked being on my arm, especially when I preened her, and she did a Benji self-scritch. When I lay down on the couch she almost literally turned my beard into a nest. I wished sometimes that she didn't preen so close to my eye, or so hard, but more than any other bird in the flock at the time, she was my companion. She died on that couch. I am glad that we later got rid of that piece of furniture, as it would be very difficult for me to lie down there without my beard's constant companion. The couch was filled with too many memories.

Tika would keep still on my shoulder for hours as I wrote books using my laptop. No other bird has ever done that, although Lime is learning. She did pull get one key off (which I saved after she died), but was generally pretty respectful of my property.

One day I saw Tika through the French windows that used to separate the living room (before it was divided in two) and the kitchen. My work table was placed so that I could look into the living room and see the birds. Here is the poem that I wrote later that same day.

> *Cockatiel Silhouette*
> Small pane of glass in a door
> one of several,
> bird for the first time
> seen black
> a majesty that her usual yellow
> does not allow.
> The light in the living room is off
> I stand in the darkened kitchen
> I look back
> and see her perched
> as I am ready to leave for work;
> straight and spectral
> grasping the thin wood
> and looking out at me.
> I don't know
> what she sees,
> but I do feel
> she has given me something,
> I can take with me
> outside of home
> and my own
> internal darkness.

Tika Lays Eggs

I couldn't find Tika. She had run somewhere along the floor, deliberately seeming to try to hide from me. This was uncharacteristic behaviour for her. After searching for a few minutes, I looked underneath the big cabinet, and there she was. Her body looked fluffed up, bigger than normal. How long had she looked that big? I couldn't remember. She was laying eggs. It was a wonderful moment. No matter how uncomfortable I was lying on the floor on my left side, I could not take my eyes off her. After a few minutes, four ovals lay next to the wall. She couldn't really sit on them, but she covered them as best as she could with her wings and her fluffed up body. I was so proud of her. I felt kind of like a mammal grandfather to an avian daughter's children.

Curious Louis would investigate, and she would chase him away, stretching out those long wings of hers (their length when extended always came as a surprise when you are accustomed to the wings-tucked-in size of a cockatiel's body). She was serious, and as often as he would try to approach the eggs, he knew not to stick around once she started to chase after him. She was ferocious in defense of her infertile eggs.

What would she do once she discovered they were infertile? For that matter, would she discover they were infertile? I felt sorry for her doing all that work for no living result. It seemed unfair somehow. I read up on what to do with a female cockatiel who has laid eggs. The sources I consulted tended to be manipulative works on how to shape the behaviour of your parrot. Behaviorism didn't work particularly well on humans, rats or pigeons, so why would it work for parrots? The books spoke of replacing the eggs with hard, round objects like stones or marbles so that eventually the little would-be mothers would have to give up their maternal behaviour. I didn't do that.

Tika would not return to her cage. And although she would let me come near, unlike poor Louis, I could not coax her to return to her cage, where there was food and water. I left food and water near her on the floor. She slept with her unliving children, a little mother whose dedication nearly brought tears to my eyes. She was so determined to take care of them.

Eventually, she was there less often, and I took the eggs away. I felt like a thief, a fox in a chicken coop.

This would not be her last brood. She would go through the process again not very long afterwards. No wonder cockatiels are so inexpensive, although that has nothing to do with their intrinsic value, their spirit—the equal of that of any large $2,000 parrot. This time, Louis wouldn't come near her, but even Angie was chased away. Tika would begin to chase me away and then stop, realizing that she could let me get close to her new brood with no harm coming to them. These eggs were in the corner of the room, still underneath the cabinet. I saw her sleep with them. I felt closer to her than I had before. My sister Ann thought that Tika was my favourite bird, as I so often sent e-mails describing the activities of my little mother. She was a natural mother, but would have no children. I took this batch away too, and we did not get another. After we lost her, I wish that one had somehow defied the laws of reproduction and had hatched.

I was often told as a lad, and I imagine that you've been told this as well, that you should never touch a baby bird that has somehow fallen from its nest, as its mother will then reject it because it smells like a human. I want to challenge that claim. I have seen the strength of Tika's mother bond with eggs that were to never hatch. I know it would not have mattered to her one bit if I had touched her children, other than the threat she might think I posed—it wouldn't have mattered how much they smelled of me. I can't imagine wild cockatiel moms would be any different. We are talking about a very powerful biological drive. I now suspect that our parents told us that story because they didn't want us to bring baby birds home so that we, and ultimately they, perhaps, would have to take care of them. I wonder whether anyone has ever written a scientific paper on the subject. Somehow I rather doubt it. If some scientist does, I hope the person reads this first and makes scientific reference to Tika.

Reminders of Tika

Finn used to remind me of Tika, when she would say, "One, two, three, Tika". There were times that I could hardly bear to hear those words

One day, one of the birds called to me in a way that made me stop what I was doing. I don't know which bird it was but it caught me off guard. It sounded just like Tika when she would call to me from the living room, before we even had an aviary. I suspect it was Sam, as he imitates well the calls of the other birds.

I've been learning to appreciate mourning doves. I think that Tika helped there. Today I saw one sitting in her nest in our cedar hedge. The nest is not so high up or deep that I couldn't reach it (barely) by stretching on my tip-toes. I sensed her trust. She didn't move as I looked up at her. I would protect her at my own risk. Tika taught me about the relationship between little feathered mothers and their eggs.

Remembering Tika

When I was going through drawers and things frantically looking for my birth certificate, I found the receipt for our purchase of Tika in August 2010, the equivalent of her birth certificate. She was referred to as a "pied cockatiel," one of the main variations or "races" of cockatiel. Gus is a pied cockatiel, too. I conjure (not conure) up a picture of her in my mind of when I would scritch her around the neck. She would open her mouth wide; you would almost think, and several times I *did* think, that she was trying to cough something up, a behavior she shared with our other lost girl, Finn, when I scritched her the same way. I think now that it was a yawn of pleasure. She never failed to do it in response to my scritching her, and I never failed to feel joy that I could give to her as she did to me, and that her trust in our connection was monumental.

The Story of Gus

In volume one of his *Parrots in Captivity*, published in 1884, W. T. Greene wrote of cockatiels: "Taken, when about half-fledged, from the next, and brought up by hand ... the young male Cockatiel becomes the most charming pet that can be imagined." Our experience with Gus has proven this to be true.

Shopping for Gus

The day after Tika died, we went shopping for Gus. You can't say that we wanted a cockatiel to "replace" Tika. We just needed someone to help fill the hole that her passing left in our hearts. The emptiness without her was huge. There are times when I still feel it, particularly when I write about her. Fortunately Gus now fills another large space I can retreat to.

We didn't have much of a game plan for our search. We went to Newmarket, northeast of where we live, saw a cockatiel in a store, but ended up being more interested in the Quaker they had. For the first time in my life I touched a macaw, a big red one who apparently has been there for a long time. Despite its huge, finger-crunching beak, he or she was very friendly with me. If Angie had enabled my parrot addiction at that time, we might have brought it home. I liked stroking its beak. But there seemed to be something wrong with the cockatiel. It had a deformed beak, and we suspected that there might be other things wrong with him, too. He wasn't very responsive. Alas, he wouldn't be coming home with us.

We drove south down Yonge Street looking for pet stores, not the best of strategies as on a busy multilane street you have to be aware of where you are going so you can prepare for your turn, especially if it's a left. I'm sure I wasn't popular with some of the drivers behind me.

Finally we came upon a small pet store that sold cockatiels. There were other birds there, but I cannot remember what kind they were. On this day they were invisible to me. There were four cockatiels in a cage, all looking strong, healthy and happy—two males and two females. It was going to be a hard choice, as all of them were beautiful and friendly. But one of the males was a little more aggressive than the others, a little more curious, and seemed to be saying "Pick me, pick me." So we did pick him (or so he let us think).

We didn't have a name in mind, so it took us about as long to choose a name as it took to choose a bird. The name Gustaph came to mind, Gus for short. It seemed right, and we took Gus home.

We had thought that Gus would be the only cockatiel in the world with that name (like our cat called Brenda). It turns out that the mother of one of the waitresses who serves us breakfast every Saturday has had a cockatiel by that name for 18 years. He was named after the mother's husband, Constantine, who was always called Gus. At least we were right in thinking that it was name of proper distinction for a bird of definite distinction.

The first night we had Gus, I took him into the bathroom with me, as I didn't want to abandon him to the whims of the other, bigger birds so soon in his new life with us. That was when I first heard him articulate his thoughts with cockatiel sounds of his own choosing. There were no (human) words but it was clear that he had something to say. He and I bonded in that moment. I knew that he and I would become good buddies.

Cockatiel Story Time

When Tika sat in or near my beard as I lay on my back on the couch, I told her stories in the same way I would a very young granddaughter. As I told the story, the angle of her head would tell me that she was listening intently. The story was always the same, about a beautiful and intelligent young female cockatiel who was the queen of a flock of cockatiels who all looked up to and admired her. I would tell the story when I needed a distraction from the concerns, stresses and pressures of my own life. Telling her the story made me feel good. It was then that I felt that Tika was my favourite bird, because she would listen to my

Gus

stories and always wanted to be with me. Thinking of that as I write this, I miss her terribly. Tears lurk in the weeds, like northern pike looking for minnows of emotion.

And then I think of this morning. The scenario I just described came to mind while I was in the aviary. I talked to Gus. Before I left, Gus started a short whistle-singing session directed at me. I stood still and listened, then said to him, as I so often do, "You've earned your seeds today, young man." Only Gus can help me deal with this particular brand of sadness, and did so again in the same manner when I was doing the final editing of this chapter.

Male Cockatiels' Displays of Anger

One characteristic of male cockatiels that I have never seen in female cockatiels (but then my selected memories of Tikka are all positive) is a display of complete, crazy anger. Don't let that keep you from having a male cockatiel, as these fits of pique appear more display than actual threat. Gus does this when I put my hand (in a fist) near him. He attacks me in a frenzy of strikes, but it does not hurt at all. I feel that he is holding back on the biting action. I am not over-generalizing from Gus. As Esther Woolfson writes about her daughter's male cockatiel, Bardie: "Nor could I have imagined, before becoming acquainted with Bardie, that the anger and passion displayed by doves [her first birds] was not only common behaviour in birds but could be surpassed and extended by a capacity for irritation allied to frank displays of uncontrolled rage."

I was researching this topic, and came across a so-called "expert" who tried to pathologize it as something wrong with the relationship between human and bird. Gus and I are very, very close, and I know what a male display looks like in humans, dogs and cockatiels (as well as larger cockatoos). It is normal and psychologically healthy male behaviour, not a problem to be fixed with sticks and carrots.

My favourite writing about the behavioural distinction between male and female cockatiels comes from Diane Grindel's aptly titled "Male versus Female Cockatiels." As she describes it, females are "more likely to be gentle and not as attention seeking" (or maybe they are just more subtle?) and "male cockatiels are in your face." Male cockatiels are very cockatoo-like in that way. When we first entered the World Parrot Refuge building, there were cockatiels in a room-wide cage opposite to where cockatoos and other larger species were kept. A not-so-easily countable group of what I am pretty sure were male cockatiels were all vying for our attention.

Now Gus has me wondering about the crest and emotions. Yes, it sticks up when he is attacking my hand, and in other times of wild emotion. But I feel that there are two other crest positions to consider. Sometimes his crest is pressed down flat, slicked down upon his head. I believe that this has meaning, too. My analogy is to a car's automatic transmission, with drive, neutral and reverse gears. I am beginning to believe that "slick-down" is *not* neutral. When his crest is somewhat but not fully up—that's neutral. What does it mean when his crest is fully down? When I gave Gus his morning Cheerio today, his crest was slicked down. Maybe it's a sign of pleasure. But I would have to observe cockatiels and other cockatoos for a long time to prove or disprove this theory.

Whistling and the Male Cockatiel

Gus's main medium for verbal messages is through whistling. The following are a few stories that relate to his use of that medium.

A Male Cockatiel Needs Someone to Sing to

Lime and I were in the aviary exchanging two-note whistles. It was a little strange as she normally only does that only when I'm not in the aviary. Gus was on top of Lime's cage and looked like he wanted to step up. I read him right: he stepped up to my hand and I transferred him to my shoulder. But then, when I offered to take him to the mesh, he was happy to stay on my shoulder, not his usual response. He started to reply to my whistling with a song of his own. When Gus sings, he usually sings directly to someone, not to the world in general. He looks upward at the other bird or human and sings straight at them. The upper part of his beak rises with the higher notes. On this occasion, he looked at me and sang, first whistling high and low notes and then making his cheeping sound. He went through pretty much his entire musical repertoire, looking straight at me as he did so. Then, when Louis landed on my head, Gus started to sing up at him. When Juno, our parrotlet, tried with his little voice to sing back at Gus, imitating his brother bird as closely as he could, Gus looked back and sang a bit to him, too, facing in the direction of Juno's cage.

Gus took a brief break and started preening the left side of my face, quite tentatively, as if he was worried that he would get it wrong. That was a rare treat. I can count on both hands the times he's preened me. He was caught up in the excitement of the music.

When I want Gus to whistle, I can get him going just by whistling myself. This isn't just copying (or that dreaded verb "parroting") on his part. He *wants* to whistle back to me, to further the contact that I have initiated. I am as sure (or unsure) of that as I am about human speech and interaction. Gus looks me in the eye, unlike many humans, and whistles variations on a theme. I hate to leave the aviary when he is partway through his whistling songs. It seems rude when I was the one who started the communication. I should wait for the completion of his response.

I discovered one day on the basis of a non-deliberate experiment that Gus would rather whistle than eat. He was singing to me one Sunday morning when I offered him a bauble (that is, a Nutriberry), something he loves to eat with attacking beak blows. He kept on singing, completely disregarding the proffered food. You are a true artist, Gus. You will stop singing when the song is over, and no sooner. When he felt he was finished, then he went for the bauble.

A Song and Dance Bird

On Saturday mornings, Gus is often a song and dance bird. Wiikwaas, our border collie cross, permits me (sometimes) to sleep in until seven o'clock on Saturdays and Sundays. In the springtime, that means I can lie in bed and listen to Gus as he greets the day with song. I hear wild birds sometimes, too, but it's Gus I am listening to. There is great comfort in those songs for me.

I walk Wiikwaas, and after he and Trudy, our dachshund, are fed, I go to the aviary to "release the birds." They all greet me in their own ways, Juno with a birdie smile, Stanee with a burst of flight out of her cage, Tikkifinn with words soft and low, Louis with enthusiasm, Quigley with an energetic bite off the apple slice I offer him, Sam with a small peep in quiet moments of apple-eating reflection, Lime with a baby-bird call. But it is Gus who greets me in a way that touches me this morning. He is dancing on his perch, so excited to get out and get on with the day. His talons move up and down, his little body moves side to side, and he hardly even nips me (his usual response) as I offer him a finger ride to the outside. He does a "happy dance," something he usually reserves for Lime's return to the aviary. Today he is just celebrating another day of living.

Gus's Gift

One Monday morning, facing marking and all the other strains of the week ahead, Gus gives me a gift. Usually when I take him from the cage in the morning, he bites my step-up finger a bit, I set him on his stick perch, and then move on to the other birds. This morning was different. Gus remained on my finger and clearly wanted to stay. So I went through my cage-opening rounds with Gus on my arm. It had been a long while since he had travelled with me like that. As I went to leave the aviary, intending to put him on one of the feeding perches on the aviary mesh, he refused the offer of the perch, and moved up my arm. Louis flew to my shoulder and Gus began to sing. He stood a little more than two inches away from Louis and sang to him, while Louis preened my right eye. For once I did not rush to leave the aviary to get my breakfast, but stood motionless while my two birdie boys, brothers laid by other mothers, did their best to make me feel better. As Gus sang, Lime occasionally mimicked his voice, repeating some of his whistle notes as a quiet commentary: "I'm listening to you." Even Louis followed the odd note in a casual way. I kept silent. For about five minutes we all kept to that musical script, and my morning mania slowed down to a livable level. But Gus had not completed his gift to me. As I came back with my cereal, sharing Cheerios with Gus and the gang of conures, Quakers and Sam, Gus preened himself and dropped a feather. That feather is beside me now, waiting for me to put it in a place that will trigger memories of Gus's morning gift.

For the rest of the week Gus travelled with me as I let the others out of their cages. I had a new routine, and a new assistant. Unfortunately, it ended with that week—who knows why.

Gus Sings to an Audience

I was in Angie's room watching television. Gus started to sing. When the show was over I walked over the aviary to respond to Gus's song. He was on the metal television cabinet, singing away. When I stood in front of him, he looked me straight in the eye and sang and sang and sang his whistle song. There always seems to be a privilege in that. When he stopped for a while and moved his feet up and down, I had him step up and carried him over to the mesh wall of the aviary. He resumed his singing. Louis quickly climbed to a spot a hand above Gus and about three hands to the left. Gus looked up to him and directed his serenade Louis-wards. Louis repeated a few of the notes. Behind and above, by the window, Lime too echoed some of the notes, but not very often. Then Quigley flew over to the other end of the perch upon which Louis stood. He spoke back to Gus, but not in any way that sounded anything like Gus, or anything even mildly tonal. It was a gruff Quaker sound (they do not generally imitate other birds in our experience, except for Tikkifinn's amazing imitations of Sam), but the rhythm was right. Gus definitely had an audience.

Bravo, maestro cockatiel. Bravo.

Gus Completes a Song

It was Sunday night. I really could use one of Gus's songs. I was taking garbage out the front door, and Gus began a song. I walked up to the aviary cage wall and listened to his song, praising him for helping me out with a song. He sang for a few minutes, looking right at me. Then he stopped. He fluffed up his face a bit and looked proud of what he had just done. I swear I have never seen him make that exact face before, but it definitely showed pride. Gus, you've done it again, helped me when I needed it.

Gus and Lime
Singing Up to a Friend

I was sitting in the aviary watching Blue Jays baseball. Quigley was chased off the mesh by Stanee and flew to my shoulder. Stanee went to my other shoulder, and with Tikkifinn's help they bullied Quigley off me and onto the mesh. Quigley, angry and frustrated, took it out on Lime, a bird that he used to preen. She flew off the mesh to her bicycle tire by the window. He isn't usually this aggressive with her and she was clearly unhappy with him. So she called to a friend, making a sound that swirls around the notes that Gus usually whistles. She did this several times. Gus responded with a little whistle-singing. She repeated the swirling sound a few times and Gus kept responding, looking across the room, whistle-singing to her directly. I couldn't help but feel that was the effect she wanted to achieve, a little vocal reassurance when another friend had betrayed her.

As the two extremes in the aviary, big and little, outside the "norm" of the "cool kids", the conures, Quakers and a Senegal, Lime and Gus seemed have found each other. The outliers have united.

Gus Invents a New Preen

Gus doesn't have a mate, but as you've seen, he does have a special relationship with Lime, our yellow-headed Amazon. He sometimes sings to her, looking way up at her as he stands about two inches away, bringing to mind the words of the 1960 song about the 20-foot woman: "Take me to your ladder. I'll see your leader later." When he sings, Gus has a way of looking at her and at his human companions that tells them, "This song's for you."

Recently, I saw Lime walk up to Gus, face him, and bow her head down, way down in the classic "I want to be preened" pose. I thought this odd, as there is no easy way that Gus could reach up that far, given his small beak and short height. I failed to recognize Gus's ingenuity. He started to climb up the back of her bowed head like he was trying to escape her looming presence. But then he went back down, as if recognizing the recklessness of his move. He did it again and again. This slow human mind finally realized what he was doing. He was preening her with his talons, a cockatiel solution to an Amazon problem. You have my respect, Gus. You are creative.

In the weeks that followed, I saw Lime and Gus hanging around each other more and more. It is mostly him, I think, but with her singing her echo chorus to his whistling, it clearly had two sides to it. I believe she likes the attention. When Lime is locked in her cage for misbehaving or if there is a potential that she could attack Angie, Gus flies across the aviary, not an easy task for him, and settles on the top of his cage. His loyalty is commendable, particularly as sometimes she pulls his tail. The only time that I have ever seen him pull her tail is when he wants to drink from the communal water dish, and she is not only hogging the water, but is literally sticking her tail in his face as he waits at a nearby perch. .

I wondered later whether I might just have imagined his new way of preening Lime. But months later I saw Lime standing on the communal water dish with her head bent way down. Gus was on a perch slightly above it and to the right. He used one talon to scritch the back of her head and neck a few times and then the other, with one talon always on the perch. He had refined his technique so he was less likely to fall.

Improving on the Preen

Still later I noticed that Gus and Lime had improved their preen, that is, his preening of her. Gus was standing on a higher perch, Lime was standing on a lower one. She put her head down and he was lifting his feet up and down, as he does when he is excited. Then he led with his left talon, scritching the top of her head. He followed this up by preening her with his peak, directing his attention to the top of her head and the area around her beak. He appeared to be a little nervous concerning how she might react (I would be, too), and there were brief pauses between sessions. Then the whole sequence started over again.

A Half and Half Preen

About six months later, I saw Gus preening Lime for the first time in months. I had just taken them out and was coming back with my breakfast of cereal. He was on a higher perch, she on a lower one with her head bent down. He had his right talon on her head, the left talon on his perch, and was preening her with his beak. This seems to me to be the most efficient method of preening he has developed to date. There is a lot of smart in Gus's crested head.

I Will Follow Her

And then I experienced another first. I went into the aviary to say hello to the birds. Gus was singing up to Lime, while both were on top of her cage, he on the "roof," her on the perch above it. Lime then flew out towards the kitchen, as she often does, before I closed the door. You have to be very careful closing that door. As I went to get the communal water dish to refill it with fresh water, there was a wild, mad flapping sound from the same area as the door. I looked into the kitchen and saw Gus beginning what was to be a very awkward landing on a pile of books on the floor. When I got to him, he looked up at me, and I put down my hand for him to step up. Then I went to get his "girlfriend" from the plastic container with the big wooden spoons that she likes to gnaw on. When I returned to the aviary, I put her in her bicycle tire, him in the wreath beside the tire. After 10 minutes, they were both still there. Gus obviously wanted to be with her. He had never flown out like that before. It was a first. I haven't seen it happen since.

I Am Your Protector

Gus initiated something else new in his relationship with Lime. Whenever I approach Lime and he is near, he lets out an aggressive peep. If she is in the bicycle tire by the window and he is to the left of her in the wreath, and I approach her, he peeps in protest. If she is perched on the aviary mesh wall and he is close by to her left of her (the proper position for the queen's consort), I expect now to hear that sound. To me it says, "Watch out. She is not alone. She has a tough, male cockatiel protector."

A few weeks after I first observed this behaviour, he stepped up his warnings a notch. The peep became a hiss, a sound that male cockatiels are well known to make when they are feeling aggressive. It reminds me of the sound that a male swan makes. His is scaled down in volume, but not in intent.

Tandem Flight

When I walked into the aviary Gus and Lime were close together. He was on his corner on top of Lime's cage and she was on top of the metal television cabinet. When I came in, they both flew, taking off at the same time, to the aviary mesh. It was like it was a planned move. This was the first time. I have experienced it several times since.

She Returns!

Friday night, and I had to do some last-minute writing. Lime had flown out of the aviary, sneak that she is, and I had her on my shoulder for about 15 minutes. When she returned, Gus was clearly excited. He chirped in response to her coming back. He also stretched himself up tall several times, as if to show her that he really wasn't that short after all. I hope that she appreciated the grand greeting her return received.

The next morning, Lime was on my head as I was working on revisions to my sociology textbook. Occasionally I could hear his little chirps, I suspect calling to her.

Well, she pooped on my head, so I got up to find a paper towel (they always disappear when I have urgent need for them). I went into the living room and saw Gus not only chirping but presenting in full male cockatiel display, his head bobbing and his long wings partially lifted as if in preparation for take off. He doubled his chirp rate and was clearly excited. I had to give Lime back to him. He is now a very happy bird.

Gus is always happy when Lime returns to the aviary. Often he dances on his perch attached to the aviary wall, making happy sounds. "She's back, she's back!" he was saying in so many gleeful ways. It seems a trifle one-sided. She does not seem to reciprocate, but maybe she gives back some subtle signs that

I can't see, that only Gus can perceive. I don't believe that the relationship is completely one-sided.

One Bird Parrot Chorus

As I write this, Gus is singing one of his whistle-songs. When I hear them I get the distinct feeling that I am being told a story, like a grandparent telling a story to a small child. One of the things I love to do when I am in the aviary is start Gus singing by whistling a short tune to him. He always picks up on it, and starts his own tuneful storytelling. Recently, Lime has been adding her two seeds' worth. She picks up two or three of the notes and imitates them tonally perfectly, but not with a whistle. There is a rhythm to it, as if she is singing the chorus of a song every other bar. Gus and Lime are very much like mates. Gus often watches intently when I play with Lime. It reminds me of how intensely social parrots are. Sometimes you see the two of them together on top of Quigley's cage, an unusual place for her, but not for him; he often goes there in the morning, I think as an escape from some of the other birds who pick on him.

The Balcony Scene

Picture the balcony scene from *Romeo and Juliet*. Now change it a bit. Romeo is a handsome male cockatiel standing on ladder-like steps leading to a perch at the top of a large bird cage. Juliet is a much larger yellow-headed Amazon busy eating from a bowl attached to the perch. Romeo the cockatiel walks up the stairs and starts singing up to her. Juliet the Amazon eats. Romeo the cockatiel steps up almost to the top of the ladder still singing, until his face is about an inch away from Juliet the Amazon. She continues to eat while serenaded by the handsome young Romeo. Eventually she eats her fill and flies away, to land on her perch on the aviary wall. Our hero then follows her in a mighty feat of flying with his damaged-feather wings. He situates himself nearby. The scene has ended.

Calling to Her

Two more indications of the close relationship between Gus and Lime have revealed themselves. When I took Lime with me into my office, Gus whistle-called to her, wanting to know where she was. Later, when I brought her back to the aviary and had to put her in her cage, because I was leaving for work, he quickly flew from his perch on the aviary mesh wall to a spot on the left side of Lime's cage, above where I put her. He is loyal to her. It doesn't seem to me that she does much if anything to deserve his loyalty, but she definitely has it.

Lime Responds to Gus

Angie was cleaning up the aviary and Lime and I were in Angie's office, watching *Coronation Street* and interacting with each other. Lime was walking up the suspended cage, climbing up to the curtain rod, and then walking back down to play with daddy. What I was not listening for, but it was there, was Gus' whistling out to her, to find out where she was. I heard it a few times, but didn't pay it any attention. Then she stopped on the curtain rod and whistled with the two-tone call that she uses with me when I am out of sight in the bedroom, the bathroom or Angie's office, a call that asks for—demands—a response. She was telling him where she was. I had never heard her respond to him outside of the aviary before.

Gus Sounds the Alarm

Gus was loudly chirping, and it was not his usual message of happiness. It did not take long to determine the cause. I saw that Sam and Stanee were by Juno's cage, so I had them step up on the stick and took them inside the aviary. But Gus was still sending off his alarm. Then I noticed that Lime was not to be seen. A quick look into the kitchen and I spotted her on top of the basket with the wooden spoons, her favourite spot. After I took her back to the aviary, Gus could relax.

Gus and Louis

Gus and Louis are buddies. It is a different relationship than that Gus has with Lime. First off, Louis preens Gus, the only bird who does so. Gus will sometimes whistle to Louis in such a way that his buddy comes over to visit. This sometimes leads to Louis preening Gus. Now Gus is kind of a fussy "preenee." He doesn't like to be preened very long or too roughly. After a relatively short period of being preened, Gus often drives Louis away. On a few occasions, Louis has responded by pulling Gus's tail. I have to side with Louis on this one.

The best demonstration of the close buddy relationship between the two male birds I have seen was described in chapter two. Gus had been bullied several times by other parrots, and Louis came over to preen him, to show him that he was not alone. That's what friends are for, bird or human.

Gus Makes a New Sound

One night, after I put Gus in his cage, he started making a sound I had never heard from him before. It sounded exotic and Australian. There were two notes, the first lower and longer than the second. He kept repeating this sequence for about 20 minutes after I put him in his cage, including after I had left the room. I have no idea why he made that sound, or what it might have meant to him. For days afterwards, I heard it. Never uttered outside the cage, the sound was made only when Gus is newly in his cage at night.

Gus Is Bullied But Not Beaten

Later that same day Gus had a hard time. Twice he was bullied to the floor. I am glad I was able to have him step up to my down-stretched hand. The second time he seemed happy to stay with me. His heart was beating rapidly. I waited a while before I moved, giving his pounding little heart time to slow down (parrots' hearts beat faster than do ours). Then I took him to my office. He stayed there, happy to be with me. We hadn't spent time together like that in quite some time. Then, after he heard one of the birds call to him, he called back and was anxious to return to the aviary, even though he had just been bullied there.

Late afternoon, and Gus sings, determined not to be daunted by what life has dished out to him. Early in the evening, he was down on the floor again. I didn't see or hear what happened, but he ran to me as I put my hand down.

Gus Is Blooded

One of the nastier sides of having a contentious flock of parrots is that sometimes someone gets hurt. That someone today was Gus. He was blooded on his left wing, and the blood flowed. He could still fly, but only barely. The blood flowed rapidly down his wing, falling to the floor. None of the others had blood on their beak, so I could not take out my anger, hurt and worry out on any one of them—although I did give Sam a dirty look. He only blinked in seeming innocence, as he always does. It was hard to clean the blood off Gus. I had to block his flight as I tried to wipe blood off and cleanse his wound at the same time. Before I left, I fed him a Nutriberry, which he first ate and then attacked, not missing out on the opportunity to get me in the finger. He was blooded, but he did not lack in male cockatiel attitude.

Later at the college, that image came to mind that I sometimes have, the one where I enter the aviary and a bird lies dead at the bottom of his or her cage. I know Gus only suffered a superficial wound, but I hated to leave my friend and companion bird wounded like that. I pictured the dead bird as Gus. When I returned home I was glad to see my little 'tiel fine and feisty again. No serious damage was done. Nothing he couldn't handle.

Gus: You've Done It Again

Sometimes you don't know that you need affection until a parrot shows you that you do. That was true this morning. I put Gus on my shoulder as I uncaged (or is that decaged?) all the birds. He is the first to be released. When all the birds are free, I usually let him walk off my shoulder onto the top of Lime's cage. This morning Gus started singing, looking right at me. I stood there and let him sing to me. It was a hot, humid, dreary morning, but I've been sung to, and I feel better for that. Thanks, Gus. You know what I need before I do.

A Favoured Perch

One morning I fetched Gus out of his cage as usual. He bit at me several times while still stepping up, again as usual. But this morning our short time together would be different. As I moved over to unleash Lime from her cage, I stopped and looked over at Gus. He was looking straight back at me. As I took Lime out of her cage, he started his whistle-song. I offered him a step over to the top of Lime's cage where he goes every morning, but he politely declined the offer. He shifted into full male cockatiel song. I stood still and looked across my shoulder at him while he sang. He was singing to me. We stood together for a few minutes, avian songster and human audience, and then I went over to the aviary wall to offer him that as an option for perching. It was declined. Then we went back to Lime's cage. There is another offer for a step over, another declining of that offer. He continued to sing his full whistle-song. I walked out of the cage and he changed his song to a series of statements telling the others where he was. He didn't seem happy, so I returned to the aviary. We stood by Lime's cage for a short while, and eventually he stopped singing and took the offer of stepping over. But for a while, I had been given a cockatiel compliment as a favoured perch.

The next day he did the same thing, only without the song. If a bond can grow, then ours is doing just that. He has done the same thing a few times since, and I always feel that he has given me a gift.

Gus Has a Plan

Gus often has trouble flying across the room, but he makes up for it with smarts. He tried to fly from the mesh to the roof of Lime's cage and failed, landing not so gracefully on the floor. I went over to retrieve him. It wasn't long afterwards that he decided that he wanted to fly back to the mesh. He made some pre-flight moves from the roof of Lime's cage, but didn't feel confident that he could make it. That was when his clever cockatiel mind clicked in. He climbed up the ladder to the high perch above the cage and then he launched into flight, making it to the other side with only a little height to spare. Where your wings won't take you, your mind will, if you are a clever cockatiel.

Starting the Week with a Cockatiel

It was a Monday morning, and I was feeling it like a curse. I walked over to Gus's cage to release him. After I put him on my shoulder, Gus decided not to leave when I offered him two perches on either side of the aviary. He wanted to stay and talk to me, using his *cha-cha-cha* sound. This worked its wonder. Once I had taken him outside the aviary, he began to signal to the others where he was. And when we returned to the aviary, he accepted the offer of a perch. But the magic had been worked, the message received that sometimes he especially cherishes my company. I was duly complimented.

Then he did it again. I was angry with myself, unhappy with what I was writing, as a writer can often be. And Lime was at her annoying best. Gus knew. He started singing to me as I was replacing the papers in the cages, his face pointed directly at mine. He doused a fire I didn't want to be burning, but had little control over. Again, Gus, you saved me from myself.

Gus Tells Secrets

Sometimes when Gus is chirping and I'm standing right beside him, he cocks his head slightly, like he is telling me secrets, or at least gossiping about the other parrots, particularly about how they drive him off of a perch or pull his tail. Either way, there is a definite feeling that he is sharing something with me that he wouldn't share with the others. I have never pulled his tail.

A Rare Treat from Gus

Tonight I received a rare treat from Gus. I put him on my shoulder. He usually flies away, but not this time. I whistled to him and he whistled back. Then he started preening my moustache, the only place where he will preen me. He's never touched my beard. A couple of times, his preening followed whistling from me. Gus's preening is rather like one of his multiple, mad-male cockatiel attacks. Two things were unique about tonight's preening. One was that he preened me in at least four sessions. He had never done it that often before. Second was the fact that he preened around my eyes, as Quigley and Lime do. I was a little nervous about that, as he had never done that before, but I had nothing to worry about. Relationships with parrots sometimes grow with small events. This appears to me to be one of those small events that make a parrot and a human grow closer.

Summarizing Gus

As you have read in the little vignettes that have comprised most of this chapter, Gus can communicate a lot, although he speaks no human words. His whistle songs delight his humans, and, I suspect, his avian mates. They are his way of letting others know that he is happy and often that his happiness springs from the company he is with. Like the big cockatoos that are so popular on Facebook (and are shared with people known to have parrots), Gus dances, although not to music that I have ever seen. His dancing is triggered by eager anticipation. He dances when he is on his perch at night and wants me to give him a ride over to his cage for his night's rest. He could fly there himself, but expects that his dad will give him a lift. His talons are likewise animated when I come into the aviary early in the morning, and am about to release the birds from their cages—usually he is first. And they drum in excitement when I am bringing Lime back to the aviary, and into his presence. Like many a human, he has a happy dance.

Gus can put on a display of apparent anger, when I get closer to Lime than he is happy with at the time, when I put my fist near to him when he is on a perch, and when he steps up before being taken to his cage at night. But it is more display than anything else.

He has two bird friends, one a much bigger female Amazon (a fellow blonde and outsider apart from the 'cool kids' of the conures, Tikkifinn, Poccopeck, and Sam), and the other a slightly larger conure. Gus preens the former, and allows the latter to preen him ("but not so tough now or I'll complain"). He sings to both, and to me, when the mood strikes him.

Gus sitting on his tire-perch

Chapter Seven
Juno the Celestial Parrot

This is the shortest chapter, but that seems reasonable as Juno is our smallest bird, and we have known him the shortest amount of time of all but one of our current flock. But like him, this chapter has an inner bigness, a *lot* of inner bigness. And it is also fitting that this chapter includes several passages written by Angie, Juno's best friend.

Meeting Juno
by Angelika Steckley

In our favourite pet shop, I headed towards the birds for sale, but only to visit, as we already had seven parrots. As I peered into their cage, the busy chatter and fluttering and preening of the budgies froze for a second. I greeted them, they acknowledged me, and resumed their business. In a cage all to himself, a sprite-like bird caught my attention. With his big beak and stout tail he looked like a clown-like version of his busy neighbours, the budgies. Although I'd seen celestial parrotlets before, this one enchanted me by his curious interest in me. He demanded my attention as he flew to the cage bars, hung upside down, and peeped excitedly. He fluffed his feathers, adding nominally to his size of five inches. There was something so familiar about the feathered fellow! "Finfin," I said to myself. Could he possibly be a reincarnation of the beloved blue Quaker parrot that we had lost three months earlier? John, who had come into the shop ahead of me, found me staring in wonder at the parrotlet. I shared my sudden notion and he said he had thought the same thing.

We giddily interacted with our newfound friend. When the shop clerk seemed to suddenly appear out of thin air, we laughed and smirked at each other, already knowing what destiny would bring. I dared to ask, "Could

Juno the Parrotlet

we please see the parrotlet?"

The store clerk warned us that he was not very friendly and it would be hard to get him out. She opened the door. He dashed out, his rapid flight reminding me of a hummingbird, and alighted on a shelf. The clerk said he'd be a challenge to catch so I approached him carefully. But one jump on his delicate, long-toed feet, and he was on my shoulder. The clerk said, "He's never done that before."

I was holding back tears. John was already thinking about a cage for him. The parrotlet was born in June. Finfin, the Quaker, had died in June, so we named him "Juno."

We quarantined him in my office just to make sure he was healthy before we introduced him to the bird room. On that first day, he sat on my finger, looking up as I sang songs to him. It was difficult for me to sing "Twinkle, Twinkle Little Star," as it had been Finfin's favourite song. Three-month-old Juno had never heard it before. Juno was all ears, his twinkling eyes blinking intermittently as he listened. A few hours later, as he was settled into his new home, I could hear Juno singing in his sweet, high-pitched way, "Twinko, Twinko, li-il stawr." He had picked up the same riff, the same intonations as Finfin when she had sung the song. For a week, he sang the song and then suddenly he stopped, never to sing it again.

He may or may not be Finfin, come back to us, but he is his own bird, full of love and curiosity. When memories of Finfin bring tears, I bring him out of his cage, and my heart is mended.

[A note from John: I would only add to this that he likes to play "Gotcha," as Finn did.]

Parrotlets

Like "conure" and "parakeet," *parrotlet* is not a precise scientific term. There are three different parrotlet genera: *Forpus*, *Touit*, and *Nannopsittaca* (literally, "very small parrot"). All parrotlets share two main characteristics: they are all very small, and they all live in the area from Mexico south to South America. The genus of parrotlet that has been domesticated is *Forpus*, which is also the one discussed in this chapter. Our Juno is a *Forpus*.

You may not have previously heard of parrotlets, as, compared with the other parrots discussed in this book, they have only recently become popular in the northern hemisphere as pets. I myself had never heard of them until we saw the sign on Juno's cage. One of my editors with another publisher even thought that I had made the term up when I sent him an e-mail in reply to his often-asked question, "How many parrots do you have now?" It's a question that Angie and I are frequently asked by friends and family. It is not as annoying a question as "Do your parrots talk?" but the unspoken suggestion that we have no sense in acquiring ever larger numbers of parrots is not well received by us, even though there is some truth to it.

Something else people regularly say when they find out you have parrots is: "I hear they live a long time." This forces you into presenting the person with a verbal chart about the lifespans of the various species of parrot you have. For parrotlets, there is not great certainty, owing to their relatively recent entry into aviculture ("bird raising"), but 10 to 20 years sounds a reasonable rough estimate from the varying numbers that I have read.

Pacific Parrotlets

As aptly described on one website, www.parrotletbirds.com, Pacific parrotlets are "feisty little buggers." They are tightly packaged little balls of energy indigenous to Peru and Ecuador. Their flocks (I think gangs might be a more appropriate word for a collection of parrotlets) range from as few as four to as many as 100. Pacific parrotlets belong to the sub-family *Arinae*, and their scientific name is *Forpus coelestis*, the species name relating to their alternate common name, "celestial parrots." The name fits Juno as he is various shades of blue, all of them seen in the sky at various times. And he seems truly a sky creature when he flies all over the place at once. Powder blue is his default colour; a streak of a darker blue that leads back from his eyes like a thin strip of dramatic makeup tells you that he is male. A similar streak on his wings confirms that gendering. Subtle shades in between decorate and describe the colouring of his tiny body.

The genus name comes from its scientific "discoverer," Forpus F. Boie, who wrote about them in 1858. No Internet search I have engaged in mentions anything about him other than his name, the year 1858 and the parrotlet genus. Type in "Forpus" and you only find discussions of parrotlets. His name seems unusual, perhaps a Latinization of a more recognizable name, a not uncommon practice of early scientists, the most famous of whom was Carl Linné, who wrote as Carolus Linnaeus. There was a German scientist, Friedrich Boie, who lived during the appropriate time period (1789–1870) and who studied bugs, reptiles, birds and the law. He is attributed as naming several genera and species of birds, but none of them of parrotkind. Maybe Forpus was an alias or a discredited cousin.

Parrotlets have some large relatives. The sub-family, *Arinae*, to which they belong includes the big guys, the macaws and the Amazons, as well as the smaller (though still much bigger than Pacific parrotlets) members, the conures and the Quaker parrots.

Descriptions of parrots on websites are usually dry, but that is not always the case for Pacific or Ceparrotlets (a short form for the more common term, celestial parrotlets). As stated above, they are definitely feisty. This means that they don't always play nice with other parrotlets, and they even bite and sometimes attack humans. "Nippy" is a much favoured adjective on websites describing them. But if you are right for them, they are great pets. They are easily worth a few scars on your hands.

One way to describe parrotlets is to say that they are the dachshunds of the parrot world. We have a crafty female dachshund named Trudy. This is why I make this analogy. When we were interviewed prior to being permitted to adopt a dog from Canadian Dachshund Rescue, we were asked, "Do you know what they're like?" with slightly sinister undertones. I would ask the same question of a prospective Pacific parrotlet owner. "You do know what they are like, don't you?"

While celestial parrots are not the smallest parrots on earth—the pygmy parrots of New Guinea hold that title—they are still tiny for parrots, typically stretching between 4½ to 5½ inches (roughly 11.4 to 14 centimetres) top to tail-end. They weigh about 33 grams or 1.1 ounces. If parrotlets cost $100 a pound, then you could get one for $7. It is only a bit of an exaggeration to say that if my thumb grew feathers, fluffed up a bit and grew a tail and a beak, it would be roughly the size of a Pacific parrotlet.

This small size has earned them the alliterative nickname, the "pocket parrot." That would only be true if you were wearing old farmers' pants with big pockets and the denim was very, very thick, as putting one in your pocket would be a bad mistake. As mentioned earlier, they can bite. Maybe "purse parrot" or "backpack parrot" might be more fitting.

Two aspects of their bodies are disproportionate to their small size. They have big beaks for their bodies (all the better to nip you with), and their talons look big enough to be parrot-sized snowshoes, making them well-suited for life in Canada.

Juno: Drawer Explorer
by Angelika Steckley

We are in the kitchen and after a moment Juno starts: "Woi-tee-tee, woi-tee-tee, tee-tee-tee-tee." He flutters in a circle in front of me. OK. I get it. I open the utensil drawer and he zips down to it. Don't need to take this guy to the movies. Each time, he's fascinated. He full-fluffs up, repeats his excited "Woi-tee-tees" and prances back and forth along the edge of the drawer. If I put my finger anywhere near it, he bites. Inside, the silverware and cooking utensils seem to take on more of a glitter. He settles down and silently inspects the contents of the drawer. At first he just perched safely on the edge of the drawer, peering at its contents. I say, "What's in there?" and he peeps. Gradually he's ventured further and further in his exploration of the drawer. Once he was bored with just looking in from outside, he bravely flew into the drawer and perched on the utensils there, but he still stayed safely in the outer part of the drawer—in the light. After two years of exploring the familiar, he's finally crept into the back of the drawer, into the darkest depths. We have to watch that we don't accidentally shut the drawer he is so quietly engrossed in, searching for who knows what. But when my hand wanders into the drawer, he is always on the alert to bite my finger. Eventually he must come out. He has learned that when I flutter the bottom of my shirt, it's time to fly out and leave drawer exploration for another day.

[A note from John: Despite the new adventure of delving into the drawer, Juno still seems to prefer just to look at it, fluff up and chatter at a rate of more than one comment a second. Perhaps the view is better from the ledge. Who wants to look around in the Grand Canyon when the view is much more spectacular from the cliffs above?]

Juno: "Mister Bluebird's on My Shoulder"

Juno is remarkable in that he has the spirit and intelligence of the bigger birds. He is nothing less than they are, only smaller. I like the fact that on one website they say that parrotlets have "the same size personality as an Amazon" (www.all-pet-birds.com/parrotlets.html). I have observed the truth of that, having both an Amazon and a parrotlet, and often having both of them on my shoulders at the same time: not for the faint of heart.

He is so light that sometimes when he is on your back you cannot feel him through your shirt, and wonder whether he has flown away. But do not take him lightly. He can bite your nose so that it hurts. How do they learn that that is a good target on a human? Senegal Sam learned it as well, to my great pain.

Time for a Little Science: Contact Calls and the Parrotlet

There's a population of green-rumped parrotlets (*Forpus passerinus*) living in Venezuela that can be rightfully called the most studied and best-known wild parrot population in the world. They have been the subjects since 1987 of nearly three decades of research by Steven Beissinger of the University of California at Berkeley, and following him Karl S. Berg and others. Data exists on over 8,500 of these wild birds. Berg's work is discussed at length in Virginia Morell's *Animal Wise: How We Know Animals Think and Feel*, in the chapter entitled "Parrots in Translation."

One of the key concepts explored in this research is that of the *contact call*. Contact calls are used by social animals to establish location and other important information. The "honks" made by Canada geese as they fly overhead are contact calls. Lime's two-note or three-note whistle call when I am out of my office and more obviously her calls of "Where are you?" are both contact calls with essentially the same meaning.

Berg noted that the green-rumped parrotlet's contact call was unique to each bird, and in a way functioned as the bird's name. That's not just a peep you hear, that's a contact call: "Hello, I am Juno." As a socially active parrotlet, you learn your own contact call and those of other birds that you know. Berg noted in his research that when a female hears its mate's contact call/name, she is much more likely to respond than when other males uttered theirs. Mated pairs have as many as 15 different calls that they use when interacting with each other. Berg believes and is trying to prove that these contact calls are given to a bird by its parents, just as we give names to our children.

Contact Calls and Juno: The Password is "Three"
by Angelika Steckley

When Juno says "Three!" I know he definitely wants out. One of our language learning exercises is to count to three. I say "one," and he has learned to say "two." I say "three," and he often repeats it with fervour, for which I praise him. So now, when he wants out of the cage, he says, "Three!" It works almost every time.

I clean Juno's cage every day and yet each time it's as though it's a new ordeal for him. He has spent a whole day making his home comfortable by piling up the bits of paper he has chewed off the newsprint on cage floor. The blackberry juice and the fleshy bits of the fruit are nicely spread all over. Chattering noisily, he chases after my hands as I roll up the soiled newsprint. He hangs onto it with his talons as I pull the rolled-up paper out of the cage. I say, "I'm cleaning up the poopoo," and he flies off, landing on top of the cage, chirping excitedly. He watches intently, head tilted, spying on the activity as I vacuum, wipe down the cage, and put in clean paper. The food dish is the highlight of the chores, and when I pick it up, he perches on my finger and munches away on the leftovers, peeping between bites. I wonder if perhaps he thinks we are dining together. The refreshed bowl of food is explored and tasted as we head back for his cage. Seemingly unaware as he is perched on the bowl, he and the bowl are put into his cage. As if I tricked him, after a few seconds he loses interest in eating and demands to come out again, twittering "Three! Three!"

Juno's Other English Words

While his strictly parrot utterances have meanings that we are still learning to decipher, I would say that Juno has at least one other contact call that we know of: his name. He utters it once or twice in short succession. Sometimes, when Juno is flying free and Angie calls his name, he not only comes when he is called but says his name in response as well, sometimes twice in a row ("Juno, Juno"). This behavior is very much in line with what Berg is finding out about the contact calls of the parrotlets that he is studying.

Once Juno has made contact with us, he sometimes uses other English words. While on your shoulder or other parts of your body, "pretty bird" is often part of his fast-flowing articulation. Sometimes he says "ouch" just after he bites Angie on the nose. He has never done so when he has bitten me, but then I have never said "ouch" to him either.

You have to listen carefully when Juno speaks, as he does not have the loud broadcasting system that Lime, Sam, the Quakers and the conures have. Neither does he whistle-sing like Gus. The following situation is a case in point

I was sitting on the plastic chair, watching *Murdoch Mysteries* and eating raisin-bread toast. I now rarely eat in the aviary—too many experiences of parrot swarming. I had Lime on my head, Tikkifinn behind my back on top of the chair, Quigley on my right forearm, Stanee on my upper right bicep and Louis on my shoulder—a man at home with his parrots. I heard Juno speaking rapidly, but which language was he using?

At first I thought I heard "di-di di-di di-di gotcha," but was that just because that was what my mind wanted to hear? I finished the toast with some parrot help, got up, shook them off and went closer to Juno, who was in his cage on the other side of the aviary mesh. His articulations sounded clearer now. It was definitely "di-di di-di di-di … gotcha," repeated over and over. This is what he sometimes says when I am playing the gotcha game with him. I was pretty sure I knew why he was doing this. He wanted to be let out to play, so he was using the words of our game. My mind flashed back to another blue bird now gone, another gotcha, but I didn't feel sad for long. Juno was speaking to me and got excited when I repeated his words back to him. Angie then came into the room and took him to her room. She got the message, too. Thanks for that, little man. You have made my night with your words.

In a follow-up to the section of "Mr. Bluebird on My Shoulder," we usually begin his time on my shoulder, by my saying "diddle, diddle, diddle, gotcha", with both of our gotchas spoken at the same time.

But most of Juno's speech consists of his chattering in his own language, a good indication of excitement on his part, and also that he is male. Male parrotlets are more likely to speak than females. Given the rapidity with which he speaks, perhaps the poor females don't have a chance to get a word in edgewise.

Juno Learns Calls from the Other Birds

Not surprisingly, Juno is a good imitator of other birds. I have heard him make sounds associated with four other birds. He can issue the non-whistle chirp that Gus uses. He articulated one of those when he was on my left shoulder, trying to get my attention away from Lime who was then sitting on my right shoulder. One night he was on my right shoulder when Sam was on my left knee. I made the vocal clicking sound that I use to speak to Sam, and twice it was imitated by the little guy. Even with his little voice, it was not difficult to know the sound that he was making. I had gone to fetch him because I heard him call to me with his small version of "A Wiggle and a Peck," a verse of the song that Angie taught the Quakers. It was soft-sounding, but still clearly his imitation of what Quigley does when he sings a longer version of the song. Right now, Lime is on my head making baby-bird sounds of endearment, and Juno, who is on my right bicep, is imitating her. It took me a while to realize what he was doing. It would be easy to underestimate the capacity of a celestial parrot for human speech if you don't listen carefully.

Juno and Friends

Juno's first friend when he came to our home was his mirror, a kind of security image for him. Early on, he also established a sleeping spot in his cage close to the mirror, where he now regularly goes. We kept him at night in Angie's room, the auxiliary parrot room, but he liked the presence of the other birds so much, and they liked his presence so much, that his cage is now on the other side of the aviary.

An English aristocrat, Hastings William Sackville Russell, the 12th Duke of Bedford (1888–1953), who bred parrots (though not parrotlets), succinctly described *Forpus vividus*, cousin of the Pacific parrotlet: "It … is quite good-tempered with other birds, but it fights most savagely with its own kind and does so from pure love of fighting." The duke's words apply to parrotlets, too. We considered getting a parrotlet "friend" for Juno, but we have since thought better of it.

The duke also seems to have been right about parrotlets getting along with other species.

Louis was Juno's first bird friend—no real surprise, as Louis also first befriended Tikkifinn and Gus, and is usually the bird in our flock that humans connect with first. Juno can be a loud bird, and certainly is the fastest utterer of bird sounds; rapid-fire machine-gun speech is his specialty. And he does not fear the other birds. Parrotlets are known to be fearless, and are sometimes reported to attack other pet parrots, as well as cats and dogs. But after more than four years with Juno, and his having numerous visits with the other parrots in the aviary, I have never witnessed him acting aggressively towards the other birds. If another parrot comes close to him in the aviary, he takes off. He is the most acrobatic flyer that we have, so he has little to fear about being attacked in the air.

But there is the danger for his toes. I wrote earlier than Juno has, proportionately, snowshoe sized talons. Unfortunately, this makes them fairly easy targets for being bitten by bigger birds. Poor Juno has had his toes seriously bitten twice. This happened when he was on the aviary wall, and someone on the other side took exception to his presence there. The first time he lost his toe. The second time, he had his toe and a good section of one of his talon's wrapped up in a two-layer cast. He definitely does not baby it. After Angie set up his cage so he wouldn't have to fly or land to get food, he still did both. It is amazing to see him adjust himself, as well as climb up the cage wall, dragging his right talon. You can see his trial and error process, his thinking. Early on he learned that he could put seeds on the cast and use it as a plate as he did his wings. And he refuses to let his handicap restrict his movements. This is not trying to look strong, not weak in the face of imagined predators. It is important to him to be as fully functional as he came be because it makes his life easier, and he gets a sense of pride from it. He reminds me of my three months on crutches. I kept trying to see where I could go. We went for a visit to two different parks for a dog walk, and I would not let the crutches keep me from going where I wanted to, even in taking a short cut through mud and snow rather than taking the long way a round along the sidewalk. I think he could relate.

Lime and Juno

I am sitting at my computer with Lime on my right shoulder and he flies to my left, he makes no show of aggression towards her. Both seem to be content to get half of my attention, meaning, of course, that I have little left for writing. Interestingly, Juno seems fascinated by Lime. When he is was first permitted to enter the aviary, he often flew near to her and stared. In return, she did not move aggressively towards him with her beak. When he gets what I suspect is "too close" in her view, she puts out one of her talons in defense.

These days Juno and Lime are friends. When he is in the aviary and she is in her cage, he is always less than two parrotlet lengths away. When she escapes the aviary, he follows close behind. They are the two extremes of our birds, by far the largest and by far the smallest, and yet they have clearly bonded.

Quigley is Juno's Hero

Quigley was engaged in one of his male-display feats of ferocity. There are three rubber triangles linked to each other and suspended from a perch attached to the aviary mesh wall. He attacks them with great sound and beaky fury. Sometimes either Angie or I will run into the room to see if everything is all right, to determine whether there are bird battles to break up. We have learned that this is a sound that he makes when he is feeling his seeds (not oats). Today I noticed that he has a big (but physically small) fan in the cage across the mesh. As Quigley demonstrated his birdly manliness, Juno was hopping around close by, trying to get the best view of the scene before him. He couldn't sit still, he was so filled with excitement. It very much put me in mind of our watching the young fans of the Toronto Marlies, the American Hockey League affiliate of the Toronto Maple Leafs, as their heroes did battle with the villains (called the Admirals, but with pictures of pirates on their chests). The kids could barely contain themselves, especially when the announcers told them to "get loud." We didn't need to tell Juno to "get excited." If sweatshirts were issued to birds, Juno would want to wear one with a picture of a big (to him) green Quaker parrot who was clearly his hero on this day.

Juno Has Imitators

Juno is a source of almost constant fascination for the other birds. This can be heard in the imitations made of the sounds that he makes. Sam often makes Juno sounds. Sam has fooled me more than once into thinking that Juno is in the aviary. Tikkifinn also seems fascinated by him. Like Sam she is good at imitation, and does a passable Juno. Our parrots vary in how good they are at 'parroting.' What is surprising is that Gus, who imitates no one else, can do a decent Juno sound himself. And the two of them are rivals for Lime's affection.

Wings of Wonder
by Angelika Steckley

I have learned that Juno often utilizes his wings to express himself. When Juno is excited, his wings lift up and flutter slightly but rapidly two or three times, adding to his repertoire of communicative gestures.

Unlike the rest of our flock, who scratch their heads by exposing their scratching talons out front from under the wing, Juno draws his foot over his tucked wing. He tilts his head way down and scratches his head. It is comical to watch.

The other parrots are able to hold their food in their talons while eating. But the talons of Gus the cockatiel and Juno the parrotlet are not well designed to hold food. Where Gus lets the food drop from his talons, Juno creates a plate out of his wing. It's ingenious. He gets a piece of food, holds it under his wing and breaks it down to more manageable bits, keeping them there as he consumes each morsel.

[A note from John: It would be interesting to see whether this is a general parrotlet practice or the product of Juno's clever celestial mind, possibly an adaptation to confined living arrangements before he came to the store. Either way, it is unique to him among all our parrots.]

Personal Pictures of Juno

Juno has a way of moving his head when he is excited that is very hard to describe. It bounces up and down and around like a bobblehead, a sure sign that he is "over the top" about something. He is often super-excited about what he does and what he sees and hears. I sometimes wonder whether he breaks into a coffee jar and fills himself up to the brim with caffeine.

I have an image of peace or tranquility, that "happy place" that therapists annoyingly tell you to go to when you are justifiably upset. For me, that image is of Angie lying on the cot in her office asleep, her cupped right hand near her face and Juno cuddled, nestled (in a very "nesty" way) in her hand. He closes his eyes for a while, but energetic boy that he is, keeps opening them again. Life does not look more beautiful than that for me.

Reacquainting Myself with Juno

For a week or so after our rescue kitten, Brenda, came into our house in the late spring of 2014, I hadn't spent much time with Juno. I would talk to him through the cage and through the aviary, but not much more. What I didn't realize was how much he had missed me. Angie had him out while she prepared the morning dishes for the birds. He flew over to my shoulder, and speaking in a very rapid, high-pitched way (the usual tone, but fast even for him), he walked from one of my shoulders to the other, right to left. He was clearly excited to be with me. I had to take some garbage out, but he was having none of it. I put him by the dishes, showing him which one was his, but that didn't work. He flew back, speed-talked and walked from shoulder to shoulder by way of my back. Eventually I had to put him back in his cage, along with a dish filled with fresh fruit. But we both realized how great it was to be with the other. He made my day. He knows how to make a human feel appreciated. Afterwards he would often greet me with excitement when I arrived home from work. It reminded me of when we had one dog, a border collie, and she would greet my arrival with energy and excitement.

Growing in Colour: After Five Months

Juno seems to me to be growing in colour over time, with each new shade of blue—really more an extension of a hint of a shade—marks an experience with us and a growing relationship. It is like Lime's growing extension of yellow on her head, and maybe the red that surprises me when I see her fallen feathers. Who knows how colourful he will be in a year of so. He is not getting larger. He still looks to us to be the same size that he was on the first day that we got him. We wondered, as with puppies, whether he would grow into his feet, but no, the proportions have stayed the same.

The Last Thing to Learn about Flying

The last thing to learn when acquiring flying skills is how to land. That is one indication of how much your young bird has advanced in his or her flying skills. Juno is a great little flyer, able to turn in midair on a wing and a whim. But his landing skills took a little longer to develop. He once came out of nowhere and flew directly at me, landing on my nose and grabbing on for dear life. "Juno, did you not see that large landing field/runway that is my bald head?" Maybe that is why Pacific parrotlets have big talons. Maybe they do not tend to land softly (victims of their speed and level of excitement), so they need to grab ahold of something before they slide off.

Juno and John

Juno is spending more and more time—and more and more *times*—with me. He stays on my shoulder, back and arm most of the time. Maybe only once or twice over a long period does he fly to the aviary wall as he did more frequently the first few times we tried this. I get to scritch the back of his head several times during the course of one of these sessions. I originally thought that I would not be able to break the sheath of his pin feathers, but with practice and a few bites I managed. And, as I scritch him, his mouth opens in pleasure, putting me in mind of Benji and Tika.

A Peaceful Time with Juno

A relatively peaceful time with Juno is a rare bird (from the Latin *rara avis* meaning something unique or exceptional). One day with Juno on my shoulderJuno stayed with me after Angie left for a rehearsal of her play. He did not move much, just seemed happy to be there. We shared a quiet peaceful time. Occasionally I would move to play with him, but it was clear that he was happy simply to stay where he was. That is a beautiful event with any of our birds, but special in this case because our wild and crazy bird was quiet, as content to be with me as I was with him. Since that time he has engaged in this quiet pleasure a number of times. In fact, he is doing so as I write this.

Juno is becoming more and more of a good "shoulder bird." His trust in me is growing. He spends ever more times on my left shoulder, sometimes walking across my back to see the sights from another perspective. He also lets me preen him more often, and for much longer periods.

He has even let me break his pin-feathers, which I think of as a powerful sign of trust. I haven't done that for the others in a while.

The Gentling of Juno's Kisses

I've known for a while, but am always wonderfully reminded, that Juno is excited when I return home. I didn't fully appreciate it before, as he would bite my face a few times hard if he was outside the cage and coming to greet me. But today as I write this, he flew to me and I found out that the bites might really be "Juno kisses," and that they were meant as a friendly greeting, a form of tough parrot love. For some reason he prefers the left side of my face, above the beard. He very gently bit/kissed my face a number of times, for the first time, without any flinching on my part. It didn't hurt. He had learned to greet more gently. I could fully appreciate his greeting and how glad he was to see me. I couldn't be better made to feel welcome in coming home. Parrots are the equals of dogs at doing that.

Juno Stages a Break-In

We went out for breakfast one Saturday morning, as is our custom, bringing the dogs with us so that they would not make a mess in our absence. What we did not know was that we had accidently left one of the doors to Juno's cage open. When we returned, we could not find him. It usually does not take long to locate him as he usually finds *us* in these circumstances, making sounds so that we know where he is. He would be no good at the "hide" part of hide-and-seek. He would give his location away. But this time he didn't. And then Angie looked inside the aviary, and there he was, on the mesh, and of the aviary, on the other side for the first time. He wanted to be with his big feathered friends. He was about two parrotlet lengths away from Gus—not surprising as the two often imitated the sounds made by each other, and knew one another by sight. Juno made Gus look big, and was also probably the only bird never to pick on him. Clearly he does not see Juno as a threat, and Juno seems to like the bird who is closest to him in size.

Juno flew to Angie's hand and we inspected him. There was no damage. We never learned the clever little fellow accomplished the break-in. Never judge the intelligence of a parrotlet by the small size of his brain.

We still keep Juno's cage outside the aviary. We think he is safer that way, and it enables us to spend more time with him.

Crinkling Plastic: The Ultimate Excitement in Being a Parrotlet

If there is anything guaranteed to drive Juno completely chattering crazy, it is the sound of crinkling plastic. His commentary turns on full speed. He is by far the fastest talker that we have. I wonder where that strange fascination comes from. It puts me in mind of the hares at Edinburgh Airport that would hang out around the runways and run around like crazy whenever a plane took off. One television commentator (who coined the term "hareports" for this phenomenon, which is found at a number of airports in Britain) suggested that because hares have such sensitive hearing, the noise of planes taking off created a sensory rush that they actually liked. Perhaps with Juno's brain so attuned to sound, this multitude of little sounds made by crinkling plastic comes together in a brain rush for him. In any case, the sound of crinkling plastic never fails to excite him. There could be a subtlety of appreciation of the sound that we humans lack, similar, perhaps, to how we can't appreciate smells the way our dogs do.

If you want to see a good example of male parrotlet behaviour in connection with the crinkling of plastic, watch (and more importantly listen to) the YouTube video entitled "Simon the Parrotlet Loses his Mind over Plastic Bag. Kevin the Aracari Vaguely Interested." An aracari is a type of toucan. Not being a parrot, perhaps its interest in sounds and capacity for being absolutely fascinated by them is considerably less. Still, our other parrots don't share Juno's crazy response to the crinkling of plastic.

Juno Hangs Around

Juno is the most upside-down bird that we have—by far. He especially likes to hang upside down in his cage so that he can look at you and swing like a pendulum while chattering away. He does this hanging from the bottom rung of the cage, so that you can see his face in the clear side of the bottom of the cage. This is a definite sign that he wants to be let out of the cage to spend time on your shoulder, and he will keep this up until you let him out.

Juno Wants to Have Sex with Angie

We were sitting in Angie's office watching television. She had Juno on her shoulder. He had been with her a long time. He ran from her shoulder down to her hand, and looked to us to be trying to have sex with her hand; not knowing what to do, he would alternate that with running around like crazy. He approached her hand in several ways, got confused and frustrated in what he was trying to do, and then ran around some more.

She loves you, Juno, just not in that way.

Preening and Talking to His Feather Friends

A strange, but very endearing aspect of Juno's behaviour is the way that he interacts with the vase of feathers on my table/writing desk. When he flies into my doorless office, he almost always visits his feather friends—rearranging them and speaking rapidly to them. It might be my imagination, but he seems particularly fond of Lime's brightly coloured feathers.

All Told

All told, then, both Angie and I would recommend the purchase of and relationship with a parrotlet. Just do not expect them to be like similarly sized birds, such as canaries and finches, who seem to me to be a lot less excitable and active.

Chapter Eight
The Whole Flock

In this chapter I will look at some of the socializing and social behaviour of the flock (including their humans). I will begin with one of the first aspects of parrot interaction with humans: stepping up.

Stepping Up: the Opening Gambit

"Step up" is the first command that a parrot learns—or ignores. The response to this command can tell you a lot about the parrot and his or her relationship to the people in his or her life. As far as our parrots are concerned, Louis will almost always step up. As you have read, he is very affectionate and generally eager to please. At night, right after I have put Stanee to cage and I have closed the door on the cage just above his, he will often fly to the perch (if he isn't already there) from which I usually ask him to step up.

Gus will always step up, too. I think that he doesn't refuse the offer because it has helped rescue him from the floor. His flight feathers are damaged and he finds it very hard to take off from the floor. And he steps up when I open up his cage in the morning and put him to cage at night. While he doesn't refuse the step up, he will still usually demonstrate to me, sometimes resulting in a little finger pain, that he is a ferocious male cockatiel and not to be messed with. It is part of the in-your-face nature of a male cockatiel.

Stanee will usually step up, and always does so when it is time for her to go to cage at night. She steps up in a way that I would describe as dainty. She reminds me then how light she is, and how beautiful her combination of different coloured feathers make her look. She has, however, on two occasions savaged my finger after stepping up. One instance occurred when she was nearly buzzed off my hand by Lime and she became upset. The other time I have no idea why she did it, but she must have been bothered about something. After that, I had her step up on a stick for about a week as I didn't trust her. Trust has since returned.

Juno, too, will usually step up, and will sometimes even say the words "step up" as he does so. He is the only one who steps up with verbal accompaniment. Sometimes, he gives us a nip during the process, particularly when he is excited. The nip can be a form of greeting for him.

Lime will usually step up. She always does so when I open up her cage in the morning.

A few times she has bitten my finger when I took her out of the cage in the morning. I have learned to watch for any suspicious signs of dangerous emotional states before I put my finger into her cage in the morning. Recently, about an hour or so after breakfast, when she has been screeching and I've come to take her to my office, Lime has rejected the words and the hand and started climbing up the mesh of the aviary wall. It seems that she is not yet quite ready for committing to going to work with me.

The instance in which she will reject a step up is when she has flown up to land on a box that lies on the top of the cabinet in the living room. She knows that I can't quite reach her there. I need her to take a few short steps in the direction of my hand before any stepping up can take place. A few times she has rejected both the hand gesture and suggestion (I can't really call it a command). In that case, I have to tilt the box upon which she is standing. As she begins to slide, Lime has to take wing, and typically lands on the roof of Juno's cage. Once she is there she quietly resigns herself to stepping up.

Quigley is more likely to step up with Angie than with me. He will sometimes step up with me, but usually not, and often lightly bites me instead. The best two locations to try a step up with him are on top of the back of the chair, and on top of the door of his cage. When he needs emotional support, or when I have taken someone else out of his cage, he is more likely than usual to step up with me. And once Stanee has been put in her cage for the night and he is perched just outside it, he is very likely to step up.

Tikkifinn has never stepped up for me, but she will gently (though firmly) push my hand away with her head, a very Quaker gesture. When I put her to cage at night with Louis, she will step up on a stick with no problem, although she will generally look a little wild first. She often opts for a flight to the cage instead, going to her cage on her own terms.

This is in stark contrast to Poccopeck. She will always step up. But then, she is not a rescue, like Tikkifinn, who came from a place where she had very little interaction with her owner. Poccopeck was well taken care of at the pet store. The people there, like us, could not resist her charm

Then there is Sam, who came from a very bad place. I wouldn't even think about putting my finger out for him to step up on. He would most certainly bite it, and maybe hang on. He is good about stepping up on a stick, but he will grab it with his beak first before putting his talons on the wood. I can just imagine that stick being my finger.

Shoulder Bird Relationships

As I have already mentioned earlier, shoulder bird relationships with parrots are gifts. When a bird wants to be on your shoulder, it is a feather-wrapped present of trust and affection. It is not, as I was more than once told, something that will make your bird think that he or she has the upper hand or talon over you. That has never happened to me. As you read in the first chapter, Benji was the first bird ever to fly to my shoulder, the first to give me serious shoulder time, and that will stay in my heart forever. I learned first from him the true beauty of such a relationship.

Of our current flock of nine, seven have a shoulder bird relationship with me: Lime, Louis, Stanee, Juno, Quigley, Poccopeck and Gus.

The bird who now spends by far the greatest amount of shoulder time is Lime. She usually perches on my right shoulder. And you have to add head time to that, as she is perched on my head making soft sighing sounds as I write this sentence. She was going to climb onto my head from my shoulder, but given her sharp talons, that is not a lot of fun for me. So I offered, and she accepted, an elevator ride on my index finger to the penthouse perch. She will sometimes spend between one and two consecutive hours on my shoulder and head. Other times it is only a few minutes. It depends on her mood. She flies off to the plastic basket of spoons or to the bookshelf when she wants to leave. Often her tail is flared out and her head feathers are raised. Leaving her perch would seem to be an emotional decision.

Number two in my perch parade is Louis. When I used to have breakfast in the aviary, he would perch on my shoulder and continually harass me for Cheerios. As he typically dropped just about every Cheerio that I gave him, there was a lot of beard- and hair-pulling on his part, an aggressive form of begging on his part. When he perches on my right shoulder, he generally preens my right eye. At night, when I am reading or watching hockey, he prefers to perch on my head. If I am lucky, and most of the time I am, he will preen my forehead when he spends time up there. My brain cranks out a lot of endorphins when he does that, and—rare for me—feelings of relaxation come to the fore.

Number three on my right shoulder is Stanee. This is a relatively new development. She has recently decided that we need to renew our relationship, after a few years in which she rarely approached me. Usually she flies to my arm, shoulder, head or back after Louis has done so, or when Sam is on one of my knees. But increasingly she is the one who flies to my shoulder first. I am still surprised when I look to my shoulder to find that it is her and not Louis. One of the good parts of this renewed relationship is the fact that I am hearing more articulations from Stanee when she is on my shoulder, trills and trillish sounds. It brings to mind how much I like how she speaks to me. A conure's trill is a lot like a cat's purr.

Juno is often on my shoulder now. We play the gotcha game when he is there. When he first started doing this he required a lot of stimulation and entertainment, as he is young and very energetic. He can bite hard, but I put it down to youthful enthusiasm, not nasty intent. He just gets so excited. As he and our relationship mature, he is more content to just perch on my shoulder, with occasionally gotchas, and with him sometimes allowing me to preen him, with a great deal of fluffing up on his part.

The only shoulder time I get with Gus is when I take him from his cage in the morning to the top of Lime's cage. It is a travelling relationship. It is very rare for him to be on my shoulder otherwise, although one night I put him on my shoulder while I was watching a hockey game. I know that he wanted to go to the mesh so that he could be with Lime, but I wanted him to spend a little time with me, so I sat down with him on my shoulder. He looked over to Lime, then to me, and several times he preened my moustache a little bit. He is the only bird that does that. As you have read, Gus has preening manoeuvres with Lime that are all his own. Gradually, his desire to be on the aviary mesh became so strong that I had to take him over there before he flew away. Still, I got a little preen, and I felt quite close to the little guy, even after he left my shoulder.

Quigley sometimes lands on my shoulder or head. It is almost always a surprise to me, and it is a powerful statement from him. Perching is on his terms. It is typically followed by his preening me. I know that when he does this, he really wants to be with me. It is a conscious choice. In the chapter on Quakers, I referred to his doing that three times in one day. The next day, I was putting Lime into her cage because she was screeching too much. I had to fight off Stanee, who bit me hard on my left forearm because I wouldn't let her attack Lime for being "bad." After I yelled at Stanee, Quigley came to the rescue. He seems to me to be a peacemaker at heart. He must have known that I was angry at Stanee, so he flew to my shoulder and immediately began to preen me. Louis joined him, on the opposite shoulder. Thanks, boys.

Sam certainly wants to be a shoulder bird, and tries to be one every day that I spend serious time in the aviary, but I keep him as a knee bird, my only knee bird. It has to be knee time or no time for me. The reason for that should be fairly obvious to the reader by now. If I let him up on the shoulder, eventually, when I least expect it, I will get bitten. On my knee, I stroke his beak and he doesn't bite me. Both of us are reasonably happy. Sit there on my knee, Sammy boy. You're banned from my shoulder, Sammy boy.

It's the exact opposite case with Tikkifinn. I would love for her to land on my shoulder, but it has only happened a few times. It doesn't last long; it seems as though she is caught up in the spirit of the moment, which overrides her usual caution in dealing with me. She gets close when the conures are on my arms, shoulder or head and Sam is on my knee, usually flying onto the back of the plastic aviary chair. She wants to be part of things, part of what the gang is doing, but is still not completely willing to fly to my shoulder or head. I encourage her presence with a deedle-deedle-boop, even though it involves an awkward turnaround and Sam is out of sight, which is always a little dangerous when he is close by. It would give him an opportunity to creep up to my shoulder.

Again, Poccopeck, is the opposite of her blue Quaker sister. She often flies to my shoulder, complete with her apparently commenting on the events of the day, and a little beard preening.

The Full Parrot Treatment

It was one of those days in which pretty much anything that could go wrong did go wrong: photocopiers, printers, and, more seriously, Angie was attacked around her eye by Lime. It is hard for me to think that this was the same bird whose beak preens right beside my own eye. We had to go to the eye doctor to have Angie's eye checked. Afterward, I was sitting with the parrots in the aviary around 9 p.m. It began with Stanee. For the second night in a row, she gave me a preen around the side of my head. There was no biting of my nose or cheek, just good preening. This was the longest preen I had ever received from her. Louis then flew to my shoulder, followed by Quigley, who came to my right forearm to let himself be petted. He even clacked into my hand, something I know is a sign of Quaker endearment. But the least expected event was yet to come. Tikkifinn flew from her usual place on the back of the chair to land on my arm behind Louis. We engaged in some deedle-boop for a while, until jealous Louis drove her off. I fully believe that they knew that I needed some parrot attention and care: the full parrot therapy treatment.

Of Parrot and Human Gender Bonding

As a sociologist, I have been trained to look for patterns in society. Here is one pattern I have observed, though I don't know whether I can prove its existence or not. It goes like this. In general (a good opening for a sociological sentence), male parrots seem to me to become closer to women than to men. Remember the discussion in the chapter on Amazons of the birds that Elizabeth Taylor, Stefanie Powers and Elizabeth Hurley had. The reverse also appears to me to be true. Female parrots seem to me to be generally closer to men than women. Of course, exceptions exist. How does that work with our birds? While all of our birds like both of us, there are in some cases preferences on their part:

Steckley Family: Parrots and Humans

Bird Name	Gender	Preference
Quigley	Male	Angie
Stanee	Female	None
Louis	Male	None
Lime	Female	John

Bird Name	Gender	Preference
Tika	Female	John
Finn	Female	John
Misha	Male	Angie
Gus	Male	John
Tikkifinn	Female	None
Juno	Male	Angie
Poccopeck	Female	None

What patterns do I see? Of the six females, only two have preferences, and they are for me. Of the five males, four have preferences, three for Angie, one for me. And with the six cases of preference, five accord with my hypothesis. Maybe the exception exists because I have some kind of cockatiel appeal.

I have noticed that in five books I've read about individual parrots and their humans, all of the writers were female, and four of the parrots were male. Here is my chart:

Writer	Gender	Bird	Species	Gender
Arlene M. Pepperberg	Female	Alex	African Grey	Male
Georgi Abbot	Female	Pickles	Agrican Grey	Male
Jessica Hagedorn	Female	Ben	Amazon	Male
Joanna Burger	Female	Tiko	Amazon	Male
Betty Jean Craige	Female	Cosmo	African Grey	Female

I should point out that in the case that's the exception, the owner at first thought her bird was male. Of course, in these cases, it could be the human doing the gender selecting, not the bird.

The sociologist in me says that the sample size is way too small to be considered proof, but it is at least slightly suggestive. And then there is my Aunt Nell with her succession of budgies called Richard. I don't think that she would have accepted a free female budgie. Again, it is human choice that is involved.

Now, if what I see could be proven to be true more generally, the next question would be: "Who does the choosing?" Do humans tend to gravitate to parrots of the opposite sex? Do I need to ask a statistically significant number of people, say one hundred or more, that if they were to have one parrot, would they want one of the same or different sex? My hypothesis would be that most would prefer a parrot of the opposite sex, but that remains unproven.

But maybe it is the bird that chooses, at least some of the time. Can parrots distinguish gender in humans? What about visual clues? Even though in North America women tend to wear more brightly coloured clothes than men, this is probably not a factor. Men have deeper voices on average than women, but that distinction doesn't exist insofar as parrots are concerned, so sound is probably not a factor either. That's unfortunate, as parrots are so perceptive with sounds. What about smell? I would think that however different males and females smell, that would be something that might be species-specific. But maybe there is a warm-blooded species consistent smell to hormones.

So I would say that I think I have seen a gender pattern with regard to parrots and their human friends. I have played with the idea a bit. Now it is up to you, the reader, to take it and walk with it a bit, or drop it.

Parrot Patterns of Interaction

How Do You Get Five Parrots on the Floor?

Here is the solution to the problem posed in the first chapter: In what order and for what reasons did the five parrots on the floor get there?

Today I walked into the aviary and found, one by one, five parrots on the floor. How did this happen? I didn't have to watch it to be able, with almost absolute certainty, to correctly identify the sequence of events that created this situation. The first one on the ground would unquestionably have been Sam. He is the most comfortable there, as there are dark places to be found on the floor, along with newspapers to rip up. Sam wouldn't have to be there very long before Stanee would have flown down to see that he was okay and properly protected. This would be followed by her frequent companion Louis hitting the ground as well. He often follows were Stanee goes. Tikkifinn would have moved in afterwards, as she is often interested in getting involved with what the conures are doing. She otherwise would not care where Sam was. She has no interest in him. Finally would come Quigley, wondering what the trouble was and wanting to be in on the action. There is no way that the outliers, Lime and Gus, would be found on the floor. Most of the time, they only want the gang of five to be out of their feathers. Then there is the little blue boy in the cage outside of the aviary, Juno. Even had he been in the aviary, I doubt that he would have ventured down to the floor to see what was going on. While he sometimes lands on the floor, I have never seen him do so when others are there. Had Poccopeck been in the aviary at the time, she would undoubtedly have followed Louis to the floor, and there would have been six there

Parrot Interactions with Parrots

Tail-Pulling

The ultimate parrot trick to (literally) pull on someone else is to pull another parrot's tail. I have seen all of the parrots do it at some point. Poor Gus is the most common victim because of his size; on the other hand, I have never seen anyone even try to pull Sam's tail, the consequences would be so dire. I have seen everyone else have their tail pulled. I can't even say that Juno is an exception because the others have tried to pull his tail through the aviary wire, and he himself has tried to get Louis by the tail, again through the aviary wire.

Why do they do this? Tail-pulling can be an act of jealousy. I came up to Stanee and let her go for my thumbnail, because I know that she likes that. Then Quigley strutted over and I began to pet him, which I have been doing a lot of recently. Well, Stanee seemed to feel that that was taking my attention away from her, so she pulled his tail.

Recently I have discovered that this avian behaviour is not limited to parrots. Angie and I really like going to Stratford, Ontario and not just for the plays. We love the water birds that live on the Avon River there. The swans, geese and ducks never fail to charm us, and we hardly ever fail to bring some cracked or frozen corn for them to eat. Once when we were feeding by hand all the birds that had swum in our direction, there was a swan standing on land, quietly minding its own business, looking for some food in the grass. Another swan came charging towards him or her—swans tend to charge full-out, none of the trickery and subtlety of our parrots—and rose up and pulled the tail of the other swan, then turned around and then escaped back into deeper waters. There was ample food around, and we weren't paying any attention to the victimized swan. Perhaps it was part of an ongoing swan game of "I got you last."

I have seen pictures on the Internet of corvids such as magpies and crows pulling the tails of eagles, hawks, even cats and dogs. I guess they have an advantage of quick take-off not available to their tail-pulled prey. Tail-pulling would seem to be a trait of intelligent birds, then. I have never once seen the mourning doves, sparrows or chickadees in our front yard pull each other's tails, and can't imagine them even trying. I suspect that the blue jays we occasionally see and hear would be up for it, however. They are big, smart and aggressive. I'll have to watch them around the feeder to see if they partake in any tail-pulling. Usually they just bully the other birds off of the feeder with a loud announcement of their arrival. But what if there is a blue-jay rival for the food? Again, further observation is necessary.

Eating and Hanging Out in Another Bird's Cage

There is something about the food in another bird's cage that makes it so attractive. So why not go over and eat it? I saw this first when we had only two birds, Quigley and Stanee. They would regularly get into each other's cage and eat each other's seeds.

Like other behaviours of our little flock, there are clearly demonstrated patterns of who eats in whose cage. This is part of a general personal invasion or intrusion into another bird's cage. When I started taking notes early in 2015, before we moved Stanee and Sam in together, the following patterns were observed.

Cage Owner	Parrot Intruders
Stanee	Sam, Louis and Tikkifinn
Louis and Tikkifinn	Sam

Cage Owner	Parrot Intruders
Quigley	Louis, Sam, Stanee and Tikkifinn
Sam	Gus, Quigley, Stanee
Gus	Louis, Sam
Lime	Louis, Sam, Tikkifinn

You can see the patterns here. Sam was the main intruder, willing to fly into anyone's cage to eat their food. Louis took second place, not wanting to cross Sam by flying into his cage, but okay with trespassing into everyone else's home and food dish. Tikkifinn is the one female who is comfortable in the others' cages. She just avoided the side-by-side cages of Gus and Sam, but was willing to fly into the cages of the other two female parrots. And, because she is fascinated by everything Quigley, she liked to spend time in his cage. She also spends time in the confined space between the top of the cage space of Quigley's cage and the top of the whole cage.

Poor Quigley is the most victimized by cage intrusion. Sometimes Tikkifinn, Stanee and Louis gang up on him and drive him out of his cage. That used to automatically bring on shouting matches; it still sometimes does. However, now he seems strangely quiet about this intrusion, and just leaves. When I see the three of them in his cage and Quigley perched on his open cage door, I drive the others out and let Quigley return to his home. Quigley is a rare cage intruder. He only went into Sam's cage. He is also aggressive with Sam, jealous of the time that the latter spends with Stanee.

Gus is not an aggressive bird, but Sam's cage was next to his and he seemed to feel comfortable there. Stanee went there as Sam is her son, and she could claim parental rights.

Lime is by far the largest bird and has the largest cage. It would be a tight fit for her to enter one of the smaller cages. She rarely voluntarily goes into her own cage during the day. As well, she must know that the other birds, except for Gus, would drive her out. She is an outlier.

A few months after drafting this section, I saw something new. Gus has been going into Lime's cage to feed there. This can't be considered surprising—their relationship has been getting closer and closer, so it is to be expected that he would now feel comfortable enough in his relationship with her to go into her cage.

A while after this passage was first written, we moved Sam and Stanee in with each other, into the top half of the big cage. Only Tikkifinn has the nerve to go in and eat the food in that cage.

The Second Time Around: Who Regurgitation-Feeds Whom

"In the human world vomiting all over your date is not considered a pleasant end to a perfect evening, but in the avian world it could mean true love." —Alyson Kalhagen

One indication of closeness is regurgitation-feeding another bird. Parent parrots feed their young in that way, and it can be part of courtship. Stanee, the mother bird of the flock, is the one most likely one to be involved with this behaviour. I noted in the third chapter that she fed Quigley this way. Louis does this with her too, and she reciprocates. And then there was the night of what I call "re-gifting." Tikkifinn went down to Sam's bucket, where Stanee was standing on the rim. She regurgitation-fed Stanee, and then, a short time later, Stanee brought up food for her son, Sam. The conures seem the most involved with this as Louis gets fed this way by Stanee and Tikkifinn, and returns the favour to both. Poccopeck, who spends a lot of time with Louis when she is in the aviary, and preens him, still has not regurgitation-fed him, or been so fed by him. Maybe she is still too young.

Regurgitation

Giver	Receivers
Tikkifinn	Stanee, Louis
Quigley	Stanee
Stanee	Sam, Louis
Louis	Tikkifinn, Stanee
Sam	Stanee

This doesn't just happen between parrots. Sometimes parrots do it with their favourite humans and toys. I mentioned in chapter four that Lime may have come close to trying to feed me in that way. I suspect that Rita the wreath has received such tokens of affection from the Quakers, but I haven't witnessed it yet.

Bird Bathing

The best description of bird bathing that I have ever read comes from Chris Chester's book about his sparrow, which was called B:

He begins by landing on the edge of his large plastic water dish, and circumnavigating the miniature lake it contains. There's a sort of droll poise in the way he dithers, stalling for time while he searches for the optimum entry point as divined through the principles of avian hydrology. I imagine him evaluating currents and tides that are obvious to him but are invisible to me. Or maybe he just thinks the water might be cold. These are times when I'd like to dress him in an 1890s-style full-length bathing suit. (Chester 2004:28)

Not all of our birds bathe, or take to it right away. Tikkifinn was with us for over a year before I saw her bathe. That activity is generally confined to Stanee (our cleanest bird), Louis and Quigley. In what appeared to be her first time,

Tikkifinn engaged in her bath in two tentative goes. There was a bit of shivering involved, but she took it like a Quaker.

When we first got Juno, he bathed a bit in his water dish, but I haven't seen him do that since. Every once in a while, though, he gets the wet, slick and punked look as though he is using some form of gel. It's a good look for him. I hope that Lime, the main object of his affection, appreciates it.

It would be difficult for big Lime to bathe in our bathing bowl, but she does like a full shower with a water bottle, to the accompaniment of Angie singing "It's raining, it's pouring…." Lime loves it, lifting her wings over her head in a Dracula-like move, making sure that she is wet all over. I once took her in the shower with me, but it was too complicated and awkward as I didn't want her to feel the full flowing force of the shower head.

Even if we got her a special bathing dish her size, I suspect that she might not bathe. Amazons, like a few species of macaws, do not have the uropygial or preen gland that produces an oil that, among other things, has a kind of waterproofing effect.

Gus has sometimes responded well to the shower, but sometimes he looks like a wet, unhappy bird. This is not strange as—unique among our birds—Gus as a cockatiel is a "powder down" or "dust" bird. This is a kind of bird dandruff appears in all species, but in especially large amounts with cockatoos (of course including 'tiels) and African Greys. Although Sam, as a Senegal, is related to the bigger birds, he is not a powder down bird.

However, while Gus does not bathe, except for a strange one-off occasion in 2017, several times he has come very close to the bathing bowl when someone else is bathing. The splashing gets him a little wet. I think that is what he wants. He will often stretch his wings over his head, like Lime does when she is being sprayed. Gus is doing it on his own terms, a very male cockatiel thing to do.

One of the funny things about birds bathing is how tentative that they are at the beginning, much like a human being jumping into a lake at the very beginning of the summer when he or she knows that the still-cold water will be a shock to the system. The parrots enter into their bathing a little bit at a time and then fully commit to as full a bath as they can manage in the shallow waters of the bathing bowl. Watching parrots bathe is when you first notice that birds can be clumsy, just as humans are. It's part of recognizing their personhood, something that never leaves you once learned.

There are a few rules in bird bathing. The water in the communal water dish attached to the aviary wire wall must be clean. Sometimes, when I take the dish out to have it cleaned during the middle of the day, the bathers wait for me to return so they can bathe. There might be a little dance of etiquette (or power) concerning who gets the first bath, with Quigley taking precedence over Louis, and, of course, Stanee having precedence over everybody else. It is not unusual for one bird to bathe, then for another (and a few times another) to quickly follow suit.

Three Variations on Spring Bathing
Three Birds in a Tub

As I write, it's a sunny day early in March, looking more like spring than what we have seen in quite some while. I changed the water at about four o'clock, and the birds were waiting for me to return with the clean water. First Louis took a very long bath, as he tends to; then Tikkifinn made her way into the metal water dish. The water level was running low as the quantity splashed out of the dish ran high. I went to fetch a smaller dish to bring water to refill the bathing dish. I waited as Tikkifinn took her bath, not wanting to dump water on top of her, but while I was waiting Quigley flew over to my hand. To my great surprise, he started ducking his head into this portable bathtub, but seemed frustrated by its small size. We both waited Tikkifinn out, then I poured water into the bathing bowl and let Quigley onto a perch a little bit underneath the bowl. He then could have a full bath.

Bathing is About Taking Turns

One thing that both humans and indoor parrots have to learn is that bathing is about taking turns. It was a warm spring afternoon in March. I had just dumped out the dirty old water and replaced it with fresh, clean, not-too-cold water. Stanee was in there like a shot. She got herself well and truly soaked. Tikkifinn approached for her turn. She was about to go in when Stanee returned from the wreath by the window. Though Stanee had already taken a good bath, Tikkifinn had to stand back while Stanee soaked herself again. She repeated this five or six times. Tikkifinn waited patiently, although it was apparent, as she stood on the perch right beside the bowl, that she wanted it to be her turn. It was almost like a show of power for Stanee, or perhaps she was thinking, "She is going to take over the bowl. I must be sure that I'm done."

Finally Tikkifinn got her turn. After Tikkifinn's relatively short bath, Lime flew onto the perch nearby, on the other side from the one that Tikkifinn had been waiting on, and Tikkifinn decided to fly away.

Tikkifinn Takes Over

It was the second communal water-dish change of the day on a bright sunny mid-March afternoon. Tikkifinn took to it right away—a full, explosive bath. She can be a violent bather, splashing water to all sides. Twice Louis came to take his turn, and twice she chased him out. Once she was finished and had flown away, Louis returned and went quickly into the bowl. The problem was that there wasn't much water left, not enough for him to be able to take a decent bath. Tough luck, Louis.

Sam Joins In

I don't think that I had ever seen Sam take a bath until one day in June 2015. But sure enough, not long after Louis took his bath, Sam was in there. He didn't get himself very wet, but it was clear from the way he put himself pretty much completely into the water bowl and moved about, ducking his head, that he was giving it a try.

It must have been an ideal sort of day for bird-bathing, humid and somewhat sticky. Even Gus, whom I thought would never even get close to taking a bath, tentatively approached the water bowl as Louis came out, though he thought better of it in the end.

Within the week Sam tried again. He circled the water bowl, as if contemplating the best angle for bathing, then suddenly ducked his head in. He didn't go any farther than that. He circled again, then ducked his head in once more. After that he flew away, content that he had done what the others have done at other times.

There's a Parrot Down
(with thanks to Mike Myers' "So I Married an Axe Murderer")

Louis is good at communicating that there is something wrong in his world. His distress call is distinctive. Today he had taken a bath, or was still in its finishing stages (it's often hard to tell with him), when Quigley must have been imposing himself, impatiently wanting to take a bath of his own. Once one bird becomes interested, the two other bathers often grow interested, too. Louis repeated his complaint/distress call rapidly, over and over. When I walked into the aviary, I found that he was stuck between the front window and the cabinet. Stanee and Sam were in the immediate area, responding to his call. Well, Stanee was certainly responding, as mother of the flock. Sam was just there because Stanee was. Stanee was there protecting Louis, but it was up to me to rescue him. I bent down, he stepped up, and I put him on a perch on the aviary wall.

A week later it happened again. I was in the aviary while Louis was taking a long bath. After left the room, he attempted to fly and ended up in the small space between the window and cabinet. Stanee flew there because she heard his distress call. Sam joined her on the floor. As soon as I heard Louis give out a distress call, I knew that he had hit the floor. This hypothesis was confirmed when I saw Stanee standing just outside the small space between window and cabinet. Louis is not especially good at learning from his mistakes.

Just Getting Your Head Wet

I just came to realize that parrots bathe in the exact opposite way than humans swimming in a relatively cold lake. Stanee showed me this. We humans go in tentatively, feet first, then we wade in a bit (or a lot) and eventually dive in, whole body. In English we use the expression "You need to get your feet wet," referring to getting involved in something for the first time. Stanee does it the opposite way. I brought in a bowl bearing the fresh, clean water. She quickly flew to the water bowl. She walked around the rim a bit, and then decided to try the water out. She started the process by getting her head wet. She moistened her head tentatively, then pulled it quickly back out of the water. Then she put it in more boldly, drawing it back out again. Okay, this water isn't so bad; it is time to make the full commitment. She dipped most of her body in, and pulled it out. Stanee was ready to bathe. She jumped in "full bird" and got her whole self wet. Then she jumped out, shook herself a bit and repeated the action. Finally she came out, gave herself a quick shake and flew away a cleaner bird.

A Sunny Spring Bath

It's late Friday afternoon, a sunny, spring day at the end of a week marked by a blizzard and intense cold. The sun shines brightly through window of the aviary. I go in to clean a few things up and replace the communal water bowl. As soon as I bring the bowl in, complete with fresh water, Stanee climbs her way across the mesh to have a bath. There is no mistaking her purpose. I sit down in the plastic chair to be part of the scene. She takes a complete bath, going out for a bit and returning perhaps seven or eight times. Her lovely trilling comes out as a verbal smile when she leaves the bowl.

Tikkifinn stands on the edge of the bowl like a personal lifeguard, almost going in; but Stanee returns again and again. She can barely fly, but still she takes short, strategic flights, only to return to the bowl. When Stanee leaves, Tikkifinn, a little more tentatively, takes her bath. After each splashing session she stands tall above the bowl. I bring some more water as there is little left after Stanee's vigorous bathing. Tikkifinn doesn't mind, in fact seems to enjoy the fact that she now has a full bowl. She flies away once, as Sam has invaded her cabinet territory, only to return once he has been chased away. She doesn't take as complete a bath as Stanee did, but she seems satisfied with the process.

Meanwhile, Quigley has been waiting patiently on the back of the plastic chair, fluffed up and ready for his turn in the bath. After Tikkifinn leaves, he enters the bowl. There is only a little water left, so I go fetch some more for him. "Shall I draw your bath sir?" He, too, is not disturbed by the pouring water during his bath, and is only too happy to have a good full bowl in which to do his ablutions. When he leaves, I look to Louis, who often enjoys a bath, but he will have none of it. Maybe he has memories of the last time he crashed on the floor. Maybe he distrusts the weather. Thanks, guys. My mood had been down and you brought it back up. You have earned your seeds this sunny spring afternoon.

Preening Behaviour

A very important form of social behaviour for parrots is preening. A few years back, I wrote a piece for the newsletter of the World Parrot Trust on what I referred to as the parrot sociology of preening. It is interesting for me to look back, note what has now changed, and see if my analysis has held up.

The seven parrots we had then were Quigley, Finn, Stanee, Louis, Lime, Tika and Sam. Here is the way that the preening worked then:

PREENER	PREENED
Quigley	Stanee, Finn, Lime, Sam
Stanee	Quigley, Louis, Sam
Louis	Stanee
Finn	Quigley
Sam	Stanee
Tika	No one
Lime	No one

The arrangement was a fairly simple one. Males preened females and females preened males, except for Quigley preening Sam, something he no longer does. The more "socially mature" parrots, Quigley and Stanee, whom I deemed the father and mother of the flock and who had been with us the longest, were the most active preeners, and were themselves preened by the most birds. All preening relationships were reciprocal except for the socially immature (he still is and may always be) Sam.

With the deaths of the two beautiful souls, Tika and Finn, and the introduction of Gus and Tikkifinn, the configuration changed somewhat:

PREENER	PREENED
Quigley	No one (but see below)
Stanee	Louis, Sam (and possibly Quigley again, see below)
Louis	Stanee, Tikkifinn, Gus
Sam	Stanee
Tikkifinn	Louis, Stanee, Gus
Gus	Lime, Louis
Lime	No one

With Finn gone, Quigley lost his main preener. His growing separation from Stanee, due mainly to the amount of attention she gave her "child," Sam, caused him to lose Stanee as a preener, too. He sometimes attacks Sam out of jealousy. Yesterday, he blooded the big guy's talons. It is a sad situation for him, and when he is sad, he goes to his humans for preening. He will always preen me when I bend my head down in front of him. I very much appreciate that. He's a bit of a rough preener sometimes, but definitely a caring one. And I preen him whenever he lets me. A sign of his availability is where he is perched. You cannot preen him when he is on any of the perches attached to the wire aviary wall. He will bite your fingers. The most likely spot is when he is on the back of the chair.

Stanee still preens Louis and Sam, both of whom reciprocate. She overdoes it on the top of Sam's head, so he looks to be a trifle feather-balding. Louis, who was Tikkifinn's first and still dearest friend, expanded his list of preened to include her. We had hoped that she would take to Quigley. She is fascinated by everything he does, learned building from him, hangs around his cage a great deal, and responds with Quaker sounds to his Quaker sounds. But, like everyone, she was charmed by the friendly ways of Louis. Louis had tried with Tika to be friendlier to her than she wanted. When she had a clutch of eggs, he regularly went over to observe, and she just as regularly drove him back. Gus is more open to be preened by Louis, and is the red-headed conure's good friend, even though Louis sometimes pulls his tail and chases after him. Sometimes Gus feels that Louis' preening is too hard or is lasting too long, so he issues a highly vocal complaint. Sam has socially matured enough that he reciprocates the preening that Stanee does to him. Gus's monumental efforts to preen Lime have been recorded elsewhere.

Parrots Arrange Their Own Relationships

We have learned something about parrots that we should have known beforehand. It is not easy to set up "arranged relationships" among them. Joanna Burger notes that in her book, commenting that personality match seems to be a factor. Complications also involve same-sex couples (which are found in the wild as well) as well as what may happen if a parrot already feels already bonded with and mated to a human. Concerning the latter, Burger notes that "parrots bonded to human beings typically disdain other parrots. Friends have acquired second parrots with horrific results; the two birds detest each other, screech nonstop, and need to be caged in separate rooms. Parrots are emotionally fragile. Breaking Tiko's [her male red-lored Amazon] bond with me and inducing him to bond with a female parrot would be risky and an enormous investment of time."

Let's look at the Steckleys' record here. Our first parrot was Quigley, a handsome young Quaker parrot (SGM—single green male). Our second parrot was Stanee. She came from the same store, so when we brought her into the house, the two of them fell fast in love. Unfortunately for this relationship, we were smitten by Louis when we met him, a very charming rose-crowned conure, and when he came into our house he and Stanee became mates. Further complicating this was the entry into our home of Sam, a rescue Senegal. Stanee literally took this abused and shattered young male under her wing and became his mother.

Quigley would look on longingly whenever Stanee was preening Louis or Sam. When we got Finn, the two would preen each other, but they didn't really pair-bond. When we put them in the same cage she crowded him out. He literally escaped through a side exit one night, which really sent a message. Enter Tikkifinn into our lives, another SBF (single blue female). We very slowly introduced her to the flock, putting her and her cage in another room (Angie's office), making sure that Quigley met and interacted with her first. Then we put her cage on the other side of the mesh and wood wall that is the aviary side of our living room.

Louis is the parrot with the greatest number of preening relationships. He is the most preened parrot we have (by Gus, Stanee, and Tikkifinn). He and Gus are close friends, preening each other, although sometimes Louis chases Gus away, and has been known to pull Gus's tail. Fortunately for Gus, he also has a close relationship with Lime, as was described earlier.

But the planned-for relationship didn't happen. Charming Louis and young Tikkifinn bonded across the mesh. When we took him to her side of the aviary, the two would spend the day together. The two of them now spend their nights together in a shared cage. However, she is fascinated by what Quigley does, and has learned a lot about Quaker-speak and basic building from him. It seems more of an uncle-niece relationship.

And when we got Poccopeck, another young blue Quaker girl, our expectations concerning a possible relationship for Quigley were lowered, and she, too, fell for Louis' charismatic charms.

The Extremes

Juno is very much attracted to Lime. They represent the two extremes of our birds, by far the biggest and easily the smallest. When he is out of his cage and on the aviary mesh, he is on a perch across the mesh from Lime. When she flies to a different perch on the mesh, he follows suit. We at first that this was a one-sided relationship, like the ones I am about to discuss. But more observation shows her going to align herself across the mesh with where Juno is. And sometimes she is quite content to stay on the perch nearest his cage on the outside of the aviary. She often looks at him when she is there. This is an avian 'opposites attract.'

One-sided Relationships

It seems to me that there is a pattern in the two essentially one-sided relationships of male and female: Quigley and Stanee, and Gus and Lime. First off, it is clear that they are not mates, in part possibly because of the fact that they are in different genera Also clear is the fact that the relationship in both cases is driven by the male, not the female. Quigley wants to be near Stanee, and often moves towards her when she is alone. They end up perching near each other, looking uncomfortable, a lot to me like a pair of early teens at a dance, not knowing what to do, there being no appropriate further moves that would not lead to one or both of them flying away. In this case, the one most likely to fly away is Stanee. Then there is Quigley's flying toward his own cage once I have put Stanee in hers for the night. His protection or possible company no longer needed or possible, he flies to his cage, often walking in the door: "My work here is done."

With Gus, he is the one who approaches. When Lime is put inside her cage after she has made threatening gestures at Angie, he makes his way over to her cage to stand on its roof, directly above where she is, on the left-hand side. When I return home and Lime is still inside her cage, Gus is to be found at that position. I can't really say that his intent is to protect her, but he does want to be with her. And, at night, when I go to put him in his cage, he is often on the circle suspended to the left of the bicycle tire that is one of Lime's favourite places. When he is not there, it is because there is someone bigger there already..

These two relationships are quite different from that between Quigley and Tikkifinn. Tikkifinn is fascinated by what Quigley does, particularly building. She likes to go into his cage, even when he is in it, to eat his food, but also to scope out the results of his building efforts. She appears mystified by the process. She can insert sticks into the mesh wall, but that is far as she can get. She has not yet started building inside her own cage, even though we sometimes put sticks inside there. She has reached a certain level in her building ability and seems to have plateaued there for a while. She appears to listen carefully when Quigley starts to sing, talking in what a primatologist might refer to as a "long call," a behaviour that she was not earlier much involved with. The two of them sometimes are perched close to each other in a position of combined discomfort and interest similar to that currently shared by Quigley and Stanee, but yet different in ways that I have not yet figured out how to describe. The two Quakers speak the same language, and that seems to mean something to both of them.

The Next Night

The night after I wrote the paragraphs above, I received a pleasant surprise. I saw a hint of something going on when I was changing the water. Stanee and Quigley were on the two perches on the door, a few inches apart. When I came back they were on perches that were even closer. Then in a flash, she preened him for just about a second, and he preened her back for about twice that long, both of them looking like they acted on impulse. Then they stood, a few inches apart, Quigley making soft sounds and being fluffed up. Stanee was looking down at him, her perch slightly above his. Nothing much happened after that but it was an amazing moment, a moment of rediscovery perhaps. Certainly it appeared that they both wanted to be there with the other; there was just the uncertainty, much like what happens at the door on a first date, wondering whether or not to kiss. I told Angie about what I had seen, and she said that she had seen the same thing happen not too long ago. I hope that these attempts to reconnect continue. Quigley could certainly use some preening from another parrot.

Later that same night, Quigley and Stanee were standing on top of Sam's cage a little more than a hand's distance apart. There were looks shared between them. She looked straight at him. He flew up to the lower right-hand front corner of the slanted roof of the double cage. She stood there for a few seconds, then took big steps to the right-hand side of the top of Sam's cage. She then took a few big steps back across the cage. She flew up to stand close beside Quigley. Probably remembering times when she did that to chase him away, he flew to the door of his cage. I truly believe that he misread the situation. Quigley, you need to pay closer attention to her body language. She seems to me to be looking less aggressive. Having been bit by her several times, I watch that language very carefully.

Quigley and Lime

It was not just my imagination; Quigley and Lime are often close to each other these days. I just saw them on the same perch, about a human hand apart. He is fluffed up as he sometimes gets when he wants attention from a human or a female bird. I have seen him recently close to all three of our female parrots at some time or other. Perhaps he is going through a sexual time, something like what the females do, only a male version. Yesterday, he had fairly loud sex with Rita, his wreath. It had been a long time since I heard that. I don't listen for it, as I am not some kind of bird pervert, but you hear it whether you want to or not. I didn't want to hear it but I did.

A few days later it seemed to have ended. Lime was on an upper perch, Quigley on a lower one. He raised a beak to challenge her, and then Stanee flew in to drive her away. This was in part to protect Quigley, but I also think it was part of her continuing battle with the bigger bird.

A Matter of Gender

One issue that often arises with parrots is that of gender. Is my parrot female or male? They are not, as a rule, sexually dichromatic, that is, with different colours and colour patterns for males and females. Males are not as a rule bigger than females, do not have a larger beak or exhibit other clear signs of being different from females. Of course, the birds know. I believe the clues are through smell: pheromones.

If you really want to know, there is always the blood DNA test. But that seems unnecessary and cruel. We have had birds take blood tests for health reasons, and we would not like to inflict that on them just to determine their sex.

Quigley, we were told, was male, although I don't think a test had been performed. He reveals his maleness in other ways. His attachment to Stanee is a clear sign. He definitely wants to be her mate. There is also the matter of how he had sex with Rita, his wreath. Let's just say that he did so in a way that indicated that he was a male. His most significant relationships have been with females: Stanee, Finn and Tikkifinn, and, for a short while, Lime.

Stanee was thought to be male by the pet store people, I think because she is so tough. It was when she got broody that we first believed that she was a female. Her pairing off with Quigley and Louis, and her very maternal relationship with Sam, added to that conviction. And her head is rounded on top. Angie and I believe that male parrots tend to have flatter heads than females do.

There was never any doubt with Louis. Of course, the pet store name for him, which we kept, provided a big hint. His early infatuation with Stanee told a story, as did the fact that he also initiated relationships with three other females, Tika, Finn and Tikkifinn, despite the fact that we wanted the last two to pair off with Quigley. And he has spent time with Rita the wreath.

We weren't sure at first with Lime. The name could apply to either sex. Her attraction to me, complete with the sexual shaking and clucking, and her jealousy of Angie, sealed her gender identity for us.

Tika was easy, as cockatiels have two signs of sexual difference. Cockatiels generally look like females from the time they hatch to when they have first moult at six to nine months (after all, they are chicks). Females then maintain the horizontal barring of the chicks. Males get a bright orange patch on their cheeks. Tika was very attracted to me. And there was the little matter of the laying of eggs, a sure sign.

There was no question with Gus, as he clearly has the bright orange patch and his tail is not barred. His strange attraction to Lime adds to this. His friendship with Louis is really just two birdie buddies hanging out, sometimes playing rough games (Louis pulling Gus's tail) as boys do, parrots or humans.

Tikkifinn was difficult. We went back and forth on this one. She hung out with Stanee (what is it about conures that make them so attractive to Quakers?), a relationship which later became more distant. She will lurk near Stanee, but her preening relationship is definitely only with Louis. She used to live in the top part of the big cage, until she suddenly decided, as Quakers do, that she was going to occupy the bottom part, but not alone. Louis was going to be with her. That was months and months ago. Finally, she, like Quigley, had sex with Rita the wreath, in such a way that her gender was no longer in question.

Now we believe that Juno is a male. It's partly because he has the "striking cobalt rump" that is said to be typical of the male Pacific parrotlet, as well as the darker blue stripe behind his eyes and on his wings. He doesn't really have a relationship with the other birds. But Tikkifinn often hangs around the cage on the opposite side of the aviary wall. Maybe she sees him as her child, as they are both predominantly light blue. It does not take much imagination to see him as a smaller version of her. And he likes to hang out near Lime when he is in the aviary, as was already point out.

There is whole other question in this regard. Do you really need to know the gender of your bird? Is it important that we know to say "he" or "she," "him" or "her"? Does it change the way you interact with your bird? Does it affect how you name your bird? For a while, when we didn't know everyone's gender, it was different and interesting not to know.

Conclusion

So that is the flock among us at the Steckley household. As you have seen, they form patterned relationships, as humans do, and those relationships are dynamic, subject to change, as human relationships are. The flock among us has taught me a great deal about birds. I hope that in reading this book you have learned something as well.

Bibliography

Abbot, Georgi, n.d., *Pickles the Parrot: A Humorous Look at Life with an African Grey*, CreateSpace Independent Publishing Platform.
Beaudoin, Terry, n.d., "An Introduction to Senegals, " *Companion Parrot Quarterly,* https://companionparrotonline.com/Senegal_Terry.html.
Berg, K. S., S. Delgado, K. A. Cortopassi, S. R. Beissinger & J. W. Bradbury, 2012. Vertical transmission of learned signatures in a wild parrot. *Proceedings of the Royal Society, Biology*, 279, 585-591.
Berg, K. S., S. Deglado, R. Okawa, S. R. Beissinger & J. W. Bradbury,2011. Contact calls are used for individual mate recognition in free-ranging green-rumped parrotlets, Forpus passerinus. *Animal Behavior*, 81, 241-248.
BirdLife International (2015) Species factsheet: *Amazona oratrix*. Downloaded from http://www.birdlife.org on 02/12/2015.
Bittner, Mark, 2004, *The Wild Parrots of Telegraph Hill*, New York: Three Rivers Press.
Blackwood, Algernon, 1929, *Dudley and Gilderoy*, E.P. Dutton and Company.
Boehrer, Bruce T, 2004, *Parrot Culture: Our 2,500-Year-Long Fascination with the World's Most Talkative Bird,* Philadelphia: University of Pennsylvania Press.
Burger, Joanna, 2002, *The Parrot Who Owns Me: The Story of a Relationship*, New York: Random House.
Burns, Bill, 1999, *Raising Susan: A Man, a Woman, and a Golden Eagle*, Toronto: Stoddart.
Chester, Chris, 2004, *Providence of a Sparrow: Lessons from a Life Gone to the Birds*, New York: Anchor Books.
Corbo, Margarete Sigi and Diane Marie Barras, 1983, *Arnie the Darling Starling*, Boston: Houghton Mifflin.
Craig, Betty Jean, 2010, *Conversations with Cosmo: At Home with an African Grey Parrot*, Sainte Fe, NM: Sherman Asher Publishing.
creagrus.home.montereybay.com/parrots.html.
Defoe, Daniel, 1994 (orig. 1719), *The Life and Adventures of Robinson Crusoe*, New York: Norton Publishing.
Darwin, Charles, 1839, *The Voyage of the Beagle,* The Electronic Classics, Pennsylvania State University, http://www2.hn.psy.edu/faculty/jmanis/darwin/voyagebeagle.pdf.
De Waal, Frans, 1997, "Are we in anthropodenial?", *Discover* 18 (7), 50-53.
Fossum Karin, 2002, *Black Seconds*, Boston: Mariner Books.
Greene, William Thomas, 1884, *Parrots in Captivity*, vol. 1, London: George Bell and Sons.
—————, 1924, *The Grey Parrot and How to Manage It*, Dutton.

Grindel, Diane n.d., "Male Versus Female Cockatiels", www.birdchannel.com/bird-magazines/popular-birds/cockatiel-male-female-aspx.
Hagedorn, Jessica, 2010, *Life with Ben: A Story of Friendship and Feathers*, CreateSpace Independent Publishing Platform.
Heinrich, Bernd, 2006, *Mind of the Raven: Investigations and Adventures with Wolf-Birds*, New York: HarperCollins.
Johns, Linda, 1993, *Sharing a Robin's Life*, Halifax: Nimbus Publishing.
Jonson, Ben, *Epigrams*, www.hollowaypages.com/jonson1692epigrams.htm.
Kalhagen, Alyson, www.birds.about.com/od/behaviorandtraining/qt/regurgitation.htm
Lambert, Megan, Amanda Seed, Katie Slocombe, "New evidence of tool use discovered in parrots: First evidence of tool use by greater vasa parrots (Coracopsis vasa), *Biology Letters*, vol. 11, issue 12, DOI:10.1098/vsbl.2015.0861.
Leopold, Aldo, 1937, "The Thick-Billed Parrot of Chihuahua," *Condor*, pp. 9-10.
Lofting, Hugh, 1988 (orig. 1920), T*he Story of Doctor Dolittle: Being the History of His Peculiar Life at Home and Astonishing Adventures in Foreign Parts. Never Before Printed*, Bantam Doubleday Dell, New York.
Lorenz, Konrad, 1952, *King Solomon's Ring*, New York: Thomas Y. Crowell Co.
Macdonald, Helen, 2014, *H is for Hawk*, New York: Penguin Books.
Morell, Virginia, 2013, *Animal Wise: How We Know Animals Think and Feel*, New York: Broadway Books.
Pepperberg, Irene, (1999), *The Alex Studies: Cognitive and Communicative Abilities of Grey Parrots*, Harvard University Press.
—————, 2008, *Alex and Me: How a Scientist and a Parrot Discovered a Hidden World of Animal Intelligence—and Formed a Deep Bond in the Process*, New York: HarperCollins.
Rothenberg, David, 2005, *Why Birds Sing: A Journey into the Mystery of Bird Song*, New York: Basic Books.
Russell, H.W.S (Duke of Bedford), 1969, *Parrots and Parrot-Like Birds*, Neptune Cith, NJ: T.F.H. Publications.
Sculer, Phillip L., and William H. Hudson, 1889, *Argentine Ornithology: A Descriptive Catalogue of the Birds of the Argentine Republic*, vol. 2, London: R. H. Porter.
Stanger, Margaret, 1966, *That Quail, Robert*, New York: Ballantine Books.
Steckley, John, 1986, *Winter Birds of Ontario*, Ontario Ministry of Natural Resources, Poster 3423.
—————, 2011, *Introduction to Physical Anthropology*, Toronto: Oxford University Press.
—————, 2015, *Gibbons: The Invisible Apes*, Oakville, ON: Rock's Mills Press.
Stevenson, Robert Louis, 1883, *Treasure Island*, London: Cassell and Company.
Woolfson, Esther, 2008, *Corvus: A Life with Birds*, London: Granta Books.
www.all-pet-birds.com/parrotlets.html.
www.birdchannel.com/bird-species/profiles/green-cheeked-conure-2.aspx.
www.birdchannel.com/bird-species/profiles/poicephalus.aspx
www.moonsgarden.com/12_5dbfa03576668b01_1.htm.
'Mona', "Senegals as Pets", November 17, 2009; taken from an article in *Pet and Aviary Birds Magazine*, February/March, 2004, www.parrotletbirds.com.Pacific_Parrotlet_Information.html.
www.thepetpress-la.com/stefanie-powers.html.
"Simon the parrotlet loses his mind over plastic bag. Kevin the aracari vaguely interested," www.youtube.com/watch?v:5CI6-BWJL1U.

Index

Africans (parrots), 88ff.; classification, 89
Alex (bird), 1
Alex and Me (Pepperberg), 89
Alex Studies (Pepperberg), 89
Alvin (bird), 71
Amazons, 68ff.; as pets, 70–71; classification of, 69–70; whistling by, 78
Anthropomorphism, 7–8
Arne the Darling Starling (Corbo and Barras), 6
B (bird), 21
Bathing (by parrots), 157–161
Benji (bird), 22
Berg, Karl S., 138
Boie, Forpus F., 136
Boie, Friedrich, 136
Books on parrots, 8–10, 16–18
Cages, 14–16
Calls (bird/parrot), 10–11
Churchill, Winston, 77
Classification, scientific, of parrots, 2
Cockatiels, 108ff.; books on, 114; classification, 113; history, 113–114; singing by, 121–122
Cockatoos, 108ff.
Contact calls, 138–139
Conures, 20ff.; classification of, 20–21, 35
Cook, James, 113
Critical anthropomorphism, 7–8
Dogs, differences from parrots, 13–14
Duffy, Deborah, 1
Epigrams (Jonson), 18
Fiction about parrots, 16–18
Finn (bird), 49–51
Gender (of parrots), 166–167
Gibbons: The Invisible Apes (Steckley), 6, 40
Gus (bird), 118ff.
History in Canada, of parrots, 4
Human-parrot interaction by gender, 152–154
Hurley, Elizabeth, 71
Intelligence, of parrots, 1

Island of Adventure (Blyton), 16
Juno (bird), 133ff.
King Solomon's Ring (Lorenz), 12
Koko (bird), 19
Leopold, Aldo, 10
Lime (bird), 71ff.
Linné, Carl (Carolus Linnaeus), 136
Lorey (bird), 77
Louis (bird), 23, 25ff.
Lucky Lou (bird), 109–112
Mammals, compared to birds ("parallel lives"), 6–7
Mechanomorphism, 7
Mimicking (by parrots), 11–12
Mind of the Raven (Heinrich), 1–2
Misha (bird), 89–90
Moralia (Plutarch), 1
Ornithology (Scluler and Hudson), 42
Papuga (bird), 71
Parrot Who Owns Me, The (Burger), 8, 13, 69
Parrotlets, 135ff.; classification, 136–137
Parrot-parrot interaction, 154–156, 163–166
Parrots in Captivity (Greene), 11–12, 40–41
Pepperberg, Irene, 1, 89
Pets, parrots as, 4
Ping Pong (bird), 71
Poccopeck (bird), 66–67
Powers, Stephanie, 71
Preening (by parrots), 161–163
Quakers, 39ff.; banning of, 41–42; building by, 55–60; classification of, 40–41; territoriality of, 64–66
Queen Victoria, 77
Quigley (bird), 42ff.
Richard (bird), 18–19
Robinson Crusoe (Defoe), 17–18
Russell, Hasting William Sackville (Duke of Bedford), 141
Sam, 88ff.

Senegals (parrots), 91ff; classification, 91–92; threat to habitat, 92
Shoulder bird relationships, 150
Sparrows, 9–10
Stanee (bird), 23ff.
Status of parrots, in North America, 3–4
Stepping up (by parrots), 148–150
Story of Dr. Dolittle, The (Lofting), 9
Talking (by parrots), 10–12
Tango in America (Baldwin and Evants-Fragele), 41
Taylor, Elizabeth, 71
The Grey Parrot and How to Manage It (Greene), 3
Tika (bird), 114ff.
Tikifinn (bird), 52ff.
Tool use, by parrots, 26–27
Treasure Island (Stevenson), 16–17
Voyage of the Beagle, The (Darwin), 42
World Parrot Refuge, 109–112

www.ingramcontent.com/pod-product-compliance
Lightning Source LLC
Chambersburg PA
CBHW070859080526
44589CB00013B/1128